Samba

Primer Plus

Matthew Gillard

Sams Publishing
A Division of Macmillan USA, Inc.
201 West 103rd St., Indianapolis, Indiana, 46290 USA

Samba Primer Plus

Copyright ©2000 by Sams Publishing

International Standard Book Number: 0-672-31932-2

Library of Congress Catalog Card Number: 99-067619

Printed in the United States of America

First Printing: March 2000

02 01 00   4 3 2 1

Trademarks

All terms mentioned in this book that are known to be trademarks or service marks have been appropriately capitalized. Sams Publishing cannot attest to the accuracy of this information. Use of a term in this book should not be regarded as affecting the validity of any trademark or service mark.

Warning and Disclaimer

Every effort has been made to make this book as complete and as accurate as possible, but no warranty or fitness is implied. The information provided is on an "as is" basis. The author and the publisher shall have neither liability nor responsibility to any person or entity with respect to any loss or damages arising from the information contained in this book or from the use of the CD or programs accompanying it.

ASSOCIATE PUBLISHER
Michael Stephens

EXECUTIVE EDITOR
Rosemarie Graham

ACQUISITIONS EDITOR
Angela C. Kozlowski

DEVELOPMENT EDITOR
Clint McCarty

MANAGING EDITOR
Charlotte Clapp

SENIOR EDITOR
Karen A. Walsh

COPY EDITOR
Margaret Berson

INDEXER
Erika Millen

PROOFREADERS
Bob LaRoche
Matt Wynalda

TECHNICAL EDITORS
Mike Ciavarella
Steve Epstein
Robert Rati
Dallas Releford
Jason Wright

TEAM COORDINATOR
Pamalee Nelson

SOFTWARE DEVELOPMENT SPECIALIST
Dan Scherf

INTERIOR DESIGN
Gary Adair

COVER DESIGN
Alan Clements

COPYWRITER
Eric Borgert

LAYOUT TECHNICIANS
Ayanna Lacey
Heather Hiatt Miller
Stacey Richwine-DeRome

CONTENTS AT A GLANCE

INTRODUCTION   1

PART I: Setting Up Your First Samba   3
    CHAPTER 1   What Is Samba? 5
    CHAPTER 2   Compiling and Installing Samba 15
    CHAPTER 3   Basic Samba Configuration 31

PART II: Integrating Samba into Your Windows Network   57
    CHAPTER 4   Understanding Windows NT Networks 59
    CHAPTER 5   Integrating Samba into an Existing Windows Network 75
    CHAPTER 6   Using Samba with Windows 95/98 97
    CHAPTER 7   Samba in a Windows NT/2000 Domain Environment 111
    CHAPTER 8   Using `smbclient` 143

PART III: Advanced Topics   159
    CHAPTER 9   Samba with SSL 161
    CHAPTER 10   Additional Share Level Options 181
    CHAPTER 11   Tuning Samba for Better Performance 191
    CHAPTER 12   Debugging Samba 199
    CHAPTER 13   Samba Security 215
    CHAPTER 14   Third-Party Samba Tools 225
    CHAPTER 15   A Look at Samba's Future 235

PART IV: Appendixes   241
    APPENDIX A   A Sample CIFS/SMB Session 243
    APPENDIX B   Answers to Review Questions .249

GLOSSARY   261

INDEX   265

TABLE OF CONTENTS

INTRODUCTION 1

PART I: Setting Up Your First Samba   3

CHAPTER 1: What Is Samba? 5
  An Overview of Samba 5
  What Is the SMB Protocol? 6
    A Brief History of the SMB Protocol 7
  Samba's Main Functions 9
    SMB Server 10
    NetBIOS Name Resolution 10
    User Authentication 11
    Computer Browser 11
    Domain Logins 12
  What Is CIFS? 12
  Summary 12
  Review Questions 13

CHAPTER 2: Compiling and Installing Samba 15
  How Do I Install Samba? 15
  Downloading Precompiled Packages 16
    Where to Get Samba Packages 17
  Installing Precompiled Packages 19
  Downloading the Samba Source 19
  Compiling Samba 20
  Installing Samba 24
    Samba at Startup 25
  Summary 28
  Review Questions 29

CHAPTER 3: Basic Samba Configuration 31
  Samba Web Administration Tool 31
    Installing SWAT 32
    Using SWAT 32
  Testing Your Samba Configuration 40
    Using `smbclient` to Test Your Samba Configuration 41
  Getting Windows to Talk to Samba 43
    Configuring a Windows 98 Client 43
    Configuring a Windows NT Client 45
    Connecting to Your First Share on Your Samba Server 47

Basic Troubleshooting 51
   Network Adapter Problems 51
   Network Configuration Problems 52
   Name Server Problems 52
   Samba Server Configuration Problems 54
   Client Configuration Problems 55
Summary 56
Review Questions 56

PART II: Integrating Samba into Your Windows Network   **57**

CHAPTER 4: Understanding Windows NT Networks 59
Introduction to Windows NT 60
Differences Between Workgroups and Domains 61
NetBIOS Revisited 64
   NetBIOS Name Service 65
   NetBIOS Session Service 69
   NetBIOS Datagram Service 70
Browsing on a Windows Network 70
   Possible Computer Browser Roles 71
   Master Browser Elections 72
Tasks a Windows NT Server Fulfills 72
   The Login Process 73
Summary 73
Review Questions 74

CHAPTER 5: Integrating Samba into an Existing Windows Network 75
Requirements Samba Can Fulfill in Your Network 75
Samba and WINS 76
   `lmhosts` 76
   WINS 77
   Gathering Information from Samba WINS Servers 78
Browsing with Samba 78
   Samba in a Windows Workgroup 78
   Samba in a Windows NT Domain 80
   Configuration of the Browsing Clients 81
Choosing a Password Server 82
   A Problem with Using Password Servers 83
Samba and Encrypted Passwords 84
   `smbpasswd` 86
   Migrating Existing Windows NT Encrypted Passwords to a
   Samba Server 88

User Home Directories 89
  Restricting Home Directory Users .90
Samba as a Print Server 90
  UNIX Side Configuration 90
  Samba Printing Configuration 91
Broadcasting Messages to Your Windows Clients 93
  Receiving Windows Messages on UNIX 95
Summary 95
Review Questions 96

CHAPTER 6: Using Samba with Windows 95/98 97
Samba's Role in a Windows 9x Network 98
Workgroups and Domains Revisited .99
Configuring Samba as a Domain Login Server 101
Configuring Roaming User Profiles .105
System Policies 107
Troubleshooting Samba as a Domain Login Server 108
Summary 109
Review Questions 110

CHAPTER 7: Samba in a Windows NT/2000 Domain Environment 111
Adding a Samba Server as a Domain Member 112
  Configuration Details to Make Samba a Member Server 112
Samba as a Primary Domain Controller 114
  Understanding Trust Relationships 115
Samba as a Login Server for Windows NT Clients (PDC Role) 117
  Creating a PDC `smb.conf` 118
  Creating Machine Trust Accounts 118
  Setting Up Your Windows NT Clients 120
Windows NT Functionality Available on Your Samba PDC 121
  File Permissions 122
Adding Samba Users and Groups to ACLs on NTFS File Systems 130
  Server Manager 130
  User Manager for Domains 134
Roaming Profiles Under Windows NT 136
`rpcclient` 139
Summary 140
Review Questions 141

CHAPTER 8: Using `smbclient` 143
The Purpose of `smbclient` 143
Common `smbclient` Options 143
  An Example of an `smbclient` Session 144
  Connecting to a Share as Another User in Another Domain or
  Workgroup (`-W`) 147

Sending WinPopUp Messages (`-M`) 147
Debugging `smbclient` Connections (`-d`) 148
Specifying the IP Address of the SMB Server (`-I`) 150
Specifying a NetBIOS name (`-n`) 150
Default Directory to Change to (`-D`) 150
Commands to Run (`-c`) 151
Tar Options (`-T`) 151
Environment Variables 152
Using the `smbclient` Interface 152
Using `smbclient` to Print to a Windows Print Server 154
A Common Use of `smbclient`—Backing Up Windows Machines 155
Summary 156
Review Questions 157
Exercises 157

PART III: Advanced Topics   159

CHAPTER 9: Samba with SSL 161
What Is SSL and How Does It Work? 161
Certificate Signing Explained 164
How Does the Client Verify a Server-Side Certificate? 164
Creating SSL Certificates for Use with Samba .166
Setting Yourself Up as a CA 168
Installing the Certificates 171
Compiling Samba with SSL Support 172
Samba SSL Configuration 172
Using Samba with SSL 173
Other SSL `smb.conf` Parameters 175
Client Support for SSL-Configured Samba 177
Summary 177
Review Questions 178
Exercises 178

CHAPTER 10: Additional Share Level Options .181
`preexec`, `postexec` 181
What Is "Name Mangling"? 182
Parameters That Control User Access to Resources 183
`valid users`, `invalid users` 183
`write list`, `read list` 184
`force group`, `force user` 184
Parameters Related to Shares 185
`max connections` 185
`volume` 185

locking 186

copy 186

blocking locks 186

Parameters That Affect Files Located in Shared Resources 187

delete readonly 187

dont descend 187

hide files, hide dot files 187

veto files, delete veto files, veto oplock files 187

Summary 188

Review Questions 188

CHAPTER 11: Tuning Samba for Better Performance 191

Choosing a Machine to Run Samba on 191

Checking Performance 193

Samba Configuration Options 194

Compile Options 194

Socket Options 194

Opportunistic Locks (Oplocks) 195

read size 196

max xmit 196

strict sync 196

sync always 196

debug level 196

read raw 197

getwd cache 197

widelinks 197

Client-Side Tuning 197

Summary 198

Review Questions 198

CHAPTER 12: Debugging Samba 199

Common Mistakes and Troubleshooting Techniques 199

Sniffing 206

Network Monitor 207

tcpdump-smb 208

Ethereal 209

Turning On Logging 211

Samba Help Resources 213

Summary 213

Review Questions 214

CHAPTER 13: Samba Security 215

    Why Is Security So Important? 215

    Proactive Security 216

        Get the Latest Patch Levels for Your Operating System 216

        Install the Latest Stable and Secure Version of Samba 217

        Have an External Router That Filters the NetBIOS Ports 217

        Run Only the Services That You Require 218

        Implementing Security Measures on Your Samba Server 219

    Reactive Security 220

        Samba Announcement Mailing List 220

        CERT 221

        Security-Related Linux Mailing Lists 221

        BugTraq and NTBugTraq Mailing Lists 221

    Other Resources 222

    Summary 222

    Review Questions 223

CHAPTER 14: Third-Party Samba Tools 225

    `smbfs` 225

    LinPopUp 227

    The SMB Authentication Module 229

    Other SMB Utilities 230

        LinNeighborhood 231

    Summary 233

    Review Questions 234

    Exercises 234

CHAPTER 15: A Look at Samba's Future 235

    When Will Samba 2.1 Be Released and What Features Will It Contain? 235

    Operating Samba with Windows 2000 236

        New Windows 2000 Features in Samba 237

    The Future Direction of Samba Development 238

    Summary 239

    Review Questions 240

PART IV: Appendixes   **241**

APPENDIX A: A Sample CIFS/SMB Session 243

    A Summary of the Overall CIFS Process 243

    A Samba CIFS Session 244

    Summary 248

APPENDIX B: Answers to Review Questions 249
    Chapter 1 249
    Chapter 2 249
    Chapter 3 250
    Chapter 4 250
    Chapter 5 251
    Chapter 6 252
    Chapter 7 253
    Chapter 8 254
    Chapter 9 255
    Chapter 10 255
    Chapter 11 256
    Chapter 12 257
    Chapter 13 257
    Chapter 14 258
    Chapter 15 259

GLOSSARY 261

INDEX 265

ABOUT THE AUTHOR

Matthew Gillard has been working in the Information Technology field as a consultant for Cybersource Pty. Ltd. for the past five years. He has experience working for a wide range of firms, from private multinational organizations to large government departments. Matthew specializes in UNIX and Windows NT systems administration, but is becoming more involved in security-related projects. He has been a contributing author for *Red Hat Linux 6 Unleashed*, *Linux Unleashed*, and a technical editor for *Sams Teach Yourself Microsoft Exchange Server 5.0 in 10 Minutes*. Matthew lives in Australia's national capital, Canberra, with his beloved Catherine.

DEDICATION

For Catherine.

ACKNOWLEDGMENTS

I would like to thank first of all Don Roche from Sams Publishing for giving me the opportunity to write this book. I would also like to thank my Acquisitions Editor Angela Kozlowski for keeping me on track and for waiting patiently for my chapters as I finished them. Thanks to Clint McCarty, my Development Editor, for the constructive comments he provided while reviewing my work. Thanks are also due to Mike Ciavarella for being the Technical Editor. Finally, many thanks to Catherine for supporting me while I wrote this book and for her love and support.

TELL US WHAT YOU THINK!

As the reader of this book, *you* are our most important critic and commentator. We value your opinion and want to know what we're doing right, what we could do better, what areas you'd like to see us publish in, and any other words of wisdom you're willing to pass our way.

As an Associate Publisher for Sams Publishing, I welcome your comments. You can fax, email, or write me directly to let me know what you did or didn't like about this book—as well as what we can do to make our books stronger.

Please note that I cannot help you with technical problems related to the topic of this book, and that due to the high volume of mail I receive, I might not be able to reply to every message.

When you write, please be sure to include this book's title and author as well as your name and phone or fax number. I will carefully review your comments and share them with the author and editors who worked on the book.

Fax: 317-581-4770

Email: michael.stephens@macmillanusa.com

Mail: Michael Stephens
          Associate Publisher
          Sams Publishing
          201 West 103rd Street
          Indianapolis, IN 46290 USA

INTRODUCTION

Presumably, you bought this book to learn more about Samba and how you can make it work in your environment. This book is designed to complement the documentation that comes with the Samba source—in no way is it meant to replace it! The book has been written in a way that should be easy to read with real-life examples where appropriate. In my experience as a consultant, I hear the same questions and see the same mistakes all the time. I hope that I have brought the results of my experience and learning to you in a way that makes learning Samba an easier and more enjoyable experience for you.

This book was designed to benefit specific groups of individuals:

- Linux system administrators who want to be able to set up their Linux server to share files to Windows clients, rather than having to install a Windows NT server. It is likely that those companies running production Linux systems have many Windows PCs for their users. Combined, Linux and Samba provide an inexpensive way to get those users to store their data on a network server without having to introduce the cost and complexity of Windows NT servers to do this simple job that can be done for close to nothing.

- Windows NT system administrators who have heard about Linux and want to diversify their network with Linux systems to share the Windows NT load. The Linux systems running Samba can be members of an existing Windows NT domain structure, and now your Samba server can be used as a Primary Domain Controller.

- Corporate UNIX system administrators who need to provide a method of sharing resources to Windows clients. Many Oracle Financials installations require the users to export financial data in spreadsheet format and need to be transferred to the PC users. Similarly, the users sometimes have data that they need to import into Oracle, so they need to transfer it onto the UNIX server first. Samba provides an easy way to achieve this using regular Windows networking to connect network drives to the server.

Samba Primer Plus is split into four parts. It begins with three introductory chapters (Part I) to get you up and running with Samba with a minimum of complexity, moving to more advanced chapters that describe various features of Samba in more detail. This introductory section is designed to be read first. You will learn enough in this section to get Samba compiled and installed on your particular system. It then covers Samba configuration using the Samba Web Administration Tool (SWAT) including how to set up a couple of basic file-shares to get you started. The final part of this configuration chapter includes some basic troubleshooting techniques should you run into any problems.

Part II contains chapters with information on integrating Samba into an existing Windows NT environment. This section begins with some details on how Windows networking works. It covers such topics as Windows NT Domains, and unearths some misconceptions about what NetBIOS actually is and why it is used. It also goes into some details on computer browsing and the actual functions that Windows NT provides, comparing it to Samba where relevant. This background information helps you understand why Windows networking works the way it does and gives you the knowledge to implement Windows and Samba systems properly. Samba can coexist quite happily with Windows systems as you would expect. The rest of Part II goes through some techniques on integrating Samba into an existing NT environment, how to do domain logins from Windows 9x and Windows NT clients, and how to set up Samba as a Primary Domain Controller. This part ends with a discussion on a tool that comes with Samba that allows you to connect to SMB fileservers, such as Windows NT and Samba, from a UNIX (or Linux) platform.

Part III expands on the previous chapters with slightly more advanced topics. The lead chapter in this section is on using the Secure Sockets Layer (SSL) features of Samba. In a nutshell, this provides compatible SMB clients a secure encrypted channel to communicate with the Samba server. The final part goes on with more advanced options you can use when providing your fileshare resources. Next is a chapter on performance tuning your Samba server. You should note that there is not "one" method of making your Samba server improve performance. There are many variables, which include the system it is running on, what you are using Samba for, what you or your users expect out of it speed-wise, and so on. Performance tuning is a trial-and-error process. The chapter tries to convey this to you. Next is a chapter on debugging. It goes into how to use network sniffing software so you can see what Samba is doing and find out what is wrong when there is a problem. Samba security is covered next. It shows some basic security guidelines to follow when using Samba. The tail end of Part III describes some tools that are not part of Samba, but are definitely Samba-related. The final chapter describes what is planned for Samba's future.

Finally, Part IV contains two appendixes you will find useful. Appendix A is a sample CIFS/SMB session. Appendix B provides the answers to the review questions found at the end of each chapter. As one last bonus, this book concludes with a glossary of terms found throughout the book.

The aim of this book is to help you gain a deeper understanding of Samba and the underlying SMB protocol. The review questions at the end of each chapter are designed to capture the most important points out of each chapter. After reading *Samba Primer Plus*, you should be able to set up your own Samba server and troubleshoot it if you have problems. You should also be able to integrate your Samba server into a Windows NT environment, but most of all, you should gain ideas that maybe you had not thought of before that can benefit both you and your organization.

PART I

SETTING UP YOUR FIRST SAMBA

1   What Is Samba?

2   Compiling and Installing Samba

3   Basic Samba Configuration

CHAPTER 1

WHAT IS SAMBA?

You will learn about the following in this chapter:

- What Samba actually is and what it can do for you

- A history of how the SMB protocol has developed over the years

- What the SMB protocol is

- The different functions that Samba can perform

- What the CIFS protocol is

T his chapter gives you an overview of what Samba actually is, and puts into perspective how Samba fits into the "big picture" of Windows networks. At the heart of the Samba suite of programs is a free implementation of the Server Message Block (SMB) protocol. This is the protocol that is used for filesharing by the Microsoft operating systems. This chapter provides a brief history of where the SMB protocol came from and closes with a discussion on the latest incarnation of SMB—the Common Internet File System (CIFS).

An Overview of Samba

Samba is a marvelous piece of software that runs on UNIX (including the popular free UNIX implementation, Linux) and OpenVMS operating systems to allow them to function as Windows File and Print servers. This means that you can map a network drive from your Windows PC to a Samba server rather than to a conventional Windows NT server.

The first version of what we now commonly know as Samba was originally developed back in the early 90s by a man named Andrew Tridgell while he was at the Australian National University (ANU) in Canberra, Australia. He thought it would be cool to be able to use his PC to connect to a network drive that lived on one of his UNIX servers. After grabbing the relevant SMB standards (most of which are freely available) and doing a lot of reverse engineering of the undocumented parts of the protocol, Tridgell built something that was basic, but most importantly, something that worked. He found that lots of features were missing, and he slowly increased the featureset as needed. The project soon got so big that he needed other people to help, and so the Samba development team was born! After many years of development, and a great deal of reverse engineering of Microsoft's undocumented protocols, the team has built a fine solid product that has been proven in many of today's most critical commercial environments.

With the advent of Samba, if you have a mostly UNIX-based site, and there are only a few Windows desktop PCs around for specific tasks such as word processing, you can store all your files in a central location on your main UNIX server with all your other data, rather than purchasing an NT server for just this task. This provides two main advantages:

1. You can keep your organization running with UNIX at the back end but still allow easy integration with your Windows client machines.

2. If you already have a UNIX Enterprise backup system in place, you need not change anything. You just need to make sure that the new areas where you are storing the Windows files are added to your backup regime.

Today, you can build a PC file server for your site for the price of only the hardware, and of course initial system administration costs. Of course, you need an operating system, but why pay for it? An alternative that many small and large companies are choosing is Linux. If you have not heard about Linux by now, you must have been lying under a rock for the past few years! The reason this choice of operating system is so popular these days is that Linux is free and extremely stable. In fact, Linux is proven to outperform and is actually more stable than any of the Windows operating systems. This is probably the reason why two large corporations, IBM and HP, are now supporting Linux on their Intel-based servers. You will find that they will be followed by many other companies cashing in on providing commercial Linux support. Armed with the Linux distribution of your choice, it is becoming easier to install, configure, and receive Enterprise-level support (if you choose to) for a fraction of the cost of an equivalent Microsoft system, but you still have a stable box that needs little maintenance and can serve files to your Windows clients (both Win95/98 and WinNT 4.0/2000).

To make it dead easy for you, it is probably safe to say that all the Linux distributions come with Samba precompiled, and with a little configuration, Samba can be up and running before you know it. There will be more on this in the next chapter. First, it is useful to know a little history on what the SMB protocol is and why it is so important in today's corporate networks.

What Is the SMB Protocol?

The Server Message Block (SMB) protocol has been around for well over ten years. SMB is an application-level protocol that can run over network layer protocols, such as IPX/SPX, TCP/IP, and NetBEUI. In simple terms, it provides a way of giving a Windows PC the capability to communicate with another Windows machine's file system over a network. Consider the example shown in Figure 1.1.

FIGURE 1.1

The concept of the SMB protocol.

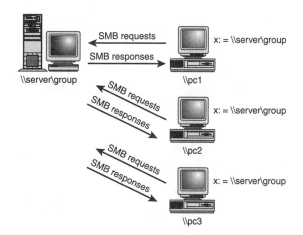

The client machine's pc1, pc2, and pc3 are all connecting to the shared resource on "server" called \\server\group. Both the SMB clients and server participate in an exchange of SMB packets with the end result being, in this case, that all the clients have drive letter X: mapped to this resource. Although it looks like a local drive, it really isn't; it is a drive letter that is redirected by the operating system to the remote machine. This simple example should give you a taste for the way the SMB protocol is used.

The SMB protocol is at work in our lives daily. Most of us have a computer on our desk with a number of network drives connected to numerous servers around the office. These servers are usually running the Windows NT operating system, and that is why the SMB protocol is in such widespread use today.

A Brief History of the SMB Protocol

What I will describe is the abridged version of the history of the SMB protocol, so you can get a feel for how SMB evolved over the years.

IBM developed one of the very first versions of the SMB protocol in the mid-80s, and then it was called the PCLAN 1.0 protocol. Microsoft and Intel obtained this PCLAN 1.0 standard and modified it for their own needs, and it then formed the core of a file-sharing protocol later to be known as SMB. They renamed it OpenNET/MSNET at that stage. This original core protocol contains the most basic SMB commands intended for use with MS-DOS such as OPEN file, CREATE file, CLOSE file, DELETE file, and so on.

Soon after, a document was released that was an extension to this OpenNET/MSNET protocol, which was in fact created for use in Microsoft's OS/2 operating system. This document was called "SMB Protocol Extensions," and the official version of the SMB protocol referenced in this document is LANMAN 1.0. This extended SMB protocol contained new SMB commands such as FIND, COPY_FILE, and MOVE_FILE. Many new commands intended for use with OS/2 were also documented. LANMAN 1.0 also introduced the concepts of share-level security and user-level security.

With *share-level security*, a resource on a server is available to anyone on the local LAN. This resource can be password-protected or not. If it is protected with a password, anyone who knows the password is granted access.

With *user level security*, a user ID and password must be entered before access to a resource is given. Of course, this provides more security because anyone who does not have a registered login to the LAN cannot access shared resources on the network at all—unless of course they have acquired someone's login name and password.

It was LANMAN version 1.0 that first used the challenge/response method of user authentication that is in widespread use by Windows NT today.

The next version that came along was the LANMAN 1.2 protocol, which extended the LANMAN 1.0 protocol. Again, it contained extensions for use with OS/2, but was designed to apply equally well to other operating systems also. This was a minor update and later known as LANMAN 2.0.

LANMAN 2.1 was released a while later and further revised the protocol to add support for Windows NT domains (domains will be described in Chapter 4, "Understanding Windows NT Networks"). The Windows for Workgroups 3.1a dialect followed, which contains Windows-specific SMB commands.

Microsoft ditched OS/2 in favor of building a new, secure operating system, which we now know as Windows NT. It realized it needed a much more secure version of the LANMAN 2.1 protocol for Windows NT to have any chance of becoming a secure Network Operating System (NOS). The old LANMAN family of protocols contained specifications not just for the SMB protocol, but also included details on methods of authentication as well. The first authentication methods sent the password in clear text, which obviously was not ideal! Later, a simple challenge/response method was used for password authentication. But still, even with the challenge/response methods, problems were identified:

- Challenge/Response authentication is susceptible to known plaintext attacks.

- It has a very small keyspace (case-insensitive passwords).

- It is susceptible to chosen plaintext attacks.

- It is susceptible to dictionary attacks.

- Part of the encryption used a known key that made it possible to reverse the encryption and find out the password anyway.

- It allows users to choose "bad" passwords.

A Word About Cryptoanalysis

Here's a short lesson in Cryptoanalysis to make sure you understand the different methods of plaintext password attacks. First, *Cryptoanalysis* is the science of recovering plaintext from ciphertext without the use of the original encryption key. However, this process commonly unlocks the key anyway. Assume you have a plaintext password that goes through a magic cryptographic algorithm and produces ciphertext, or in this case a password hash.

A *known* plaintext attack occurs when you have some given plaintext password and the associated password hash combinations, and you attempt to break the encryption using only this information.

A *chosen* plaintext attack is similar, but this time you can choose the plaintext to be encrypted. This gives you more variety when choosing the plaintext/password hash pairs; therefore, you have a better chance to be able to pick up common elements between all the password/password hash pairs.

If you are interested in more information on cryptography in general, I highly recommend you pick up a copy of *Applied Cryptography* by Bruce Schneier (ISBN: 0471117099) from your favorite bookstore. It is the industry bible on this topic.

Because of these shortcomings, an improved version of the LANMAN protocol for NT was developed, called NT LM 0.12. It contains Windows NT-specific SMB commands that map to the NT file system calls, including a much improved authentication method—and it uses a one-way function that "theoretically" cannot be decrypted.

In 1998, Microsoft addressed many shortcomings in the NT LM protocol and released a further improved version as part of Service Pack 4 for Windows NT. This is known as NTLMv2.

Table 1.1 gives a summary of all the different dialects as documented by Microsoft.

TABLE 1.1 The Various Dialects of the SMB Protocol

Dialect Name	Description
PC NETWORK PROGRAM 1.0	The core MSNET SMB protocol
PCLAN1.0	An alternative name to the core protocol
MICROSOFT NETWORKS 1.03	Extensions to the core protocol to include Lock&Read and Write&Unlock.
LANMAN1.0	Full LANMAN 1.0 Protocol (OS/2 errors)
MICROSOFT NETWORKS 3.0	Same as LANMAN1.0 except errors are mapped to DOS errors
LM1.2X002	Full LANMAN 2.0 Protocol (OS/2 errors)
DOS LM1.2X002	Same as LANMAN 2.0 except errors are mapped to DOS errors
LANMAN2.1	Full LANMAN 2.1 protocol (OS/2 errors)
DOS LANMAN2.1	Same as LANMAN 2.1 except errors are mapped to DOS errors
Windows for Workgroups 3.1a	Windows for Workgroups version 1.0 specification
NT LM 0.12	First version of the SMB protocol for use in Windows NT environments

For more technical details on these protocols, refer to Appendix A, "A Sample CIFS/SMB Session."

Samba's Main Functions

You probably want to know how Samba fits into what we have been talking about. Samba functions in five main ways:

- Acts as an SMB server

- Performs NetBIOS Name Resolution

- Performs user authentication

- Provides Computer Browser service

- Performs domain login capabilities for Windows 9x and Windows NT clients

SMB Server

The core of the Samba suite of programs is the Samba daemon, `smbd`. Essentially, Samba speaks a dialect of the NT LM 0.12 protocol, but of course can also speak all the earlier LAN-MAN dialects as well if older clients need to talk to Samba servers.

NetBIOS Name Resolution

SMB relies on some type of naming services being available so that it can map server names to a network address. For historical reasons, SMB requires NetBIOS for its name service. NetBIOS itself is not a protocol, although some people mistakenly refer to it as one—it is a network programming Application Programming Interface (API). There are even two Request For Comments (RFCs) that describe how NetBIOS should operate in a TCP/IP environment (RFC 1001 and 1002). Figure 1.2 shows where SMB and NetBIOS fit into the standard OSI network stack.

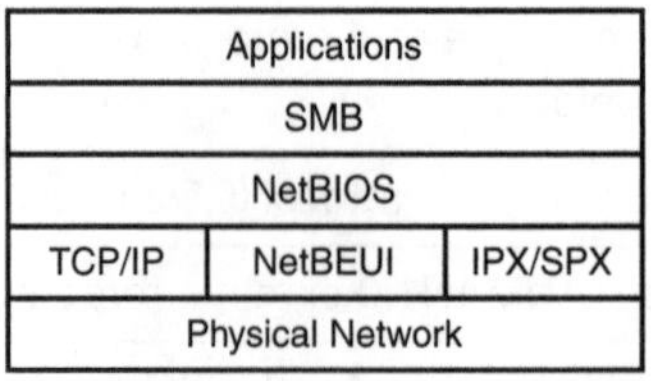

FIGURE 1.2
SMB and NetBIOS in the traditional network stack.

Applications		
SMB		
NetBIOS		
TCP/IP	NetBEUI	IPX/SPX
Physical Network		

All Windows machines have what is called a NetBIOS name, which is 16 bytes long. The first 15 bytes are an ASCII name, and the 16th byte at the end is reserved for describing the service that is advertising the name on the machine. Each NetBIOS application is assigned a number between <00> and <FF> that is unique for that application and is called a NetBIOS resource type. Each Windows machine has what is known as a NetBIOS Name Table. Entries in this name table include the domain or workgroup the machine is in, the different NetBIOS applications on the machine, which is designated by the NetBIOS resource type code, and the username of the currently logged in user (if someone is logged in at the time you do a NetBIOS name listing). You can get a NetBIOS listing of any computer on your local LAN by simply entering the `nbtstat` command and giving a `<netbios name>` as the argument, as in the following example:

```
C:\>nbtstat -a daffy
        NetBIOS Remote Machine Name Table
```

```
    Name              Type      Status
    ---------------------------------------------
    DAFFY        <00>  UNIQUE    Registered
    DAFFY        <20>  UNIQUE    Registered
    HOME         <00>  GROUP     Registered
    HOME         <1C>  GROUP     Registered
    HOME         <1B>  UNIQUE    Registered
    HOME         <1E>  GROUP     Registered
    DAFFY        <03>  UNIQUE    Registered
    INet~Services <1C> GROUP     Registered
    IS~DAFFY.......<00> UNIQUE   Registered
    HOME         <1D>  UNIQUE    Registered
    ..__MSBROWSE__.<01> GROUP    Registered
    ADMINISTRATOR <03> UNIQUE    Registered

    MAC Address = 00-C0-A8-47-F1-1E
```

As you can see, you can gather a lot of information about a computer with this command! In this particular example, the computer name is DAFFY, the user Administrator is logged in currently, and the machine belongs to the Windows NT Domain, HOME. Also, Microsoft's Internet Information Server is installed. You can tell this because the NetBIOS name, Inet~Services is registered. If you want more information on NetBIOS, skip to Chapter 4, which goes into a little more detail on NetBIOS. But for now, you just need to know that NetBIOS is implemented in Samba with the server program **nmbd**, and the accompanying client program **nmblookup** (similar in function to **nbtstat**).

User Authentication

As mentioned previously, there have been three versions of authentication protocols over the years of SMB evolution: Plaintext, LAN Manager challenge/response, and NT LM challenge/response. All these are supported by Samba through the main daemon, **smbd**.

Computer Browser

Something I have not touched on yet that is related to the NetBIOS name services is the Computer Browser service. NetBIOS is a very broadcast-oriented service, which originates from its beginnings when it was coupled with NetBEUI. Even though TCP/IP is a routable protocol, NetBIOS broadcasts go only to the local LAN. You can browse Microsoft networks when looking for a particular resource to which to connect. Browsing the network means that all the workgroups and domains are listed in a browsing screen, and you can click down each layer until you get to the resource you want. How is this browselist created—especially when today's networks are very segmented and NetBIOS broadcasts only get sent to a single subnet? One option is to allow all NetBIOS broadcast traffic through all your routers. This is most probably a bad idea. You do not want any extra traffic on your network if you can help it! Microsoft realized there was a problem here, so it introduced the concept of a Master Computer Browser. This is a NetBIOS service that can be run on any Windows machine. (This is usually self-tuning; if a machine determines there is no master browser on a subnet, an election is forced that determines who will be the master browser.) The master browser keeps track of all the

NetBIOS names on a physical LAN segment. There are other computer browsers on other physical LAN segments that do the same thing. When all the Computer Browsers share information with each other, you can see that the network effectively gets mapped so that no matter what LAN segment you are on, you can talk to pretty much any other machine by name. Samba also provides computer-browsing services via the `nmbd` daemon. More information on computer browsing is given in Chapter 4.

Domain Logins

A quite useful function is the capability of Samba to provide domain login services for Windows 9x clients, and more recently Windows NT clients. The latter is provided through Samba's experimental PDC functionality, which at the time of writing is still in Beta test, but works quite well. This domain functionality includes such things as login scripts, roving user profiles, and much more. I discuss how to use Samba's domain login functionality in Chapters 6 and 7.

What Is CIFS?

By now you probably have heard something about CIFS. In fact, many people use the term interchangeably with SMB. It stands for "Common Internet File System." Microsoft has devised CIFS to replace the NT LM 0.12 protocol. CIFS is currently an Internet Draft with the Internet Engineering Task Force (IETF), so the standard is open to review by anyone who chooses to download it. You can read it online at `ftp://ftp.microsoft.com/developr/drg/CIFS/` `draft-leach-cifs-v1-spec-01.txt`. One major feature that the draft standard dictates is that NetBIOS will no longer be a requirement for the file-sharing aspect of the protocol. Finally, this means that CIFS will be able to use Domain Name Server (DNS) to resolve server names, just as the rest of the world does! A partial implementation of CIFS is in Windows NT 4.0. In Windows NT 4.0, you can map a drive using an IP address or fully qualified domain name, but NetBIOS still has to be there. Microsoft has promised that a full version of CIFS that does not require NetBIOS will appear in Windows 2000, released in February 2000.

Summary

The aim of this chapter was to give you an introduction to what Samba is, what it does, and why it exists. You have learned that Samba was created to be able to access files on a UNIX-based server from a Windows PC. The project grew to a point where it emulates what Microsoft describes as a LAN Manager server, including many domain controller functions.

You have read that the SMB protocol as we know it today has gone through many revisions over the last decade, and the revisions are continuing to the next generation of SMB, called CIFS.

Finally, you learned that Samba performs five main functions: It acts as an SMB server, performs NetBIOS name resolution, does user authentication, provides computer browsing services, and provides domain login functions for Windows 9x and Windows NT clients. And the next area that is currently being worked on is total Windows 2000 compatibility. The eventual aim is that you will be able to plug a Samba server into your network, and your end users should not even know that the server where their files are stored has no Windows operating system on it at all.

In the next two chapters, you will be able to get your hands dirty and get a working version of Samba running on your own Linux system, be it at work or at home. If you are running another UNIX-based operating system at work, Samba will run on it as well. The practical examples in this book should work on whatever UNIX system you are using with minimal changes required.

Review Questions

1. What is Samba, and why is it becoming so popular?

2. What is the SMB protocol?

3. Samba provides five main services. Name them.

4. What is the Common Internet File System protocol?

CHAPTER 2

COMPILING AND INSTALLING SAMBA

You will learn about the following in this chapter:

- The procedure to go about installing Samba on your system

- The differences between precompiled packages and compiling Samba yourself

- How to download a precompiled Samba package and install it on your system

- How to download the Samba source

- How to compile and install Samba from the source code

I n this chapter, you will learn how to actually install Samba on your system. There are basically two methods; both will be described, as well as some hints on which method might suit your needs best. The first method is to download a precompiled package and install and configure it. Alternatively, as with most open source applications, you can grab the source code and compile it yourself. Due to the popularity of Linux, most of my examples will be based on a Red Hat Linux 6.0 system, but will probably apply equally to other UNIX systems as well. Differences will be noted where appropriate. For those of you who are interested in installing Linux, go to `http://www.redhat.com` for information on where your nearest Red Hat stocklist is.

How Do I Install Samba?

After you have read the first chapter and realized how appropriate Samba is to solve your business problems, you probably want to jump right into it! However, there is one major question to answer. That is, do you want to install a precompiled Samba package, or compile the Samba source code?

If you are running a PC-based UNIX such as Linux or FreeBSD, a precompiled package is almost the mandatory method to use. For details regarding this method, see the next section, "Downloading Precompiled Packages."

However, if you want to install Samba on a high-powered corporate UNIX server including (but not limited to) HP/UX, Solaris, or Digital UNIX (now known as Tru64 UNIX), in most cases the only option you have is to compile the Samba source code. For more information, see the section, "Downloading the Samba Source," later in this chapter.

Downloading Precompiled Packages

Your first question is probably: What is a precompiled package? The way a precompiled package works is that you download a single file (or it could be provided on a CD-ROM) that contains all the information needed to install the product, in this case Samba. To make the definition more confusing for you, almost every UNIX distribution out there has a different method of making these prepackaged files. To make things easier, Table 2.1 lists the most commonly used UNIX variants and the method of precompiled packages that they use.

TABLE 2.1   UNIX Variant and Package Format Used

UNIX Variant	Package Format
Red Hat Linux	Red Hat Package Manager (.rpm)
Debian Linux	Debian Package Management System (.deb)
SUSE Linux	Red Hat Package Manager (.rpm)
Caldera OpenSystems Linux	Red Hat Package Manager (.rpm)
Solaris	pkgadd format
HP/UX	Depot format
AIX	SMIT (ldd)
SCO OpenServer 5	SCO Software Manager (custom)
UnixWare 7	pkgadd

Precompiled packages are generally the preference when installing software today. There are a few reasons for this:

- It is easier for beginners to install a piece of software if all they need to do is download a package file and run a single command to install it.

- Both the Samba executable files and configuration files automatically get put in a consistent place.

- When a new version of software gets released, someone else goes to the effort of compiling and porting it if needed (see the following sidebar), and then packages it.

- When you upgrade your Linux or other UNIX variant operating system to a later release, vendor-provided packages automatically get upgraded as part of the operating system upgrade process. Even if some of your packages are not vendor provided, there is a good chance someone will contribute an updated version that works with the new version of the operating system.

If I Am "Porting" Some Software, What Does That Mean?

If you are wondering what "Software Porting" is all about, let me explain. John has access to a Linux box for development purposes. He develops the software on that system and it works fine. John then makes his newly developed software available for public download. Ben comes along and thinks this software looks pretty neat, and he decides to download it and compile it on his system. Poor Ben only has an IBM AIX box and finds out that John's software does not compile. Luckily, Ben has many years of experience with AIX and finds out that a system call used in the software is unavailable in AIX, but he quickly finds an equivalent. He modifies the source with his changes and soon has it compiled and ready to run. Before Ben forgets, he does a `diff` of the changes he made, and sends them to John to include in the main distribution. This means that the next person to download the software who runs the AIX operating system just has to make a change in the Makefile to tell it to compile for his particular architecture.

This process is known as "porting." It is safe to say that because of porting, Samba is available on many different UNIX platforms today. In fact, it is also available on Compaq's OpenVMS operating system.

There are also some reasons why you may not want to choose a precompiled package:

- There might be times when you want to make a feature unavailable, and the only sure way to do this is to disable this unwanted feature before compilation.

- You might want to optimize certain parts of an application for your particular server hardware. For example, a program optimized on an original Pentium system may not be totally optimized for the newer Pentium II or Pentium III architectures.

- There might be a business need to add a new feature to an application. You cannot do this if all you have is a compiled application with no source code.

Where to Get Samba Packages

When you have decided that you want to install a precompiled Samba package, you need to either download one or install it from your vendor-provided CD-ROM. The method you use pretty much depends on the variant of UNIX you are running. If you use one of the free variants of UNIX such as Linux, it will almost certainly be on your CD-ROM. However, be careful! If you have an older version of your operating system CD lying around, it most likely does not have the latest version of Samba on it. With Samba, you should try to install the latest production quality release, which at the time of this writing is version 2.0.6. There are several reasons for this:

- The latest version will generally be the most bug-free, which means you should get it up and running more quickly than it would if a bug were stopping it from working in your environment.

- A version of software, such as Samba, on an earlier version of the operating system CD-ROM may not be optimized for the newer UNIX kernel on the more recent system.

- All the latest security patches will be applied.

The version name is always clearly identified as part of the filename of the package. For example, on Red Hat Linux 6.0, the Samba package included on the Red Hat 6.0 CD-ROM is called `samba-2.0.3-8.i386.rpm` (found in /RedHat/Rpms). To make it easy to find the most up-to-date (not necessarily the latest) Samba package for your UNIX system, refer to Table 2.2. This should give you a start without having to search for it yourself. In Table 2.2, where appropriate, replace `architecture` with the hardware type of your UNIX variant, for example, for PCs use i386.

TABLE 2.2   Where to Download a Precompiled Samba Package

UNIX Variant	URL
Red Hat Linux 6.0	`ftp://updates.redhat.com/6.0/`*`architecture`*`/`
Debian Linux	`ftp://ftp.debian.org/pub/debian/dists/stable/main/`*`architecture`*`/net/`
SUSE Linux 6.1	`ftp://ftp.suse.com/pub/suse/`*`architecture`*`/` `update/6.1/n1/samba.rpm`
Caldera Linux 2.2	`ftp://ftp.caldera.com/pub/OpenLinux/updates/2.2/` `current/RPMS`
FreeBSD 3.0	`ftp://ftp.freebsd.org/pub/FreeBSD/packages/All`
Solaris 7	`http://sunfreeware.com/`
NetBSD 1.4.1	`ftp://ftp.netbsd.org/pub/NetBSD/packages/` `1.4.1/i386/All`
AIX 4.3.2 (or later)	`http://www-frec.bull.fr/cgi-bin/list_dir.cgi/` `download/aix432/`
SCO (Open Server) and UnixWare 7	`http://www.sco.com/skunkware/uw2/` `www/www/uw7/samba/`

If your flavor of UNIX is not listed, a final place to look is at `ftp://samba.org/pub/samba/Binary_Packages/`. If it is not there either, there probably is no precompiled Samba package available for your platform. If this is the case, you should probably skip to the section "Downloading the Samba Source." This is not such a bad thing because Samba is fairly easy to compile for pretty much any UNIX platforms.

As an example, I will go through the downloading and installation steps for one of the more popular Linux distributions, Red Hat Linux. You can either use the Samba package on your Red Hat CD-ROM, or download the latest one from `ftp://updates.redhat.com/6.0/i386/` `samba-2.0.5a-1.i386.rpm`.

Installing Precompiled Packages

Now that you have the Samba binaries downloaded as a package, you need to install it. If you are running Red Hat Linux, all you need to do is go to the directory to which you downloaded the package, and enter the command:

```
# rpm -iv samba-2.0.5a-1.i386.rpm
```

This command will install all the Samba binaries, documentation, and sample configurations, as well as needed directories, such as spool and lock directories.

If you are unsure of what command to use on your system if you downloaded a precompiled package as detailed in the previous section, refer to Table 2.3.

TABLE 2.3   How to Install Precompiled Samba Packages

UNIX Variant	Install Command
Red Hat Linux 6.0	`rpm -iv` *package name*
Debian Linux	`dpkg --install` *package name*
SUSE Linux 6.1	`rpm -iv` *package name*
Caldera Linux 2.2	`rpm -iv` *package name*
Solaris 7	`pkgadd -d` *package name*
AIX 4.3.2 (or later)	Use the smit interface
SCO (Open Server) & UnixWare 7	`pkgadd -d` *package name*

If all you want to do is install a precompiled Samba package, you can skip ahead to Chapter 3, "Basic Samba Configuration." Otherwise, if you are interested in compiling Samba yourself, or if that's the only option you have, keep reading.

Downloading the Samba Source

For one reason or another, you may want to compile Samba from source code. This is one of the many benefits of open source software projects—if it is not available in a precompiled form on your platform, you can compile it yourself! Remember, it does not matter which UNIX platform you are running; you still just download the one source code distribution.

The first step is to go to `http://www.samba.org` and select the Samba mirror site geographically closest to you. Then click the download link and there should be another link called `samba-latest.tar.gz`. Click that and wait for it to download.

What Do the Different File Extensions Mean?

If you are new in the UNIX world and have maybe just started using Linux, you are probably wondering what the different letters on the end of the filenames mean. As in Windows, a file extension usually is used to give you an idea of what format the file is in.

A filename called `file.gz` is a compressed file. The "gz" signifies the compressing program used was `gzip`. It can be uncompressed with the following:

```
$ gunzip file.gz
```

A file called `file.tar` is a UNIX tar archive of many different files. It was created with a program called `tar`. A tar file can be unarchived with the command:

```
$ tar -xf file.tar
```

A file called `file.tar.gz` was put into a `tar` archive first, then compressed with `gzip`. Sometimes these files are also called `file.tgz`. If you are running Linux, you can uncompress and unarchive in one step:

```
$ tar -xzf file.tar.gz
```

If you are running one of the commercial operating systems you can do it this way:

```
$ gunzip -c file.tar.gz | tar -xf -
```

The -c tells `gunzip` to uncompress to standard output, which is then piped into the `tar` command to extract each file.

After you have the Samba source downloaded, you can unpack it with the following command:

```
# gunzip -c samba-latest.tar.gz | tar -xvf -
```

It should create a directory depending on what the current version is similar to **samba-2.0.5a**.

Compiling Samba

Begin by looking at the structure of the Samba directory tree:

```
# ls -l
total 61
-rw-r--r--   1 1002     1002        17982 May  4  1996 COPYING
-rw-r--r--   1 1002     1002         3311 Nov 24  1998 Manifest
-rw-r--r--   1 1002     1002         6569 Jul 21 11:23 README
-rw-r--r--   1 1002     1002         2402 Feb 26  1999 README-smbmount
-rw-r--r--   1 1002     1002            0 Aug 21  1997 Read-Manifest-Now
-rw-r--r--   1 1002     1002         1891 May 15 12:03 Roadmap
-rw-r--r--   1 1002     1002        19494 Jul 22 12:06 WHATSNEW.txt
drwxr-xr-x   7 1002     1002         1024 Jul 21 11:23 docs
drwxr-xr-x  12 1002     1002         1024 Jul 22 12:07 examples
drwxr-xr-x  12 1002     1002         1024 May 20 05:32 packaging
drwxr-xr-x  25 1002     1002         1024 Jul 22 12:15 source
drwxr-xr-x   5 1002     1002         1024 May 20 05:33 swat
```

The README files generally give important information regarding the release of Samba. They also detail any important changes since the latest release, including mentioning things that may be incompatible.

The **docs** directory is self-explanatory. It contains a lot of contributed Samba documentation, which has grown increasingly since the Samba project began. It is always the first place to look if you cannot get something working correctly.

The directory **examples** has some examples of Samba configuration files for particular environments. It is also worth a look if you are having problems.

The **packaging** directory contains scripts to help create operating-system-dependent precompiled package files (mentioned in detail in the previous sections on precompiled packages). This is useful if, after you have compiled Samba, you want to make your binaries easily usable by someone without them having to compile it themselves.

The source directory is where all the Samba source lives. It is also the directory where you compile Samba.

Finally, the **swat** directory is where the Samba Web Administration Tool lives. More on using this will be in the next chapter, "Basic Samba Configuration."

To compile Samba, you first need to change to the source directory. As with many open source projects today, a lot of the precompiling configuration required is automatically done for you with the supplied **configure** program.

How Samba Was Configured Before the Automatic Method That Is in Place Now

Previous versions of Samba (prior to the 2.0 series) required tweaking of a Makefile for certain configuration options such as the installation directory, and other options dependent on what UNIX system you were compiling it on. With the advent of the 2.0 series of Samba, this is taken care of for you by the GNU **configure** program. If you are familiar with the older Samba distributions, you will find the configure process a breath of fresh air!

The **configure** program provides certain advantages over the former method of directly editing a Makefile:

- No knowledge of any details of the host UNIX platform is required. When executed, **configure** automatically configures a Makefile streamlined for the UNIX system it is being run on.

- **configure** automatically detects what libraries and **include** files are installed on the system, and configures a Makefile accordingly. No more getting to the end of a compilation to find you have a needed library file missing.

- If **configure** detects that you do not have a needed library or other dependency that is required for a successful compilation, it prompts you telling you what it needs, and does not create a Makefile until everything is there.

In its simplest form, you just need to execute **configure** like this:

```
[root@pinkie /usr/local/src/samba-2.0.5a/source] # ./configure
```

However, there may be a few flags you want to specify to `configure`. You can get a list of the configure options that the Samba `configure` knows about with the command shown in Listing 2.1.

LISTING 2.1   Producing a List of the Configure Options

```
[root@pinkie /usr/local/src/samba-2.0.5a/source] # ./configure --help
Usage: configure [options] [host]
Options: [defaults in brackets after descriptions]
Configuration:
  --cache-file=FILE      cache test results in FILE
  --help                 print this message
  --no-create            do not create output files
  --quiet, --silent      do not print `checking...' messages
  --version              print the version of autoconf that created configure
Directory and file names:
  --prefix=PREFIX        install architecture-independent files in PREFIX
                         [/usr/local/samba]
  --exec-prefix=EPREFIX  install architecture-dependent files in EPREFIX
                         [same as prefix]
  --bindir=DIR           user executables in DIR [EPREFIX/bin]
  --sbindir=DIR          system admin executables in DIR [EPREFIX/sbin]
  --libexecdir=DIR       program executables in DIR [EPREFIX/libexec]
  --datadir=DIR          read-only architecture-independent data in DIR
                         [PREFIX/share]
  --sysconfdir=DIR       read-only single-machine data in DIR [PREFIX/etc]
  --sharedstatedir=DIR   modifiable architecture-independent data in DIR
                         [PREFIX/com]
  --localstatedir=DIR    modifiable single-machine data in DIR [PREFIX/var]
  --libdir=DIR           object code libraries in DIR [EPREFIX/lib]
  --includedir=DIR       C header files in DIR [PREFIX/include]
  --oldincludedir=DIR    C header files for non-gcc in DIR [/usr/include]
  --infodir=DIR          info documentation in DIR [PREFIX/info]
  --mandir=DIR           man documentation in DIR [PREFIX/man]
  --srcdir=DIR           find the sources in DIR [configure dir or ..]
  --program-prefix=PREFIX prepend PREFIX to installed program names
  --program-suffix=SUFFIX append SUFFIX to installed program names
  --program-transform-name=PROGRAM
                         run sed PROGRAM on installed program names
Host type:
  --build=BUILD          configure for building on BUILD [BUILD=HOST]
  --host=HOST            configure for HOST [guessed]
  --target=TARGET        configure for TARGET [TARGET=HOST]
Features and packages:
  --disable-FEATURE      do not include FEATURE (same as --enable-FEATURE=no)
  --enable-FEATURE[=ARG] include FEATURE [ARG=yes]
  --with-PACKAGE[=ARG]   use PACKAGE [ARG=yes]
  --without-PACKAGE      do not use PACKAGE (same as --with-PACKAGE=no)
  --x-includes=DIR       X include files are in DIR
  --x-libraries=DIR      X library files are in DIR
  --enable and --with options recognized:
  --enable-maintainer-mode enable some make rules for maintainers
```

```
--with-smbwrapper           Include SMB wrapper support
--without-smbwrapper        Don't include SMB wrapper support (default)
--with-afs                  Include AFS support
--without-afs               Don't include AFS support (default)
--with-dfs                  Include DFS support
--without-dfs               Don't include DFS support (default)
--with-krb4=base-dir        Include Kerberos 4 support
--whithout-krb4             Don't include Kerberos 4 support (default)
--with-krb5=base-dir        Include Kerberos 5 support
--whithout-krb5             Don't include Kerberos 5 support (default)
--with-automount            Include AUTOMOUNT support
--without-automount         Don't include AUTOMOUNT support (default)
--with-smbmount             Include SMBMOUNT (Linux only) support
--without-smbmount          Don't include SMBMOUNT support (default)
--with-pam                  Include PAM password database support
--without-pam               Don't include PAM password database support (default)
--with-ldap                 Include LDAP support
--without-ldap              Don't include LDAP support (default)
--with-nisplus              Include NISPLUS password database support
--without-nisplus           Don't include NISPLUS password database support (default)
--with-nisplus-home         Include NISPLUS_HOME support
--with-ssl                  Include SSL support
--without-ssl               Don't include SSL support (default)
--with-sslinc=DIR           Where the SSL includes are (defaults to /usr/local/ssl)
--with-mmap                 Include experimental MMAP support
--without-mmap              Don't include MMAP support (default)
--with-syslog               Include experimental SYSLOG support
--without-syslog            Don't include SYSLOG support (default)
--with-netatalk             Include experimental Netatalk support
--without-netatalk          Don't include experimental Netatalk support (default)
--with-quotas               Include experimental disk-quota support
--without-quotas            Don't include experimental disk-quota support (default)
--with-privatedir=DIR       Where to put smbpasswd (/usr/local/samba/private)
--with-lockdir=DIR          Where to put lock files (/usr/local/samba/var/locks)
--with-swatdir=DIR          Where to put SWAT files (/usr/local/samba/swat)
```

As you can see, there are many options. Many of them are for compiling with special features for testing purposes, and these options would not normally be enabled for normal production use. Also, at the end of some of the options, you see the default setting. This indicates which options are enabled by default, and where appropriate, their default values. You can override any option if needed. The most useful option to modify would be `--prefix`. The default is to install everything under /usr/local/samba. This option allows you to replace this with whatever directory path you like. For example, your site standard could be to place all third-party applications in separate directories under /opt. If this is the case, you would execute configure like this:

```
[root@pinkie /usr/local/src/samba-2.0.5a/source] # ./configure --prefix=/opt/samba
```

As the `configure` program executes, you will notice that it performs many different tasks. It should finish like this:

```
[ ... ]
checking configure summary
```

```
configure OK
updating cache ./config.cache
creating ./config.status
creating include/stamp-h
creating Makefile
creating include/config.h
[root@pinkie /usr/local/src/samba-2.0.5a/source] #
```

Notice that the very last task is to actually create the Makefile with the information collected in the configuration process.

Now that you have a Makefile, it is just a simple matter of typing:

```
[root@pinkie /usr/local/src/samba-2.0.5a/source] # make
```

Then you wait for the compilation to complete.

What to Do if make Returns an Error

If you type make and you get the following message:

```
make: *** No targets.  Stop.
```

Either you have not run the `configure` program, or the configure process did not complete successfully. If you get any errors during the configure process, make sure that you fix whatever the problem is and run `configure` again until it completes successfully. If the configure did not complete successfully, the file `config.log` is usually a good place to look for reasons why it failed.

Installing Samba

After you have Samba compiled, you need to install it. You can do this by typing:

```
[root@pinkie /usr/local/src/samba-2.0.5a/source] # make install
```

This installs all the Samba binaries and manual pages in all the right places. If the command finds any old versions of Samba files lying around, it automatically renames them with an `.old` filename extension. Should the new version break things on your system really badly, you can back out with the following command:

```
[root@pinkie /usr/local/src/samba-2.0.5a/source] # make revert
```

This will rename all the newly installed files with a `.new` extension, and remove the `.old` extension from the old files renamed when you did the original install. You will be able to return to your old configuration seamlessly, and things should be working as they did before.

Some people like installing parts of a program separately. If that's your preference, you can do this:

```
[root@pinkie /usr/local/src/samba-2.0.5a/source] # make installbin
```

to install the program binaries only, or

```
[root@pinkie /usr/local/src/samba-2.0.5a/source] # make installman
```

to install the manual pages only.

By now, you have done all the hard work. All that is left is to get Samba installed in your system startup files, but don't worry, it is actually fairly simple as you are about to find out.

Samba at Startup

It is all very well to get Samba installed on your system, but it is not actually very useful until you notify your system startup files to start Samba up on bootup. You can do this by one of two methods. You can either configure Samba to start from `inetd`, effectively running each time a session is requested, or by using a startup control script where it is running all the time as a dedicated daemon. The main disadvantage with starting Samba from `inetd` is that it takes an extra amount of time for `inetd` to figure out which daemon is to process a particular incoming connection. This is opposed to running Samba as a dedicated daemon so that when an incoming connection occurs, all that needs to be done is to begin processing the connection immediately. If you have a low-end server and are only using Samba occasionally, it probably makes sense to allow `inetd` to start it on demand, thereby saving memory that you can use for other things. On the other hand, if your Samba server will be continually getting used and Samba is effectively running all the time anyway, you would almost certainly choose to run it as a dedicated daemon.

If you are unsure of which method to use, most people generally run the Samba daemon all the time by using a startup file at bootup. The main reason for this is that the price of memory is effectively insignificant in the overall price of a server, and you can afford to have some unused network daemons running.

Running Samba from `inetd`

Running Samba from `inetd` is probably the least common method; however, it is still useful in some circumstances. Many network services are configured to run from a program called `inetd`, which listens on particular ports for activity. When activity is noticed on one of these ports `inetd` is listening to, it starts the particular network daemon that services that port. An example would be when remotely logging into a machine with `telnet`. `inetd` notices an incoming connection to port 23 (the standard `telnet` port) and starts up the `telnetd` daemon, which then services the `telnet` connection until it is disconnected.

This involves editing the file `/etc/inetd.conf` and adding an entry for the main Samba server similar to:

```
netbios-ssn  stream  tcp    nowait  root    /usr/sbin/tcpd
➥/usr/local/samba/bin/smbd
```

And also an entry for the NetBIOS Nameserver daemon, which would look something like this:

```
netbios-ns  stream  tcp    nowait  root    /usr/sbin/tcpd
➥/usr/local/samba/bin/nmbd
```

The first entry on each of the preceding two lines specifies the port you are defining for `inetd` to listen on. All ports mentioned by name in this file must also have a corresponding entry in `/etc/services`. Red Hat Linux (other UNIX systems will have similar lines) has this in its `/etc/services` file:

```
netbios-ns      137/tcp        nbns
netbios-ns      137/udp        nbns
netbios-dgm     138/tcp        nbdgm
netbios-dgm     138/udp        nbdgm
netbios-ssn     139/tcp        nbssn
```

The first entry is the name you are defining for the port that is eventually referenced in `/etc/inetd.conf`, the second entry is the port number and whether it is udp or tcp, and the third entry is another name the port can be known by, a set of aliases for the port if you like. If your flavor of UNIX does not have these entries, include them in the systems `/etc/services` file now!

Starting Samba from a Startup File

The other method used to start Samba is to create a startup file that is processed on bootup. This method is a little more involved, but is probably the most popular for the reasons mentioned earlier. Most UNIX systems these days are System V-based (including Linux), which means that they use a directory structure similar to that shown in Figure 2.1.

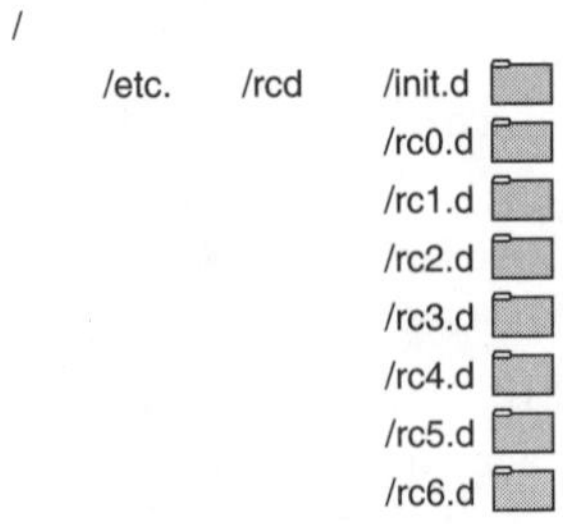

FIGURE 2.1

System V startup files directory structure under Linux.

```
/
/etc.   /rcd   /init.d
               /rc0.d
               /rc1.d
               /rc2.d
               /rc3.d
               /rc4.d
               /rc5.d
               /rc6.d
```

However, some systems, such as Solaris don't have the separate `rc.d` directory and have the `rc*.d` and `init.d` subdirectories directly under `/etc`.

There is a startup script for each different service that gets installed in the `init.d` directory. Each startup script performs both start and stop functions. Each of the `rc` directories specifies what services are to be started and stopped at a particular runlevel. The digit in the directory name specifies the runlevel, for example, `rc1.d` is runlevel 1. A link is placed in each of the `rc` directories that points to an appropriate entry in the `init.d` directory. Then when a runlevel is reached, the scripts are executed with a start as the parameter that starts each service needed at that runlevel.

Different UNIX Vendors Use Variations on the SVR4 Startup Scripts Scheme

Unfortunately, each UNIX vendor usually modifies this standard. In HP-UX, for example, all the directories mentioned previously are under the /sbin tree. However, HP also provides a control structure under the directory /etc/rc.config.d. In this directory there is usually a file for each service. In this file you can centrally control whether this service is to be started or not, or even include variables that can be used in the actual startup script. A common use of this is to specify command-line options that will be passed to the daemon when it starts.

Luckily, as part of the Samba source distribution, there is a sample script you can put into the /etc/rc.d/init.d directory. You will find this sample script at $SAMBA_ROOT/examples/ svr4-startup/samba.server. It will look something like Listing 2.2.

LISTING 2.2   Sample Samba Startup Script

```sh
#!/bin/sh
#ident  "@(#)samba.server 1.0   96/06/19 TK"    /* SVr4.0 1.1.13.1*/
#
# Please send info on modifications to knuutila@cs.utu.fi
#
# This file should have uid root, gid sys and chmod 744
#
if [ ! -d /usr/bin ]
then                    # /usr not mounted
        exit
fi

killproc() {            # kill the named process(es)
        pid=`/usr/bin/ps -e |
            /usr/bin/grep -w $1 |
            /usr/bin/sed -e 's/^  *//' -e 's/ .*//'`
        [ "$pid" != "" ] && kill $pid
}

# Start/stop processes required for samba server

case "$1" in

'start')
#
# Edit these lines to suit your installation (paths, workgroup, host)
#
    /opt/samba/bin/smbd -D -s/opt/samba/smb.conf
    /opt/samba/bin/nmbd -D -l/opt/samba/log -s/opt/samba/smb.conf
    ;;
'stop')
    killproc nmbd
    killproc smbd
    ;;
*)
    echo "Usage: /etc/init.d/samba.server { start | stop }"
    ;;
esac
```

Before you can use this script, you need to replace the **smbd** lines with the correct full path-name to where you installed Samba after compilation. Notice that the startup script is basically one large **case** statement, which executes a particular section depending on the argument. This saves having separate files for starting and stopping services. After you have made any changes to this file, copy it to your init.d directory. On Linux this will be `/etc/rc.d/init.d/samba`.

So, if it is started like this:

```
[root@pinkie] # /etc/rc.d/init.d/samba start
```

An **smbd** process will begin running on your system, as opposed to the following:

```
[root@pinkie] # /etc/rc.d/init.d/samba stop
```

The preceding command will, of course, find the **smbd** process and kill it gracefully.

Finally, you need to add a couple of links in the appropriate **rc** directories; on Linux, you would do something like this:

```
[root@pinkie] # ln -s /etc/rc.d/init.d/samba /etc/rc.d/rc3.d/S79samba
[root@pinkie] # ln -s /etc/rc.d/init.d/samba /etc/rc.d/rc1.d/K79samba
```

The first will start Samba when the system reaches runlevel 3, whereas the second will stop Samba when the system goes down to runlevel 1 or gets powered off.

You have accomplished a lot in this chapter. If you chose to install a precompiled package, you will have noticed that pretty much everything would have already been done for you. However, if you chose to take the adventurous route and compile Samba yourself, then you would have learned the entire process of compiling and installing Samba onto your system, in addition to adding appropriate directives to your startup files to begin Samba on bootup. The next chapter discusses how to configure your new Samba server and get your first Windows connection going!

Summary

By now you have learned the differences between using precompiled Samba packages and downloading the source code. You should know enough about the pros and cons of each approach to make a decision on whether to compile Samba yourself or grab a ready-made package.

If you are running one of the many commercial UNIX systems, you have learned where to go to look for a precompiled package if that is your preference. As long as you have an ANSI C compiler of some description (usually GNU GCC), "rolling your own" is probably the preferable method, unless you are running Linux, where you will pretty much always find a precompiled Samba as part of your distribution.

You've gone through the steps of downloading, configuring, and compiling Samba from scratch, and that it is not as hard as it used to be, thanks to the GNU **configure** program.

Finally, you learned the general procedure for installing Samba on your system, which you do after compiling the Samba source code. This included a discussion on the different methods to start the Samba daemon. You can either put Samba in your `inetd.conf` file, which is rarely done these days, or alternatively you can direct Samba to start on bootup so that it is running continuously, even when no users are connected. Remember that if you chose a precompiled Samba package, all this is taken care of for you.

The next chapter discusses how to configure Samba to actually use it for something useful!

Review Questions

1. How do you decide whether or not to use a precompiled Samba package or download and compile the source code yourself?

2. Where do you go for online documentation for Samba?

3. How do you configure Samba to install in `/opt/samba`, and install the manual pages in `/opt/share/man`?

4. If you have an HP-UX 11 system, how would you go about installing the Samba startup files?

   HINT: Some research may be required. Try `http://docs.hp.com`.

5. What is the difference between putting Samba in `inetd.conf` and putting it in a regular startup file in `/etc/rc.d/init.d`?

CHAPTER 3

BASIC SAMBA CONFIGURATION

You will learn about the following in this chapter:

- How to install SWAT onto your Samba server

- How to use SWAT to configure your Samba server

- How to do simple testing of your newly created Samba configuration

- How to set up Windows 9x and Windows NT to talk to Samba

- How to do some simple troubleshooting of Samba

I n this chapter, you will learn how to configure Samba so that you can connect to a share from your Windows 9x or Windows NT box. After all, this is what Samba is all about! The chapter begins by discussing the Samba Web Administration Tool (SWAT). SWAT comes with the Samba distribution, and makes it a whole lot easier to configure Samba if you are not confident with editing text-based configuration files. After that, the chapter explains the basics of setting up your Windows clients to be able to talk to Samba, so you can begin sharing files from your UNIX system. After you get that far, you'll learn how to edit the Samba configuration file directly. It really is not as hard as you might think! Finally, you may have bumped into some problems along the way, so the chapter presents some simple troubleshooting to try to help you get out of issues you might have found as you were experimenting.

Samba Web Administration Tool

Until the release of Samba 2.0, when you needed to configure Samba, you pretty much had no choice except to manually edit configuration files. There were several contributed programs that people wrote to make the configuration easier, but nothing in the official Samba distribution.

With Samba 2.0 came SWAT, the Samba Web Administration Tool. SWAT gives you a method of changing the text-based Samba configuration file easily, and greatly reducing any errors that you might make if you make changes manually.

Installing SWAT

If you manually compiled Samba, as described in the last chapter, you need not do anything, SWAT should already be installed on your system under `/usr/local/samba` if you used the default directory settings of the `configure` program.

If you installed a Samba package, SWAT may or may not be part of the standard Samba package, depending on whether the person who created the package required it. If you have installed a Samba package, and SWAT is not in the usual places, such as `/usr/local/samba/bin/swat`, `/opt/samba/bin/swat`, or `/usr/sbin/swat`, it is probably safe to say that it is not installed. As an example, to be totally sure it is not on your system, if you are using a Linux-based UNIX system that uses `rpm` for package management, you can execute the following command:

```
[root@pinkie] # rpm -qal | grep swat
```

The first section of the command before the pipe lists all files that have been installed on the system using `rpm`. Because you only care whether `swat` is installed, you `grep` for the `swat` command. If you get no results, `swat` is not installed. If this is the case, you will need to do one of two things:

1. `swat` may be in its own separate package on your Linux distribution CD. Check for something with `swat` in the beginning of the name. For example, with Caldera OpenLinux 2.2, there is a package called `swat-2.0.3-0b.i386.rpm`.

2. You can go back a chapter and read how to get the Samba source distribution and compile Samba yourself. That way, you know `swat` will get installed correctly, because you will be doing the entire compilation/installation yourself.

If you have `swat` installed, you need to do a small amount of preparation first.

You need to make sure there is an entry in `/etc/services` that looks something like this:

```
swat              901/tcp           # Samba Web Administration Tool
```

Also, you need to check for an entry in `/etc/inetd.conf` that looks like this:

```
swat    stream  tcp    nowait.400 root    /usr/sbin/tcpd swat
```

Of course, if you are not using `tcpd`, you will need to put something like this in instead:

```
swat    stream  tcp    nowait.400  root    /usr/local/samba/bin/swat swat
```

If you modify `/etc/inetd.conf`, you must restart `inetd`:

```
[root@pinkie] # killall -HUP inetd
```

Or:

```
[root@pinkie] # kill -HUP `cat /var/run/inetd.pid`
```

Using SWAT

After you have SWAT installed, you can use it! Open up your Web browser of choice and go to the address `http://unixserver:901/`. You will be prompted as in Figure 3.1.

FIGURE 3.1
Authentication to allow
Samba configuration.

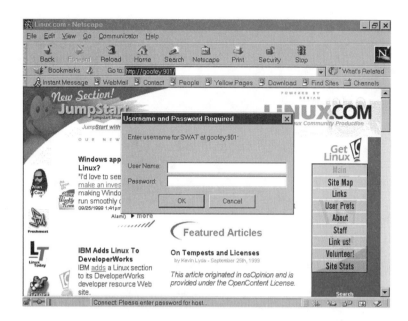

Enter **root** as the username and enter your root password. You then should get a screen similar to Figure 3.2.

FIGURE 3.2
The SWAT home page.

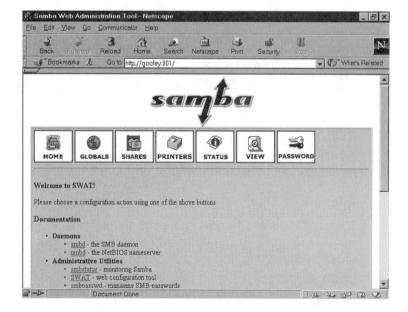

This is the main SWAT home page. In this one place you'll find all the manual pages and some other miscellaneous documentation that is useful for reference. You can navigate your way around the SWAT page using the seven buttons across the top of the page:

- Home
- Globals
- Shares
- Printers
- Status
- View
- Password

SWAT Rearranges Your `smb.conf` File if You Already Have One

If you already have a Samba `smb.conf` configuration file that you have spent a lot of time configuring, be careful! When you start SWAT for the first time, it will remove all comments and `include=` and `copy=` lines and rearrange all entries for its own use. Make a habit of always reading the README files for a new piece of software you are installing. Warnings like this are usually highlighted in an obvious place, such as a README file that comes with the software distribution.

To help you understand what each of the buttons is for, you need to know the basic structure of the Samba configuration file, `smb.conf`. The file is split into two main sections. The first is called the "Global" section where all settings that are not share-related reside, and the second is the "Shares" section, which defines what disk resources, or shares, are available for users. The "Shares" section is further subdivided into "Disk Shares" and "Printer Shares."

The following sections discuss each of the buttons in turn, including giving you some sample settings to get yourself a Samba server that does something useful with a minimum of fuss.

Home

As the name suggests, regardless of which view you are in, clicking the Home button will always take you back to the SWAT front page with the links to all the HTML manual pages.

Globals

The Globals button is the first of three buttons that are used to edit each of the sections of the `smb.conf` file. Just to point out the obvious, this is used to control all the global variables that affect how Samba is to be configured. So that you are not inundated with parameters you can change, you have the option of looking at the most often used variables using the Basic view. The Advanced view shows all parameters that can be changed. Figure 3.3 shows what this screen looks like. Notice that under the text "Global Variables," there are three buttons: Commit Changes, Reset Values, and Advanced View. The first, Commit Changes, is used to write all your changes to the Samba configuration file. If you make a few changes, but then decide, before clicking the Commit Changes button that you don't like them, the Reset Values button will reset all values back to where they were after the Commit Changes button was last clicked. If you want to see all modifiable parameters, click the Advanced View button. If you do this, the Advanced View button toggles to Basic View, so if it all looks too daunting, you can go back to Basic view!

FIGURE 3.3

The Globals view.

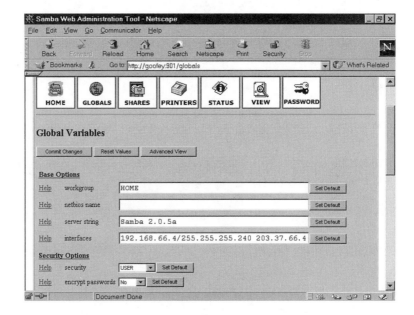

All variables can be changed in one of two ways. You can enter text, for example, if you were changing the `workgroup`. Or you can use a pop-down list of all the different values available, for instance, setting the `security` variable. At any point, you can get help on what a variable is used for by clicking the help link to the left of the variable name. This takes you to the relevant section of the `smb.conf` manual page. If you have changed a parameter at some point and you want to set it back to the Samba default, click the Set Default button and it will take care of that for you.

Here are some steps for you to follow to start configuring your own Samba server:

1. At the `workgroup` variable, enter your company name. If you are at home, enter `HOME`. You can only have a workgroup that is a maximum of 15 characters. If your company name is longer than this, abbreviate it.

2. At the `hosts allow` variable, you have the option of entering a range of IP addresses that are allowed to access your Samba server. If you are at home and connected to the Internet occasionally and all your home machines are networked without a firewall, you will almost certainly want to add something like: `localhost, 192.168.0.0/255.255.0.0`, but replacing `192.168.0.0` with your home subnet name. This disallows any connections other than the one you specified. This means any intruders from the Internet trying to break into your Samba server will be locked out.

3. Finally, if your company already has WINS set up on a Windows NT network, you can enter the IP address of the WINS NT box down the bottom at the variable `wins server`. This causes `nmbd` to register with your organization's WINS when it starts up, which allows you to browse to the Samba server using any of your Windows boxes if you are on a different network segment to the Samba server, and also allows NetBIOS names to be looked up from the Samba server using your current WINS infrastructure. If you have only a simple network at home, it is safe to leave this blank.

4. Click the Commit Changes button to direct SWAT to write your changes to the Samba configuration file.

Shares

Clicking the Shares button opens a screen where you define the disk resources you want to make available to your users. Initially this screen will look like that in Figure 3.4.

FIGURE 3.4

The Shares view.

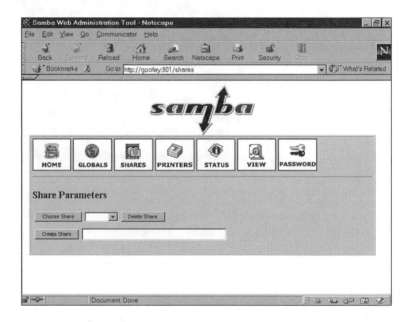

If you have not run SWAT previously, there will be no shares defined. Adding a share is simply a matter of entering the name which you want the share to be known as in the text box. For example, if I enter `tmp` (so it can be accessed later with `\\unixbox\tmp`), and click Create Share, SWAT brings up some variables I can set for this share. These are called the share level variables. This will look like Figure 3.5. As you can see, the layout is very similar to the Globals screen in that you have online help available, and an Advanced View button. The main differences are that there are different variables to set, and at the top of the screen you have a pop-down list of shares you have defined, where you can add more shares or delete existing shares.

FIGURE 3.5

The Shares view when creating a new share.

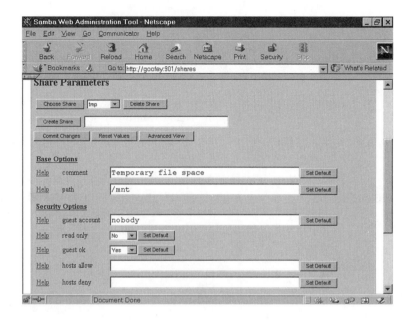

The most important part of this screen is where you define the directory path you want to make available using the sharename you defined. When you are creating the new share, make sure you click `Commit Changes` to save all your modifications!

Again, here are some steps to follow, so you can see how easy it is to set up your own Samba server:

1. Click in the text box and type `tmp`.

2. Click Create Share.

3. In the comment field, enter the following text: `This is a share for temporary files`.

4. At the read-only variable, select No. If you leave it at Yes, no one will be able to write anything to the share.

5. Finally, click the Commit Changes button to write your changes to the Samba configuration file.

Printers

The Printers button is very similar to the Shares view, which is not really very surprising because they perform similar functions. Here are some simple steps to follow to set up access to a printer from your Samba server:

1. Click in the text box and type the name of your printer, for example `hplj4`.

2. Click Create Printer.

3. In the comment field, enter some text that describes where the printer is located: HP
   LaserJet 4. Level 3, Building 10.

4. You can change the path if you like. This path is used as a spool directory where the file
   will get spooled before printing. If you do change it, be sure you have correct UNIX permissions on the directory.

5. Finally, click the Commit Changes button to write your changes to the Samba configuration file.

The Printers view should look similar to Figure 3.6.

FIGURE 3.6

The Printers view.

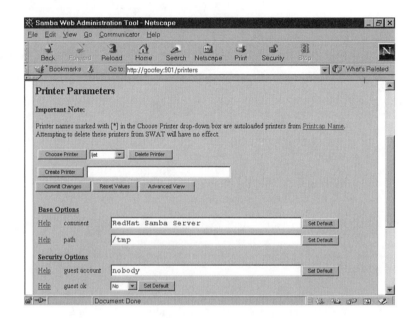

The Printers view is the last of the SWAT configuration views. The last three views deal with
ongoing maintenance tasks rather than Samba configuration issues.

Status

In the Status view, you can see the status of different aspects of your Samba server. This provides you with a central point where you can do the following:

- Tell at a glance whether or not both the main Samba processes are running (smbd and
  nmbd).

- Start, stop, or restart either process if necessary.

- See all the currently Active Connections to the Samba server by IP address, including the
  Process ID of the smbd daemon that was spawned for that process and the time and date
  the connection was made.

- Display all the shares that are currently in use. Details include which users using what shares and the time and date the connection was established.

- Obtain a listing of all open files that users are using and Samba has open. Details include which `smbd` Process ID is using the file, whether it is open for reading or writing, the filename, and the time and date the file was opened.

The information on this screen is quite valuable for troubleshooting and is probably the first place to visit in case of a problem. An example of what this screen looks like on an active Samba server is shown in Figure 3.7.

FIGURE 3.7

The Status view.

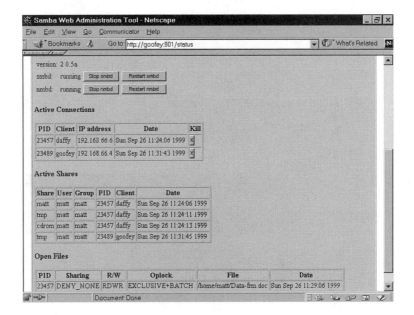

View

The View button allows you to see your Samba configuration file. If you have just started SWAT for the first time, and don't change any settings, this file will be empty, except for a few comments at the top. Your newly configured Samba server may look something like that in Figure 3.8.

Password

Finally, we come to the Password view. If you are using encrypted passwords, in this view you can perform maintenance of your Samba users. This either requires the use of an smbpasswd file, or the `security` global variable set to `Server` or `Domain`. Detailed information on setting up encrypted passwords is Chapter 5, "Integrating Samba into an Existing Windows Network." For now, you can see what the Password view looks like by looking at Figure 3.9.

FIGURE 3.8

The View view.

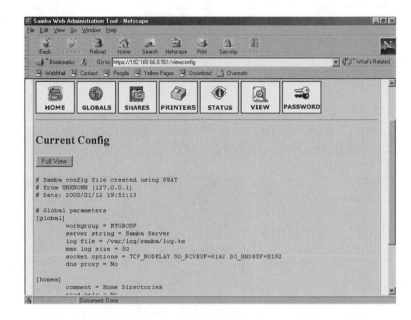

FIGURE 3.9

The Password view.

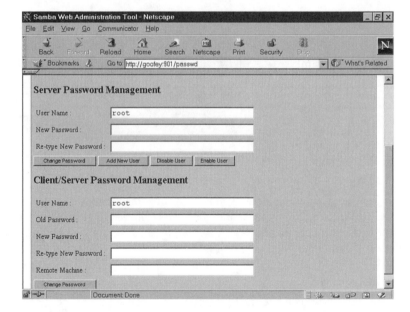

Testing Your Samba Configuration

You can test your Samba configuration without even using a Windows machine, believe it or not! Samba ships with a nifty program called `smbclient`. `smbclient` is specially designed for testing your Samba configuration without having to go to a Windows machine to do it. If you are familiar with using the command-line version of FTP, then you should quickly get used to smbclient's interface because they are quite similar. smbclient was originally created as a test tool for the Samba development team so they would not have to continually use Windows systems to test the various Samba features. You can easily use smbclient in scripts for automatic file transfers and to remotely back up Windows machines to a UNIX tape drive.

The following are some of the features of smbclient:

- It can connect to a share on any machine capable of being an SMB-based fileserver. This includes but is not limited to Windows NT, Windows 95/98, Samba servers, and any of the many commercial SMB servers available today.

- It offers an easy-to-use interface, similar to FTP, to navigate around a share's directory structure, including being able to create directories, and retrieve and send files.

- It can retrieve a list of fileshares available on a remote SMB server.

- You can connect to a printer resource with smbclient, which is handy for connecting to printers that are available only on Windows boxes.

- If you are familiar with the UNIX tar command, you can connect to a remote resource with smbclient and tar up the contents so that you can easily back up data from Windows to UNIX if you need to for whatever reason.

- smbclient functions are easily performed in scripts for unattended batch functions.

Using smbclient to Test Your Samba Configuration

It is well worth your while to use smbclient to do an initial test of your configuration before you let your users loose on it. It is a very simple process. First, log in to a command prompt on your UNIX system as a user who will have access to Samba, for example, your own personal user id.

Next, start up smbclient like this:

```
[matt@pinkie matt]$ smbclient //localhost/tmp
```

Replace tmp with the sharename you created earlier. Also, localhost may not work correctly, depending on how your UNIX machine is configured, so you may need to enter your servername instead. You will then get a password prompt. Enter your regular UNIX password. You will see something like this:

```
[matt@pinkie matt]$ smbclient //localhost/tmp
Added interface ip=192.168.66.6 bcast=192.168.66.15 nmask=255.255.255.240
Password:
Domain=[HOME] OS=[Unix] Server=[Samba 2.0.3]
smb: \>
```

You see displayed the domain the server belongs to, the operating system it is running on, and the Server comment field. You then get a prompt, not dissimilar to your regular UNIX prompt. The commands available to you are a hybrid of commands you are familiar with from both the UNIX command line and FTP clients. Assuming you have the appropriate permissions, most of the regular UNIX commands work, such as: `ls`, `cd`, `rm`, `mkdir`, and `rmdir`, as well as commands found in FTP clients, such as: `get`, `put`, `mput`, and `mget`. If you want a full list, type `help`.

When you type `ls`, you get a bunch of information:

```
smb: \> ls
  cd                                  D        0  Fri Sep 17 00:09:06 1999
  .X11-unix                           DH       0  Wed Sep 15 18:55:39 1999
  kio_0_2083_0.0                               0  Sun Sep 19 16:59:29 1999
  LST                                 D        0  Sat Sep 18 12:11:22 1999
  .initrd                             DH       0  Thu Sep 16 05:05:00 1999
  kfm_0_2083_0.0                               0  Sun Sep 19 16:59:29 1999
  jzip37E4C9520D3074A                      87343  Sun Sep 19 21:30:59 1999
  kfm-cache-500                       D        0  Wed Sep 15 18:56:08 1999
  .X0-lock                            HR      11  Wed Sep 15 18:55:39 1999
  kfm-cache-0                         D        0  Thu Sep 16 23:59:29 1999
  .MediaCon937384872                  H        0  Wed Sep 15 18:41:11 1999
  .MediaCon937385761                  H        0  Wed Sep 15 18:56:00 1999
  kio_500_961_0.0                              0  Sun Sep 19 21:56:08 1999
  kfm_500_961_0.0                              0  Sun Sep 19 21:56:08 1999
  OSL_PIPE_500_SingleOfficeIPC_2017   A        0  Wed Sep 15 19:12:39 1999
  soffice.tmp                         D        0  Wed Sep 15 19:12:40 1999
  OSL_PIPE_500_PILOT_SYNC             A        0  Wed Sep 15 19:12:40 1999

        61937 blocks of size 16384. 12262 blocks available
smb: \>
```

You get all the usual information such as filename, date/time stamp, and size. But you also get the DOS attributes on the file, such as whether it is read-only (R), a directory (D), a hidden file (H), or a system file (S). Even though you are connected to a UNIX server that has no concept of DOS-like attributes, it emulates them wherever possible. Because the user account you connected as does not have write permissions on every file, some come up with the read-only attribute set. Also, any file with a dot (.) at the start of the filename is treated as a hidden file.

When you are done exploring the smbclient interface, you can finish with the **exit** command.

Connecting to a Windows Resource as a Different User

You can specify the user to connect as from the command line when starting smbclient. This is useful if you want to log in to a share as someone other than who you are currently logged in as. For example, if you are logged in as matt, but want to connect to a share as the user jon, you would type something like this:

```
[matt@pinkie]$ smbclient //localhost/tmp -U jon
```

You need to know jon's password, because you will get prompted for it!

A detailed discussion of `smbclient` and what it can do for you is in Chapter 8, "Using smbclient."

Getting Windows to Talk to Samba

The reason you want to run Samba in the first place is so you can get your Windows clients to talk to it so your users can store all their files on your more reliable UNIX servers rather than using a Windows NT server. After all, this is what *Samba Primer Plus* is all about! To achieve this, you will need to configure all your Windows 9x and Windows NT clients to talk to the network if you haven't already. Most likely they will already be configured for network access, as this is usually done during the initial installation. This section provides you the background you need to know to be able to configure Window 9x and Windows NT clients so they are able to talk to the network if they can't already, or alternatively if they already have the appropriate network configurations, then use the example screens in this section to help you determine if your clients are configured correctly. Note that this section talks about Windows 98; however, in most cases Windows 95 configuration will be similar.

Configuring a Windows 98 Client

Configuring Windows 98 to talk with Samba is a relatively easy matter. Before you can do anything, you need to make sure that you have a working network configuration. If you are unsure as to how to do that, this section goes over the steps to achieve this with you.

First, right-click Network Neighborbood, and select Properties. If your network is configured, you will get a display like that in Figure 3.10.

FIGURE 3.10

A fully network-ready Windows 98 client.

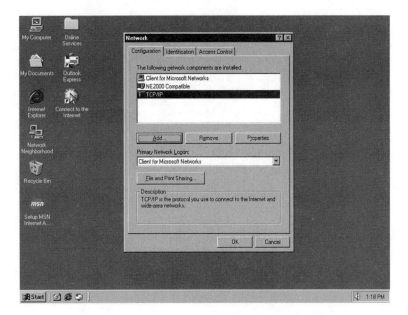

If this is the case, you probably already have a configured network client—skip down to the section "Connecting to Your First Share on Your Samba Server."

Otherwise, follow these easy steps:

1. Click Add.

2. Select Network Component Type, choose Adapter (notice that the icon next to it looks like a network card), and then click Add.

3. The adapters are sorted by vendor, so it should be fairly easy to find the correct driver for your card. When you find it, click OK. An example of this process appears in Figure 3.11.

FIGURE 3.11

Selecting the correct network adapter.

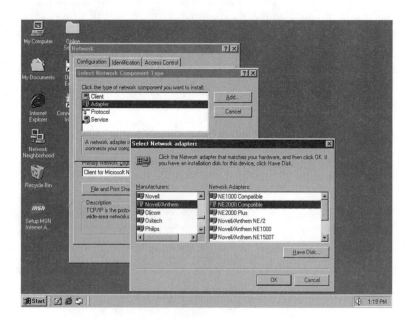

4. The system will automatically add the TCP/IP protocol, which will be bound to the adapter you just added. You now need to configure this protocol by clicking Properties.

5. Notice that you have a choice between using the Dynamic Host Configuration Protocol (DHCP) to get your IP address, or manually configuring it. Choose what is appropriate in your situation. An example is shown in Figure 3.12.

6. Click the Gateway tab, and enter the IP address of your closest gateway. This is usually a router if you are doing this on your corporate network. If you are at home, unless you have a multisubnet network, it is safe to leave this blank. After you have entered the gateway address as applicable, click the Add button.

FIGURE 3.12

Configuring TCP/IP under Windows 98.

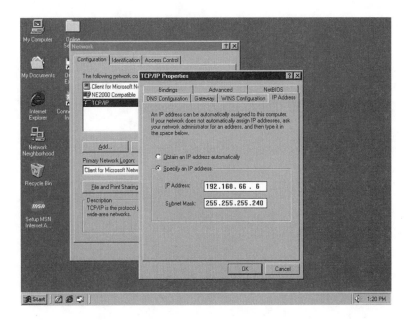

7. Click the DNS tab. Enter the name of a DNS server on your network if you have one, and then click Add.

8. Click OK and then OK again. If your network adapter needs manual configuring, a screen now pops up asking you to enter the required details, usually an IRQ and I/O Port address.

9. Finally, as with most major configuration changes in Windows, you must restart your PC for the changes you made to take effect.

When your Windows 98 machine finishes rebooting, you should get a login screen. Enter any username and password. If it is the first time you have used that username, you will be asked to confirm your password. After you have done that, you should be logged in to the familiar Windows 98 GUI.

You should now be ready to make your first client connection to your Samba server. Feel free to skip down to the section "Connecting to Your First Share on Your Samba Server" if you do not have any Windows NT clients to configure.

Configuring a Windows NT Client

Windows NT is quite a different beast from Windows 98. They may look the same, but under the covers, so to speak, they are completely different. Windows NT is a full multitasking operating system, but Windows 98 is still based on the old DOS code, and not as reliable as Windows NT. Configuring Windows NT to talk to the network is, as you may expect, quite different to configuring Windows 98. First, to check whether you have network connectivity already, right-click Network Neighborhood, select Properties, and choose Protocols. If the display looks like that in Figure 3.13, there is a good chance you already have a working net-work connection, and you should jump directly to the section "Connecting to Your First Share on Your Samba Server."

FIGURE 3.13

A fully network-ready Windows NT client.

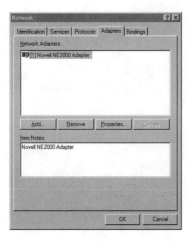

Otherwise, follow the process described next to configure your Windows NT Workstation or Server (both can follow the same procedure) for network access.

1. Click the Adapters tab, and choose Add.

2. A list of Network Adapters should appear. Choose the one appropriate for your network card and click OK.

3. If your card needs manual configuration, a pop-up box will appear for you to enter an IRQ Level and I/O Port Address. Your card probably came with a setup program on its drivers disk where you can set the IRQ and I/O Port address. When you are done, click OK.

4. Now click the Protocols tab, and click the Add button.

5. If you are planning on using the Dynamic Host Configuration Protocol (DHCP), click Yes and skip to step 11, otherwise select No.

6. Make sure the path to your Windows NT i386 directory (usually on your CD-ROM) exists, and click Continue.

7. Click Close.

8. The TCP/IP Properties window should automatically appear. Enter your IP address, sub-net mask, and gateway (if you have one). See Figure 3.14 for an example on configuring the TCP/IP properties.

9. If you are using DNS on your network, click the DNS tab, click Add, and enter the IP address to your DNS host. Then click Add again.

10. Click OK.

11. Click the Identification tab. Your computer should have a name and domain that you specified at operating system installation. If your Windows NT machine is not part of a domain, you might want to make sure that the name specified in the Domain field is the same as that in the Workgroup you specified in your Samba setup. This ensures that later on when you browse your network, you will see the Samba machine in the same group of machines that your Windows NT client is in.

12. Restart your computer.

FIGURE 3.14
Configuring the TCP/IP properties on a Windows NT client.

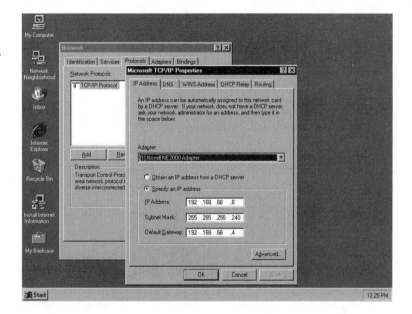

Connecting to Your First Share on Your Samba Server

You are now almost ready to start your first connection to your Samba server.

If you are using Windows 98 or Windows NT 4 with Service Pack 3 or higher, by default they send encrypted passwords when requesting an SMB share. When they were both first released it broke connections to Samba servers, since many people just set up Samba to use plaintext passwords. You have not yet set up Samba to enable authentication of encrypted passwords, so you need to force the Windows clients to send out plaintext passwords only. You can do this by modifying the registry.

A Warning About Modifying Your System's Registry

Editing the registry can cause your system to be unbootable if you are not sure what you are doing! Make sure you follow the instructions exactly as shown. If you are not confident, get your local Windows expert to do it for you. On Windows NT, you should back up the registry before you make any changes using the `rdisk` command as a command prompt.

Go to Start, Run and type:

regedt32

For Windows 98: Drill down the following registry tree:

`[HKEY_LOCAL_MACHINE\System\CurrentControlSet\Services\VxD\VNETSUP]`

And add this value:

"EnablePlainTextPassword"=dword:00000001

For Windows NT (with SP3 or higher): Drill down the following registry tree:

`[HKEY_LOCAL_MACHINE\SYSTEM\CurrentControlSet\Services\Rdr\Parameters]`

And add this value:

"EnablePlainTextPassword"=dword:00000001

You will need to reboot after making these changes.

Just to verify that you have set up your network correctly, you can do a simple `ping` test. This guarantees that your network is working properly.

If you are on Windows 9x, go to Start, Programs, MSDOS Prompt. Enter `winipcfg` and press Enter. If you are using Windows NT, go to Start, Programs, Command Prompt, and enter `ipconfig`. The adapter you chose should be there as well as the IP address that you entered, or if you are using DHCP, it will be the IP address your machine leased from the DHCP server. Now, enter

`C:\>ping 192.168.66.6`

and replace `192.168.66.6` with the IP address that was displayed with either `ipconfig` or `winipcfg`. If you get responses back from the pings, this confirms that your adapter is working correctly. Now try to ping the UNIX system you have Samba running on. If all is well, you should get a display similar to Figure 3.15. If you have any problems, skip to the "Basic Troubleshooting" section.

There are two ways of being able to connect to your Samba share. You can browse through the shares using Network Neighborhood, or map a permanent drive letter connection.

Connecting to Samba Through Network Neighborhood

This method is quite useful if you are looking for a file, but do not want to go to the effort of mapping a drive letter to every share available—especially if you need to search through multiple machines! It is simply a matter of double-clicking Network Neighborhood, and by default all machines that are browsable in your workgroup or domain show up as illustrated in Figure 3.16.

You can then select your Samba server and click down the shares. Click the tmp share you created earlier, and you should be able to see files there.

FIGURE 3.15
Verifying network connectivity with the `ping` command.

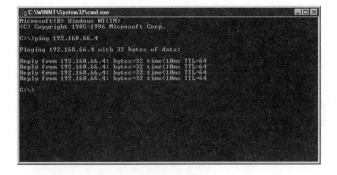

FIGURE 3.16
Browsing the network with Network Neighborhood.

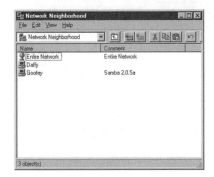

Mapping a Network Drive

Now that you have your network configuration sorted out, you probably want to know how you can connect a drive to your Samba server. You do this by instructing the operating system to connect to a remote SMB system and to a particular resource. You can do this in one of two ways: Right-click Network Neighborhood and click Map Network Drive, or open Explorer by clicking on Start, Run and type `explorer`. Click on the Tools menu and choose Map Network Drive. This is pictured in Figure 3.17.

FIGURE 3.17
Mapping a network drive with Explorer.

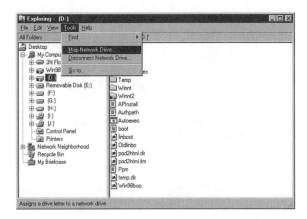

A window will pop up in which you can select a server and share to connect to.

Depending on whether you are using Windows 98 or Windows NT, you will get a slightly different screen. The Windows NT screen is shown in Figure 3.18, and the Windows 98 screen is shown as Figure 3.19.

FIGURE 3.18
Selecting a server and resource to connect to using Windows NT.

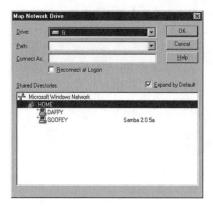

FIGURE 3.19
Selecting a server and resource to connect to using Windows 9x.

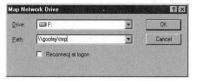

In the top half you can enter the details of the share you want to connect to. Alternatively, you can browse your network and your SMB servers (NT servers and workstations and Samba servers) will appear, and you can click them to find out what resources are available. Assuming that your Samba server is in the same subnet as your client machine, it should appear in the list. If it does, double-click it. You should get a list of shares like that in Figure 3.20.

FIGURE 3.20
Viewing shares on an SMB server.

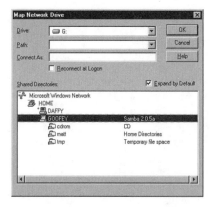

For now, click Path and enter the following path:

\\\goofey\tmp

Replace *goofey* with the name of your Samba server. Also click the drop-down drive list and select the drive letter you want to correspond with the connection you are about to make. Select T: for this example. Then click OK. You will be prompted for a password as Figure 3.21 shows. Enter it, and click OK.

FIGURE 3.21
Authenticating against your Samba server.

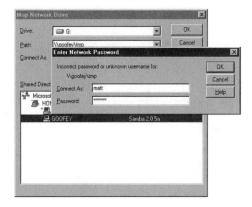

Now if you go to Explorer, the new drive letter T: should appear, and you should be able to browse through the files and directories and create new files.

Congratulations! You have made your first connection to your Samba server.

Basic Troubleshooting

Ideally, you did not come across any problems when connecting to your Samba share in the previous section. However, it is likely that something did not work quite right for you. This section describes some types of different problems that you may encounter and some possible solutions that may fix your particular issue.

Network Adapter Problems

The symptoms you will experience with network adapter problems would simply be no response from any hosts when you attempt to ping them.

- Check that the network adapter you installed is actually correct.

- In Windows 9x go to Start, Settings, Control Panel and double-click the System applet, click on the Device Manager tab, and click on Network adapters. Your network adapter should be listed with no errors. If there is an error listed, remove it, reboot, and try to reinstall it.

- Double-check the exact type of network card you have, and make sure that you have the correct driver for it. You may even have to go to your network adapter manufacturer's Web site to get the latest driver if the drivers that come with Windows do not work correctly.

- Your network adapter may have incorrect settings. If you manually configured your adapter, make sure you put the correct IRQ and I/O Port address information in. On the driver floppy disk that comes with most adapters is a configure program that you can run to check how your card is configured. Run this and make sure the settings match those you entered.

- An obvious but surprisingly common problem is forgetting to make sure the network cable is connected on your Windows machine.

Network Configuration Problems

- Try to ping other addresses that you know work and track down the problem from there.

- You may have an invalid IP address on your Windows machine. Make sure that the IP address you entered is valid on the subnet you have plugged the machine into. If you are doing this in an office environment, check with your comms group.

- If your Samba server is on a different subnet, make sure you entered the correct gateway address in your TCP/IP configuration.

Name Server Problems

You may get this message when trying to map a Samba share. This looks similar to Figure 3.22.

FIGURE 3.22
An error message when trying to connect to a Samba share.

This error message signifies a name resolution problem. If you get this error message, do not panic! It could mean a couple of things:

- You might be on a different network segment than your Samba server.

- There might be a router on your local network eating NetBIOS broadcasts.

Try opening a command prompt and entering the following:

```
C:\>tracert sambaserver
```

Replace *sambaserver* with the name of your Samba server. If you get more than one machine name coming up, your Samba server is in a different subnet than your client machine. The SMB protocol uses NetBIOS broadcasts to try to locate the SMB server. (The next chapter discusses this in more detail.) If the SMB server and clients are on different subnets, the broadcasts will not get through unless your comms group allows NetBIOS broadcasts through the routers. This is highly unlikely as it would dramatically increase the amount of network traffic on your corporate network, and probably slow it down to a grinding halt!

Similarly, if your routers actually "eat" up broadcast traffic before it reaches the Samba server, you can also get the error displayed in Figure 3.22. The client never got a response from the broadcasts sent out, so no connection could be made.

There are three ways of working around these problems, two of which will be discussed now and another that will be covered later on.

The first fix assumes that you use DNS in your environment for TCP/IP name lookups. Go to your TCP/IP Properties window, and click WINS Address. There is a check box that will probably be unchecked, Enable DNS for Windows Resolution. Check this box, and click OK as illustrated in Figure 3.23.

FIGURE 3.23

Enabling DNS lookups for Windows resolution in Windows NT.

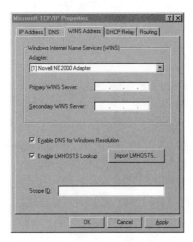

You will get a warning that at least one of your adapter cards has an empty primary WINS address. You can safely click Yes, and then click Close. Then you will need to reboot to make the changes take effect.

When you have rebooted, try making the network connection again, but use the fully qualified domain name (FQDN) as the server name, like this:

`\\goofey.mycompany.com.au\tmp`

Assuming you have entered a valid DNS name earlier, you should successfully be able to map a drive now. The way Windows can tell the difference between using broadcasts or DNS when trying to set up a NetBIOS session is quite simple. If the name you are connecting to is less than 15 characters, it is likely to be a NetBIOS name; otherwise, if it follows the rules for an FQDN, DNS is used.

An Alternative to Using DNS

If you are not using DNS, for example, most people with their home networks do not bother to run a DNS service. In this case, you can still use the first method. All you need to do is edit your system's hosts file and add an entry for your Samba server. For example on Windows NT:

```
C:\>notepad %systemroot%\system32\drivers\etc\hosts
```

Or Windows 98:

```
C:\>notepad \win98\hosts
```

In both cases, simply add a line like this:

```
192.168.66.6          goofey.mycompany.com
```

The second fix is probably more likely to be used if you are not using DNS, and is simpler to configure. For Windows NT users, open up a command prompt and enter these commands:

```
C:\>cd %systemroot%\system32\drivers\etc
C:\WINNT\system32\drivers\etc>copy lmhosts.sam lmhosts
C:\WINNT\system32\drivers\etc>notepad lmhosts
```

For Windows 98 users, open up an MS-DOS prompt, and just enter this command:

```
C:\>notepad \win98\lmhosts
```

In both cases, enter a line containing the name of your Samba server and its IP address, for example:

```
192.168.66.6 goofey
```

Save it and try mapping the drive again. It should work with no problems for you now. The reason why this works will be unraveled in the next chapter.

Samba Server Configuration Problems

This is obvious, but check that smbd and nmbd are actually running on your Samba server. You won't be able to connect if they have been stopped for some reason. Entering the following command will let you know if Samba is currently running:

```
$ ps auwx | grep -e smbd -e nmbd
```

Also, there is a command that comes with Samba called testparm that you can run which runs through your Samba configuration file and reports any errors it finds. You just run it like this:

```
$ testparm
```

All your Samba configuration variables will scroll up the screen. This is sometimes quite handy if you have a precompiled version of Samba and are not sure what the defaults compiled in were set to. Errors in the configuration file are displayed to the screen, so fix any if they appear.

Client Configuration Problems

On Windows NT you may get the message `Incorrect password or unknown username for: \\share\name`. This is usually just a simple matter of providing an incorrect username/password combination. If you are using Windows NT, and you are logged in to Windows NT as a different username or have a different password than your account name on the Samba server, you will have to enter a password. If your Windows NT username is different than the account you have on your Samba server, you must also enter a username.

If you are using Windows 98, things are a little more complicated. You need to make sure that the username you log in to at the start is exactly the same as your Samba username (the password can be different, though). The main reason for this is that when you are logged in to a Windows 98 session, you cannot connect to resources using different usernames as you can in NT. If either your username or password is different, you will get a password prompt like that in Figure 3.24.

FIGURE 3.24

Specifying a password when connecting to a network resource with Windows 98.

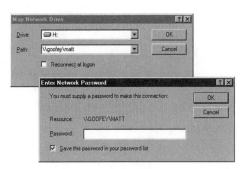

For Windows NT client systems you may get the message in Figure 3.25.

FIGURE 3.25

Windows NT trying to connect to a Samba server with encrypted passwords.

This error simply means Windows is attempting to connect to Samba with an encrypted password, and your Samba server is configured to use plaintext passwords (the default). All you need to do is enable plaintext passwords as mentioned in the previous section.

In this same scenario with Windows 9x, you will just get an access denied message, just the same as if you typed an incorrect password. If you are sure you have entered the right password, and you are using plaintext authentication on the Samba server, check that your Windows 9x system is set to send plaintext passwords as described earlier in this chapter.

Summary

This chapter started with a fairly detailed discussion of the Samba Web Administration Tool (SWAT). You were shown how to install it, if it was not already installed on your system, and included some sample settings to get a configured Samba server up and running fairly quickly.

You then learned how to set up both Windows NT and Windows 98 clients to be able to talk to your Samba server. Two different ways of connecting to Samba were explained, through Network Neighborhood or by mapping a network drive; this was a method of testing your Samba configuration was valid.

Finally, the last section describes some problems that crop up all the time in different environments, and solutions for fixing the problems you might have had.

This chapter has probably overwhelmed you with information! But if you took it step by step, you managed to get your Samba server working and talking with your Windows 98 or Windows NT client.

The next chapter goes into some more detail on how Windows networking works, and how Samba fits into the overall big picture.

Review Questions

1. How does SWAT benefit you?

2. What other methods are available to you to edit your Samba configuration?

3. How can you set up your Windows client to connect to a drive on the Samba server if you do not use WINS or lmhosts files?

4. Your Windows 98 client can talk to your Samba server (tested with a ping), but your Samba server cannot talk back to your Windows client (pings timeout). Your Samba server can talk to some network clients but not others. What could be wrong?

PART II

INTEGRATING SAMBA INTO YOUR WINDOWS NETWORK

4   Understanding Windows NT Networks

5   Integrating Samba into an Existing Windows Network

6   Using Samba with Windows 95/98

7   Samba in a Windows NT/2000 Domain Environment

8   Using `smbclient`

CHAPTER 4

UNDERSTANDING WINDOWS NT NETWORKS

You will learn about the following in this chapter:

- An introduction to what Windows NT offers and what is implemented in Samba

- The differences between domains and workgroups

- The differences between share-level and user-level security

- The different services that NetBIOS provides

- How browsing works in a Windows network

- The different roles that a Windows NT server can perform, and which of those roles Samba can do

*I*f you are serious about implementing Samba in your corporate network from scratch, or integrating Samba with your current Windows NT/2000 servers, this chapter is required reading. You will learn the concepts behind Windows NT/2000 networks, why NT is so popular, and why it's such a big task for the developers of Samba to implement all Windows NT/2000 functions. To be able to use specific features of Samba properly, you need to know how the various components of Windows networking hangs together. If you already know the basics of Windows NT networking, you can skip ahead to the next chapter, which will teach you how to implement much of these concepts in your Samba server; otherwise, read on!

The purpose of this chapter is to teach you relevant Windows networking technologies, which you will need to know for later when you are implementing your Samba servers. You will need to know about all these things so you can design your Samba infrastructure the best way that you can, making use of any available Windows NT systems and being able to link them with your Samba systems.

Introduction to Windows NT

When Windows NT was first released, Microsoft's vision was for NT to become the *de facto* standard for home and office networks around the world. After eight years, five major versions, and a huge amount of Windows NT marketing, Microsoft has certainly accomplished its original dream. However, it has not been plain sailing for Microsoft. Windows NT, until and including version 4.0, has suffered serious stability and security problems and is still trying to prove itself among the more mature players in the server operating systems market, like NetWare and UNIX-based systems. Windows NT is definitely one of the most secure network operating systems available today, but it has one major failing, backward compatibility. One of Microsoft's main marketing points for NT is that it is backward compatible with a large number of older DOS and Windows 3.1-based applications. This backward compatibilty brought with it many of the insecurities of the earlier operating systems. The main insecurity is the problem-plagued and insecure SMB protocol for file sharing. Microsoft has improved it with some security enhancements, but the whole purpose of NT being backward compatible with all those older DOS and Windows clients negates the value of that extra security—unless of course you use NT-only networks. Samba brings with it a more secure implementation of the SMB protocol than NT provides.

For those of you unsure as to the features that Windows NT provides, here is a summary:

- A fully 32-bit, designed from the ground-up, secure operating system, available for both Servers and Workstations
- Backward compatibility with 16-bit Windows applications
- Available on a choice of two architectures (until Windows 2000)
- A secure and centralized method of storing and maintaining users and groups
- Easy integration between separate NT networks using trust relationships
- A secure filesystem called NTFS
- Encrypted user authentication
- File-sharing services

Windows 2000 added to this list:

- Full directory services
- Kerberos authentication
- Much better remote administration capabilities
- An enhanced version of NTFS

There are problems too, of course:

- Price. Using Windows NT can be very expensive. And when you have the operating system, you also have to pay for every application.

- Using the tools provided with the operating system, it is impossible to fully administer remotely. This means you either have to purchase third-party applications to help with this, hire system administrators at each remote site you deploy NT to, or spend money on transporting administrators to each remote site when there is a problem.

- With many different applications loaded, NT can sometimes be quite unstable. Because many Windows NT application developers come from a DOS/Windows background where there is no concept of a secure system, many developers create software under Windows NT without using the security features and guidelines Microsoft recommends.

Because Linux and other UNIX-based operating systems address these problems, UNIX systems running Samba are making huge inroads into Microsoft's Windows NT market.

As you are aware by now from what you have read so far, originally Samba was developed to provide file-sharing services, only a fraction of the tasks that a Windows NT server provides. Coincidentally, the SMB protocol is mostly documented, which made it relatively easy to implement. As time went on, extra Windows features were requested from the Samba user community to be implemented into the core Samba product. The problem was that many of the extra features being requested were generally not documented anywhere outside Microsoft. The only way to implement such features was for the developers to study thousands of lines of network traces to find out exactly what was happening when certain tasks were performed. From this enormous amount of effort over the past few years by the Samba team, it provides a majority of Windows NT's features available for free. Many companies are either dispensing with NT altogether, or integrating it in a heterogenous environment with Linux and other UNIX servers.

Differences Between Workgroups and Domains

When you start out with Samba, one of the first questions asked by Windows newcomers is: "What is the difference between a domain and a workgroup?" Even administrators with many years of experience have had problems answering this question. This section should help unravel the relationships between workgroups and domains.

Microsoft first introduced the concept of a workgroup back in the days of LAN Manager for MS-DOS and Windows 3.1/Windows For Workgroups. A large corporation usually contains many functional areas, for example an Accounting department, an Engineering department, and a Manufacturing area. The workgroup concept was chosen to categorize computers that perform similar functions or are physically in a similar area. In this example, all the computers in the Accounting department may belong to a workgroup called `Accounts`. The Engineering department may have a workgroup called `Engineering`, and the Manufacturing area may be in the workgroup `Factory`. Back in those early days, many organizations did not have a centralized server, and resources were spread out among the different departments, especially printers. The way to find these resources, both shares and printers, was to browse the network (Computer Browsing is discussed later in this chapter), expanding the various workgroups and computers until the required resource was found.

As you can see, resources in a workgroup environment were spread out among the PCs in an organization without much thought put into it. It did get better later on, with some companies putting dedicated file servers throughout the network, but there was no central method of authenticating users or keeping track of which users were connecting to what resources. The environment was very decentralized. This level of security on resources was called *share-level security*. With share-level security, an optional password is placed on the shared resource. Share-level security is not used much any more because many sites use domains where user-level security is used instead.

Then the first version of NT was released, Windows NT 3.1. With it came the concept of domains instead of workgroups. On the surface, a domain does not look any different than a workgroup. If you are browsing a large network with Network Neighborhood, you can see that the domains are mixed up with the workgroups and you cannot tell the difference. This is illustrated in Figure 4.1.

FIGURE 4.1

A list of workgroups and domains on a large network.

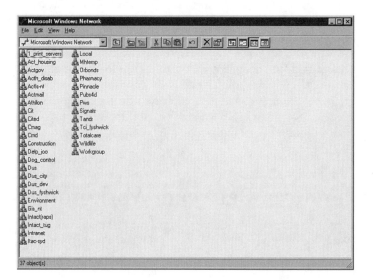

They may look similar on the browse list, but there is a key functional difference between the two. A domain provides a centralized method of security: organizing users, groups, and work-stations. Where a company may have had multiple workgroups, it usually replaced them with a single domain. For a workstation to participate in a workgroup, all that is needed is to sim-ply type the workgroup name in the appropriate network settings box, and it will appear in that workgroup. Each workstation that requires access to a domain must be added by a Domain Administrator. After a workstation is joined to a domain, the only people who can log in to it are users defined in the domain. Then when a user is granted access to a domain by a Domain Controller (DC), assuming he has correct permissions, he can access any resource on the domain. A resource again is a fileshare or printer. This type of resource sharing uses user-level security. In *user-level security*, a correct username and password combination must be given, it is verified by a special server that authenticates access to a domain called a Domain Controller (DC), and then if granted access, the resource is permitted.

There was no security with workgroups. Workgroups were just a method of providing easy access to resources on the network. Domains take that concept and extend it to include a form of access control of who actually has access to the resources on the network. All access to the domain, whether it is a user or machine, is controlled by the Domain Administrators rather than the users. A PC can only be added to the domain by a Domain Administrator, and before the user can even log in to the Domain, a user account must be created by the administrators of the domain. Figure 4.2 illustrates the differences between a workgroup and a domain.

FIGURE 4.2

A workgroup and a domain.

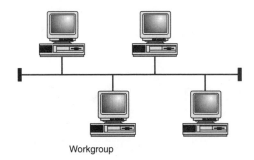

Workgroup

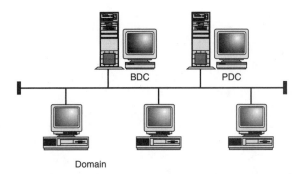

Domain

A Windows NT domain consists of these four main components:

- *A Primary Domain Controller (PDC)*. Every domain has only one of these. A PDC is the machine that holds the security accounts manager (SAM) database. Every user, machine, and group that is allowed to be a part of the domain has an account in the SAM database. A PDC is the only machine that has writable access to the SAM.

- *Backup Domain Controllers (BDC)*. There is usually one or more of these, but if the domain is small, you can get by with none. A BDC holds a read-only copy of the SAM database from the PDC. All BDCs get regular updates to the SAM, and can authenticate users to the domain. Having a number of BDCs spread out among different physical locations in the organization evens out the load for user authentication. If for whatever reason the PDC crashes, any BDC can also be promoted to PDC and then demoted back to BDC when the original PDC is recovered.

- *Servers*. These are usually where all the user's data is stored. These are also used as application servers if that functionality is required, among other tasks that you do not want a domain controller to do.

- *Workstations*. These can be Windows NT/2000, Windows 95, Windows 98, or to a lesser extent these days, Windows For Workgroups 3.11 clients. Each client can be a member of only one domain, and to get access to the resources of a domain, a user must provide the correct domain username and password combination.

On the surface, domains and workgroups seem similar and they are, but domains provide an extra level of security that should help you sleep well at night.

NetBIOS Revisited

You are probably wondering how NetBIOS is related to Samba, and why NetBIOS is being discussed in great detail here. NetBIOS is the transport layer used for the Server Message Blocks (SMBs) that are used when you connect to a shared resource on a Samba or NT server. Understanding the basics of how the NetBIOS API is used in this process helps you to be able to troubleshoot your Samba servers in the future when things go wrong. A very brief overview of NetBIOS was given in Chapter 1. This section goes into it in a little more detail.

Back in the 1980s, a transport protocol called NetBEUI was developed by Sytek, Inc. for IBM's broadband computer network. NetBEUI had a network programming interface as part of it called NetBIOS (Network Basic Input/Output System). In March of 1987, two Requests For Comments (RFCs) were released by the Internet Engineering Task Force (IETF), 1001 and 1002 (found at http://www.ietf.org/rfc/). The first, RFC 1001, describes the NetBIOS API and what services it provides to network applications. The second, RFC 1002, gives a detailed explanation of NetBIOS's implementation over TCP/IP. As the RFCs describe, NetBIOS provides the programming interface to write network-aware applications. The original NetBIOS transport NetBEUI is a very fast protocol because it has a low number of control bytes for each frame sent. NetBEUI, however, is not routable, a major disadvantage. This means that it is useful only in single subnet networks, which even then is not much of an advantage because small networks like that are almost nonexistent these days. And mainly because of the Internet, almost everyone uses TCP/IP—NetBEUI has almost become extinct.

Microsoft, counting on NetBIOS becoming a world standard for writing network applications, picked up the NetBIOS API and developed it for its own operating systems. Seeing the future disadvantages, Microsoft didn't like it being tied to NetBEUI, so it developed NetBIOS to be usable with any transport/network layer protocol. This was fairly easy considering that NetBIOS is effectively session-level-based anyway. This separation of NetBIOS from NetBEUI provides flexibility in being able to use NetBIOS over theoretically any transport-level protocol, including protocols that are routable and common today such as TCP/IP. But it also provides the flexibility of being backward compatible with NetBEUI for communication with the older LAN Manager-based networks. Figure 4.3 shows the different layers and how Microsoft networking hangs together.

FIGURE 4.3
The different Microsoft networking layers.

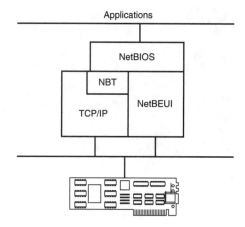

The lowest level is the Network Interface Card (or NIC), which sends the data out onto the network. The next level up is the combined Network and Transport layers. These can be non-routable protocols such as NetBEUI, or routable ones like TCP/IP. Then there is the Session layer, which is where NetBIOS sits. Microsoft wrote a mapping layer called NetBT, which is the interface NetBIOS uses to talk over TCP/IP.

NetBIOS performs three different services: a name service, a session service, and a datagram service.

NetBIOS Name Service

The NetBIOS name service is how NetBIOS names are resolved to a physical network address, in this case an IP address. NetBIOS uses broadcasts quite heavily for name resolution. Each Windows machine has a unique NetBIOS name, an example of a NetBIOS name could be ALFRED. Every time a computer boots up and accesses the network, it sends its name in a network broadcast UDP packet that is sent to every machine in the local subnet using a standard Internet port 137, which is the NetBIOS name services port. If there is another machine on the same network called ALFRED and it receives the ALFRED broadcast, it sends back a response to the machine that is booting up, which in turn will display an error message to the user while it boots up. Before any NetBIOS applications will run correctly, the NetBIOS name of the host must be changed to a unique name and the computer rebooted.

No two machines running on the same network can have duplicate names. NetBIOS names are 16 bytes long. The first 15 bytes are for the actual display name, and the 16th is reserved to identify a NetBIOS service. This 16th byte can be a hex number between 00h and FFh. Each NetBIOS service running on a machine will have the machine name as the first part of the name, and a unique hex number tacked onto the end. You can see all the different NetBIOS names running on any Windows machine by entering the command `nbtstat -n`. Figure 4.4 shows an example.

FIGURE 4.4

An example of output from the `nbtstat` command to a Windows NT host.

This is called the NetBIOS name table and shows all the different NetBIOS names, all of which correspond to a different NetBIOS application. You will notice in the list that a name can be one of two types, UNIQUE or GROUP. UNIQUE names can appear only once on the network, as opposed to GROUP names, which are shared names and can appear multiple times on the network.

You can also use the `nbtstat` command to interrogate remote machines that implement NetBIOS. You can try this by listing NetBIOS names on your Samba machine. Figure 4.5 shows the output for this command on the author's machine.

FIGURE 4.5

An example of output from the `nbtstat` command to a Samba host.

There is also a similar command in the Samba suite of utilities, called `nmblookup`. From a Samba host, you can gain information about any other SMB servers by typing the following command:

```
$ nmblookup -A 192.168.66.6
Sending queries to 192.168.66.15
Looking up status of 192.168.66.6
received 12 names
```

```
DAFFY            <20> -           B <ACTIVE>
DAFFY            <00> -           B <ACTIVE>
HOME             <00> - <GROUP> B <ACTIVE>
HOME             <1c> - <GROUP> B <ACTIVE>
HOME             <1b> -           B <ACTIVE>
HOME             <1e> - <GROUP> B <ACTIVE>
DAFFY            <03> -           B <ACTIVE>
ADMINISTRATOR    <03> -           B <ACTIVE>
INet~Services    <1c> - <GROUP> B <ACTIVE>
IS~DAFFY         <00> -           B <ACTIVE>
HOME             <1d> -           B <ACTIVE>
..__MSBROWSE__. <01> - <GROUP> B <ACTIVE>
num_good_sends=0 num_good_receives=0
```

You can also get a mapping from NetBIOS name to IP address by typing

```
$ nmblookup daffy
Sending queries to 192.168.66.15
192.168.66.6 daffy<00>
```

In this case it sent a broadcast to the local subnet, but if my Samba configuration were set up to be a WINS client (see the next chapter), **nmblookup** would have sent the request to the WINS server first.

There are many NetBIOS resource types. Table 4.1 shows some of the most common.

TABLE 4.1   An Incomplete List of the Mapping Between Some NetBIOS Resource Names and Services

NetBIOS Resource Name	NetBIOS Application
Unique Names	
\\computer_name<00h>	LAN Manager Workstation Service
\\computer_name<03h>	Messenger Service
\\computer_name<06h>	Remote Access Service (RAS) on a RAS Server
\\computer_name<1Fh>	NetDDE services
\\computer_name<20h>	LAN Manager Server Service
\\computer_name<21h>	RAS Client Service
\\computer_name<BEh>	Network Monitoring Agent Service
\\computer_name<BFh>	Network Monitoring Utility
\\username<03h>	User name for the currently logged on user

continued on next page

continued from previous page

NetBIOS Resource Name	NetBIOS Application
Unique Names	
\\domain_name<1Bh>	Registered by the domain PDC that is running as a Domain Master Browser
\\domain_name<1Dh>	Registered by the Master Browser on each subnet
Group Names	
\\domain_name<00h>	LAN Manager Workstation service—so it can receive browser broadcasts
\\domain_name<1Ch>	Used by the Domain Controllers in a domain
\\domain_name<1Eh>	Registered for browsing purposes (used in browser elections)
\\..__MSBROWSE__<01h>	Registered by the Master Browser on each subnet

If you run Microsoft applications such as Internet Information Server (IIS) or SQL Server on any servers, they register NetBIOS names as well.

For two nodes to communicate with each other using NetBIOS, the calling machine needs an IP address of the machine sharing resources. To achieve this, a NetBIOS name query broadcast is sent out from the machine requesting a NetBIOS session. This is done at the NetBT layer mentioned previously. All nodes on the subnet will receive this broadcast, but only the machine with the NetBIOS name being called will respond. If there is no machine on the network with the requested NetBIOS name, there will be no response to the broadcast.

NetBIOS name resolution can be categorized into five different types with each node on the network configured to use one method to resolve names, with one and four being the most popular:

1. *The broadcast mode, or b-node mode.* This mode is simple. The computer requesting resources broadcasts the NetBIOS name of the computer it wants to talk to across the entire subnet and waits a specified time for a response. Because most routers are not configured to forward broadcasts, this method will work only for machines in the same subnet.

2. *The Point-To-Point mode, or p-node mode.* Rather than broadcasting across the entire subnet, a requesting computer contacts a central database of known NetBIOS names on the network to find the NetBIOS name and IP address mapping. This central database is known as a Windows Internet Name Service (WINS). This method does not use broadcasts; however, if the WINS server is down, name resolution will fail.

3. *The m-node mode.* In this mode, a computer first uses b-node for name resolution. If that fails, it switches to p-node. This method still suffers from the broadcast problems discussed in the b-node, but can cross routers by consulting a WINS server if the local broadcast fails.

4. *The h-node mode*. This method uses p-node first. If that fails, it falls over to b-node as a last resort, for example, if the WINS server is unavailable. This is a good method in that it uses broadcasts as a last resort, which significantly increases LAN performance.

5. There is another method called a *modified b-node mode*, which allows the b-node method to travel across routers. This method uses a file called an `lmhosts` file. It is similar to a TCP/IP hosts file in that it contains name-to-IP-address mappings. This method works by broadcasting to the subnet first. If that fails, the `lmhosts` file is looked up. If there is no NetBIOS name that will resolve the NetBIOS Name Query, the name lookup will fail. This method was used before the WINS existed (prior to Windows NT 3.5x). This method suffers from the obvious problem of keeping `lmhosts` files updated.

After a name has been resolved to IP address, it is cached for later use and given an expiry time when it will be cleared from the cache. This allows "stale" names to be cleared out periodically. This provides fast access next time the same name needs to be resolved.

The most obvious problems with broadcast-based name resolution are as follows:

1. There is a high amount of broadcast traffic.

2. Unless specially configured, routers do not broadcast NetBIOS traffic.

3. All nodes on a subnet have to process each and every NetBIOS broadcast packet, consuming valuable resources.

That is why WINS servers are so common these days: They have decreased the amount of NetBIOS broadcasts on LANs, thereby increasing LAN performance dramatically! Samba provides the capability of being a WINS server by a directive in its configuration file. WINS functionality is implemented using the `nmbd` daemon.

NetBIOS Session Service

The NetBIOS session service is best described with an example. This section goes through the steps that NetBIOS uses when establishing a session over TCP/IP. For simplicity, assume that the client machine is using b-node name resolution. The client machine's name is PINKY and the resource PINKY wants to connect to is on machine NT001, and called \\`NT001`\`APPS`.

1. PINKY first of all uses the NetBIOS name service to send out three broadcasts one after the other to the local subnet broadcast address, to find the IP address of NT001. If it gets no response, an error message is presented to the user, saying something like: `The network path was not found`.

2. A TCP session is set up over IP to the standard NetBIOS session IP port 139 to the destination IP address for NT001 found at step 1.

3. A NetBIOS session request packet is sent over this TCP/IP connection from PINKY to NT001.

4. If all is okay, NT001 sends a positive confirmation back to PINKY.

5. SMB session setup request is sent over the newly formed NetBIOS session to connect to the share APPS on NT001.

When this NetBIOS session is set up, all NetBIOS-compliant network applications with a destination of NT001, such as SMB, are multiplexed over this already configured NetBIOS session—there is ever only one NetBIOS session between a client and server. This means that any further connections are done in the context of the user who initially established the connection. If you try to make another connection from PINKY to NT001 as a different user while the original NetBIOS session is still active, you will get an error like that in Figure 4.6.

FIGURE 4.6
Error when trying to connect to a server using a different set of credentials when there is a connection already established.

NetBIOS Datagram Service

A NetBIOS datagram again has a source and destination NetBIOS name in the header, and is sent on UDP port 138. The main purpose of a NetBIOS datagram is to send a message from one NetBIOS machine to another. The most common application that uses NetBIOS datagrams is the Windows NT Messenger application, or the Windows 9x WinPopUp program. This allows users to send short messages to each other, or a system administrator to send a broadcast message to all users notifying them to log out due to system maintenance. Of course Samba can generate NetBIOS datagrams as well; for more information, see the next chapter.

Browsing on a Windows Network

Computer browsing on a Windows network is probably one of the least understood aspects of Microsoft networking. Most people, including many Windows NT system administrators, do not understand it themselves, even though it is documented on many resources including the many articles available on the Microsoft Technet CDs. It is probably more appropriate for Samba system administrators to understand how browsing works, so they can then make sure they incorporate Samba correctly in an existing Windows network so Samba shows up on all browselists correctly.

Browsing a Windows network allows you to click your way through an organization's workgroups and domains to find a resource you are looking for. The common question that gets asked over and over is: How does a browse list get built up when you fire up Network Neighborhood? To many people, it is black magic and they don't understand how it magically appears, or, more commonly, they don't care. However, if you are responsible for your site's network, you should know at least the basics of computer browsing. Knowing this information helps you diagnose browsing problems when they do occur.

Possible Computer Browser Roles

Any one of Windows NT/2000, Windows 95, Windows 98, or Windows For Workgroups can be browsers. Further, any one of these operating systems can have one of four different browsing roles:

- Not a browser
- Potential browser
- Backup Browser
- Master Browser

But only Windows NT/2000 systems can fill this final type of role:

- Domain Master Browser

Again, Samba can fulfill any of these roles, and can also participate in master browser elections. This section describes each of the different roles in turn.

Non-Browsers

A non-browser is specially configured to not ever keep a browse list. This role works well for servers that do a lot of tasks such as file sharing or database work, and you don't want them to use additional resources to keep a computer browse list.

Potential Browser

A potential browser is capable of maintaining a browse list. It can participate in elections to be elected master browser, and can act as a backup browser if instructed to do so by the master browser. This is the default role of any Windows-based machine.

Backup Browser

The backup browser receives an updated copy of the current browse list from the subnet's master browser every 15 minutes. Backup browsers also distribute the browse list upon request to the other machines in the subnet who are members of the domain or workgroup.

Master Browser

There is one master browser per subnet. Each master browser keeps track of new machines starting up and machines being turned off and maintains the entries in the browse list accordingly. The master browser sends updates every 15 minutes to the domain master browser.

Domain Master Browser

The domain master browser is responsible for providing lists of domain resources to each master browser, and for gathering updates from each network subnet to include in the master list. As previously mentioned, the Windows NT PDC is always the domain master browser. Note that if your network already has a domain master browser, that is a Windows NT PDC, do *not* set Samba up to be one or all sorts of evil things will happen to your network, including lack of authentication and lack of browselists.

Master Browser Elections

The Master Browser role is allocated during a browser election that happens on a per subnet basis, when one of three things happens:

- A computer cannot find its master browser at startup.

- A computer determines that a master browser of a subnet has disappeared.

- A computer running Windows NT starts (Windows NT is a preferred master browser).

Each operating system is given a weighting (a host's current role is also considered as part of this weighting) and a special election is run to elect a new master browser. If you are interested, this process is in fact documented in Microsoft's Technet, which is online at `http://technet.microsoft.com` or on CD if you have that available.

Tasks a Windows NT Server Fulfills

A Windows NT server can be one of four different types:

- Primary Domain Controller (PDC)

- Backup Domain Controller (BDC)

- Member Server

- Standalone Server

As mentioned earlier, there is only one PDC in a domain. The PDC holds the only writable copy of the SAM, which is the user account database that determines what hosts and users are allowed access to the domain.

There are usually multiple BDCs that hold continually updated read-only copies of the SAM database. Any one of the BDCs or the PDC can authenticate users logging on to the domain.

A member server is a server that is a part of a domain, but sends all domain access requests to either the PDC or a BDC for verification. A member server does not hold a copy of the Domain SAM for security reasons; however, it does have its own SAM with the default accounts, Administrator and Guest. This Administrator account is known as a local administrator and can perform administration duties on this one machine only.

The standalone servers do not perform any domain user authentication; they can be file servers, database servers, Web servers, application servers, print servers, or any other type of server that an organization needs. These four types of servers are the backbone of any Windows NT Domain. Samba can perform three of these four tasks: PDC, Member server, and standalone server. BDC support is slated for version 2.1 of Samba, which should be out later this year.

The Login Process

For those who do not know how the login process works, this section briefly gives an overview of the Windows NT domain login process. If you are administering a Samba server, especially if it will take on the PDC role (see Chapter 7) it is useful to know this information for troubleshooting Windows 9x and Windows NT login problems, should you have any. Any background information always helps when troubleshooting most types of problems, but especially Samba-related ones.

1. The user enters his login credentials on a Windows NT or Windows 95/98 client.

2. The secure NT login process occurs.

3. A connection to the share `\\ntdc\netlogin` is established during the login process (`ntdc` is the domain controller authenticating the user during this particular login process).

4. If the user has a roaming profile defined, it is pulled down from the server and applied.

5. If a login script is defined, it is executed (login scripts are located on the `\\ntdc\netlogin` share).

6. The user's initial Explorer process is started.

Both the user login scripts and roaming user profiles are set on a per-user basis in User Manager for Domains. If you are using Samba, roaming user profiles are set globally which is actually easier to administer, as you will find out in Chapters 6 and 7.

For more detailed information on the secure login process, see `http://support.microsoft.com/support/kb/articles/Q139/6/08.asp`.

Summary

This chapter started by going over the main features of Windows NT and why people are moving away from NT to UNIX/Linux-based solutions with Samba instead. That discussion was followed by a clarification of what workgroups and domains are. A workgroup's purpose was to separate network resources in an orderly form for easy browsing. A domain extends the workgroup concept by adding security so that not just anyone can connect to the network and start accessing resources. Users must be authenticated and have the correct access permissions before they can access resources in a Windows NT domain. This discussion also showed the differences between share-level security and user-level security.

The chapter described the NetBIOS session layer interface, and that it is transport-protocol-independent. It also discussed why NetBIOS it is so important in Windows networks—virtually all Microsoft-provided network applications are written with NetBIOS compatibility. The discussion then went through how computer browsing works and how the browse list gets generated when you are searching the network for a particular resource. Finally, the main functions of a Windows NT server were explained, and how that compares to what Samba provides. Samba provides almost everything except for BDC functionality.

This chapter gave you an overview of the main elements of Windows networks. It is in no way intended to be a comprehensive Windows networking reference, this is after all a Samba book! For most of the topics discussed, further information is freely available from `http://msdn. microsoft.com`, `http://technet.microsoft.com`, or `http://support.microsoft.com`. These three Web sites provide quite good search engines to help you find what you are looking for.

The next chapter goes into the practical aspects of integrating Samba into your existing Windows NT network.

Review Questions

1. Why are workgroups less secure than domains?

2. What is the difference between share-level security and user-level security?

3. Name the different roles a Windows NT server can perform, and indicate which of those roles a Samba server can perform.

4. Why is it important to know the basics of NetBIOS communication?

5. Name the possible browser roles that a machine can be in.

6. If a machine is placed on the network and is marked as preferring to be a master browser, and a master browser already exists, what happens?

## CHAPTER 5

INTEGRATING SAMBA INTO AN EXISTING WINDOWS NETWORK

You will learn about the following in this chapter:

- The different roles Samba can play in your Windows-based network

- How Samba can be a WINS server

- How to set up Samba to participate in Windows computer browsing

- How to decide whether to use your Samba server as a password server, or use an existing Windows infrastructure for user authentication

- How to set up home directories with Samba

- How to set up Samba as a print server

- How to use Samba to send broadcast messages to your Windows clients

T his chapter is for those of you who are still new to Samba and unsure of its capabilities, but would like to take it for a test drive—possibly performing some tasks that some of your existing Windows NT servers are doing. There are many different jobs that have to be fulfilled. These include such things as having a WINS server for name resolution; having reasonable machines selected as master browsers; having servers dedicated for file sharing, including storing users' home directories; selecting servers to be print servers; and sending broadcast messages to your users to let them know of system maintenance periods and other important information. This chapter covers quite a lot, so don't worry if you cannot digest everything the first time through. You will probably find yourself referring to this chapter when you require help on a particular task that's covered.

Requirements Samba Can Fulfill in Your Network

Most tasks a Windows machine can do, Samba provides a way of doing also. The tasks this chapter covers are as follows:

- WINS server capability. Most Windows NT networks these days utilize what is called a Windows Internet Name Service (WINS) server. This provides a central point for NetBIOS name registration and resolution without using broadcasts (see the previous chapter). Samba can be directed by the `smb.conf` file to become both a WINS server and WINS client. WINS services are provided by the `nmbd` daemon.

- If you read the previous chapter, you are all experts on Windows computer browsing by now! Samba can fully participate in the browsing process, including becoming a domain master browser if required.

- Samba can direct all login requests to an existing NT PDC or BDC, or alternatively can handle them itself. Both methods are equally useful, and it is a simple matter of choosing the correct method for your environment.

- A feature that for some reason is not widely known to many people is that Samba *does* in fact support encrypted passwords, just like a regular Windows NT server. This chapter goes over how easy it is to set that up.

- Samba can be a full-fledged print server. This includes being able to serve printer drivers to print clients just like a normal NT server.

- When you bring your Windows NT server down for maintenance, you usually send a broadcast message to all those currently connected using the `net send` command, which sends out a NetBIOS datagram to all computers currently connected. You can do this with a Samba server too.

There are some other functions, including allowing Samba to become a login server for Windows 95/98 clients, and Samba acting as a Primary Domain Controller (PDC), but these larger issues are discussed in the following two chapters.

Samba and WINS

The WINS service was first provided with Windows NT 3.5. Since then it has pretty much become mandatory for any Windows network that spans more than a single subnet. Before Windows NT 3.5, to be able to connect to print or file servers outside your own subnet, you had to have a correctly configured `lmhosts` file. In this file were the names of all servers containing resources on your network. You can imagine how hard it would be to keep such a file up-to-date. With the advent of WINS, the `lmhosts` file became a thing of the past—although in some situations, it is still useful. Samba supports both `lmhosts` and WINS.

lmhosts

To use an `lmhosts` file for name resolution with Samba does not require any special configuration in the Samba configuration file. The only thing you need to do is create the `lmhosts` file in the appropriate directory. By default, Samba looks in the same directory as the `smb.conf` file. If you have installed Samba from a precompiled distribution, there might already be a sample `lmhosts` file installed for you.

Each entry in this file has the format IP address, NetBIOS name, optionally followed by a hash (#), and a resource type. The resource type is specified in hex. If no resource type is indicated for an entry, that entry will be returned for requests for all resources under that particular name. Some sample entries might be

```
192.168.3.4 larry
192.168.3.20 moe
192.168.1.1 mydomain#1B
```

Replace *mydomain* with the name of your Windows NT domain. The IP address you should put in is the IP address of the PDC. In this particular scenario, `larry` and `moe` are contacted whenever Samba has to resolve their names for any NetBIOS resource. The third one might look strange to you, but in some circumstances can be very useful. If for whatever reason your network does not use WINS, and you have problems browsing to your Samba server from other subnets, you need to add into your `lmhosts` file something like the third entry. For this to work correctly, your Samba server must be configured to be a local master browser (see the section "Browsing with Samba"). The NetBIOS resource for a domain master browser is 1Bh. Now, when Samba wants to integrate its browsing information into the rest of the network, it can find the domain master browser.

More information can be found in the manual page, `man lmhosts`.

WINS

Because the `lmhosts` file is a static file and requires changing each time a new host is added to the network, you need something that requires a little less maintenance. This is where WINS can help. If you do *not* already use WINS, Samba can be configured to be a WINS server on your network.

The following option must be set in `smb.conf`:

```
wins support = yes
```

With this option set, and the `nmbd` service restarted so that the option takes effect, you can set all your Windows 95/98 and Windows NT clients to point to your Samba server as their WINS server.

Don't Set Up Multiple Samba Servers with WINS Support

Do not set `wins support` on more than one Samba server on your network. Things could get a little confusing with multiple Samba WINS databases!

If you already have a WINS server on your network, Samba can be configured to use it with the next option:

```
wins server = 192.168.1.1
```

Of course, replace the IP address with the address of your WINS server.

> **Don't Set Both** wins support **and** wins server
>
> By default, if a Samba server is configured with wins support, it will automatically go to its internal WINS database for NetBIOS name resolution. If you have a Samba server configured in this way, do not also set wins server on the same system. Samba can get tied in a knot if both settings are set on the same machine!

There are a couple of other smb.conf options that are WINS-related:

- wins proxy (default no). If set with yes, this allows a Samba server configured to be a WINS server to respond to NetBIOS broadcasts on behalf of other clients. In some circumstances, this may provide better performance for older LAN Manager clients.

- dns proxy (default no). If set, this allows a Samba server currently configured as a WINS server (wins support = yes) to fall through to DNS when a name resolution request comes in that it cannot resolve through WINS itself. Samba will do a DNS lookup for the NetBIOS name being requested, and if an affirmative response comes back, the DNS IP address is returned to the requesting WINS client.

Gathering Information from Samba WINS Servers

If you encounter a problem with your Samba WINS servers, you can dump the current WINS database with the following command:

```
# killall -HUP nmbd
```

If you don't have the killall command, you will have to do something like the following:

```
# kill -HUP `cat /var/lock/samba/nmbd.pid`
```

Your currently running nmbd process will dump its WINS database into /var/lock/samba/ namelist.debug. If the file is not there, Samba was compiled to put it in a different location, and you will need to poke around a bit to find it.

Browsing with Samba

If you have not read the Computer Browsing section of the previous chapter, do so now as it will help you understand the basics behind computer browsing and you will be able to understand this section a little more easily. With a small amount of configuration, you can control how Samba or more precisely the NetBIOS daemon, nmbd, will participate in the browsing functions of Microsoft networks. Samba is always in one of two roles, either part of a Windows workgroup, or in a Windows NT domain.

Samba in a Windows Workgroup

In this configuration, WINS will probably not be configured: You have a number of Windows 95/98/NT clients all around the network, perhaps a couple of Samba servers, and maybe an NT server or two—all in the same workgroup. Most likely they will be distributed throughout your network, which is likely to have multiple segments. This network situation is depicted in Figure 5.1.

FIGURE 5.1

Browsing in a Windows workgroup.

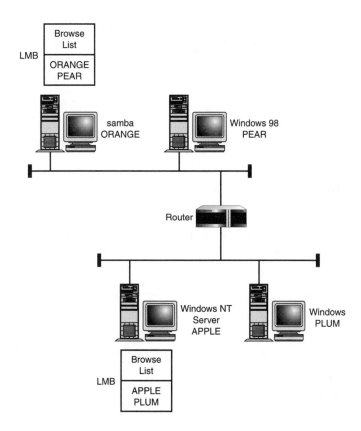

When you go to browse the network on any of the Windows clients, you will see all the machines in your segment, but cannot see all NetBIOS nodes on the network. Why? Because the NetBIOS broadcasts do not get forwarded through the routers, and there is no central point where NetBIOS names can get registered for later retrieval. Remember that to be able to browse the full network, there must be a single machine designated as a local master browser (LMB) on each segment, and also a domain master browser (DMB) that merges all the LMB's entries into one large network resource map. In this model there are LMBs allocated through browser elections, but not a DMB. In a Windows NT domain, the DMB is automatically the PDC, but in this example of a workgroup scenario, there is no PDC, so there is no DMB.

You can allocate one of the Samba hosts to be the DMB using the following **smb.conf** configuration lines:

```
domain master = yes
local master = yes
preferred master = yes
os level = 65
```

The first option, `domain master`, forces Samba to be the domain master browser for the workgroup. *Never* configure this parameter in an existing Windows NT domain. Really evil things can happen when the NT PDC discovers there is a second DMB on its network! `local master` tells Samba to participate in elections for the LMB on its network segment because the DMB is the LMB for its segment as well. The option `preferred master` tells Samba to force an LMB election every time it starts up. This parameter is essential in getting Samba to become DMB. Finally, the `os level` option is used to control what types of Windows machines it will beat during the election. A value of 65 causes it to beat any other host on the network.

Watch for Possible Performance Issues when Using `preferred master`

If you have the `preferred master` option set, and there are other Windows hosts on the same subnet as the Samba server you are configuring, be careful. If these other Windows hosts are configured to be preferred master browsers as well, an election war will occur, which will reduce network performance and fill your logs with annoying warnings.

Several other configurations are handy in certain situations. This one will allow a Samba server to become the preferred LMB in a segment:

```
domain master = no
local master = yes
preferred master = yes
os level = 65
```

You can also disable Samba from participating in browser elections completely (preferred if you already have Windows NT boxes in the same segment as Samba):

```
domain master = no
local master = no
preferred master = no
os level = 0
```

The default browsing behavior for Samba is

```
domain master = no
local master = yes
preferred master = no
os level = 0
```

which means it will try to become LMB if there are no Windows machines on the segment; otherwise, it will always lose elections to Windows hosts.

Samba in a Windows NT Domain

Configuring Samba's browsing role in a Windows NT domain is pretty much the same. You just need to make sure that you never set `domain master = yes`. It's useful to set parameters in `smb.conf` even if they are set to their default settings. This makes it easy to see at a glance what is going on. If you want Samba to become an LMB, make the following settings:

```
domain master = no
local master = yes
preferred master = yes
os level = 65
```

If you know there will always be a reliable Windows NT machine in each subnet, you can disable Samba from participating completely:

```
domain master = no
local master = no
preferred master = no
os level = 0
```

Configuration of the Browsing Clients

For the clients in your browsing environment to see the entire network, they need to be able to communicate with their LMB, which is the easy part. They can find out who that is with a NetBIOS broadcast for the resource 1Dh. However, the LMBs themselves have to be able to communicate with the DMB. A broadcast will not work for the simple reason that the DMB is more than likely located in a different subnet and would not receive the broadcast. Either each LMB needs to have an `lmhosts` file with an entry for the DMB in it, or you need to set up a WINS server. If you opt for the latter method, ensure that *all* Windows and Samba hosts are configured to register with the WINS server. For a Windows NT machine, see Figure 5.2 for the location to enter a WINS server address.

FIGURE 5.2

Configuring a Windows NT WINS client.

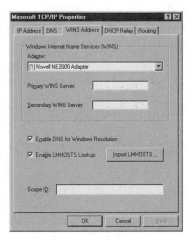

It does not matter whether you use Windows NT or Samba as your WINS server; just pick one platform and stick with it. Samba WINS configuration as both a client and server was described earlier in this chapter.

Choosing a Password Server

This section explains how to tell Samba to use your existing Windows NT SAM database. There is nothing worse than integrating a new Samba file server into an existing environment, showing the boss how cool it is, and the boss remarks, "That's great, but I don't like having to enter another password to be able to access this file service!" With Samba's default configuration, it is set up to use the regular UNIX password file as the method of deciding who can access Samba shares. In an existing environment, this provides one major problem: Each user on your Windows NT domain must have a new account created on the Samba server, complete with a new password. For an environment with many hundreds of users, this could create quite an interesting problem. You need to create all the users on the Samba server anyway, which is the easy part. But a much harder problem is to provide an easy way for the users to change their own UNIX passwords. If they have Windows desktops, changing their password is a simple matter of point and click. An entire site of Windows users would probably not be thrilled at the prospect of logging into a UNIX server just to change their password!

Luckily, the Samba development team put in a feature that allows a Samba server to use Windows NT Domain Controllers (DCs) to authenticate users. See Figure 5.3 for a diagram showing the process.

FIGURE 5.3

Allowing an existing NT server to become a Samba password authentication server.

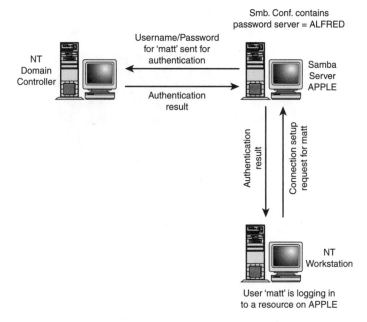

To turn this feature on, set these options in your `smb.conf`:

```
security = server
password server = NTDC1, NTDC2, NTDC3
```

The parameter `security` can be set to one of a number of different potential values: `share`, `user`, `server`, or `domain`. The `share` setting is pretty much defunct now, but it was used to provide share level security. Setting it to user is the default, and it provides user level security. The domain setting is used when you want Samba to be a member server in a Windows NT domain (see Chapter 7, "Samba in a Windows NT/2000 Domain Environment"). We are concerned with the `server` setting here. Setting `security` to `server` tells Samba to send the Username/Password pair over an encrypted channel to a Windows NT DC. The other parameter that was set, `password server`, specifies the NetBIOS names of the NT servers for Samba to authenticate against. Replace the names shown here with the names of a few of your own DCs. These NetBIOS names need to be resolvable, either in the DNS, or you must have set Samba up to be a WINS client so that they can be resolved through WINS. If their name in the DNS is different from their NetBIOS name and you are not using WINS, you will need to create an `lmhosts` file with the correct NetBIOS and IP address mapping.

Each of the password servers are tried in turn until one can be contacted, and then this one server is used for the life of the currently running `smbd` process. If, for example, NTDC2 is chosen and it happens to go down for some reason, any new authentication requests from `smbd` will fail. This is due to a limitation in the SMB protocol, the Samba developers say. However, `security = domain` overcomes this problem by making a new connection to a password server each time a new request comes in. Chapter 7 discusses this point.

A Problem with Using Password Servers

There is one problem with using password servers. Windows NT usernames can be quite long, up to 20 characters. But UNIX passwords, as you all know, are usually allowed a maximum of eight characters. How do you resolve this issue? Samba as usual has an answer! You can create a username map file that has a mapping from UNIX user to Windows NT user. This option is set by adding the following to your `smb.conf`:

```
username map = /usr/local/samba/lib/username.map
```

Now you need to create the `username.map` file to have entries similar to this:

```
mattg = "Matthew Gillard"
```

My account name on UNIX is `mattg`; however, my account name under Windows NT is `Matthew Gillard`. Listing 5.1 is a script that is useful to automatically create the `username.map` file from the entries in `/etc/passwd` in this format.

LISTING 5.1   A Sample Shell Script to Automatically Generate a Username Map File for Use with Samba

```
#! /bin/sh
#
# Author: Matthew Gillard
# Description: Example script for Samba Primer Plus which
#              demonstrates how to automatically generate
#              a username map file from an existing /etc/passwd file.
```

continued on next page

continued from previous page

```
#########################################################################

# Loop through each entry in /etc/passwd, stop when read detects
# end of file

while read passwd_line
do

# Create a line in the format username = "real name"

  line=`echo $passwd_line | awk -F":" '{printf("%s = %s", $1, $5)}'`

# Some systems allow other data in the username field, these
# are usually separated by commas. So use awk and set the field separator
# to a comma and output the first field. This gets rid of any other
# information other than the real name.

  echo $line | awk -F"," '{print $1}'

done < /etc/passwd
```

You then need to add this script to roots crontab (assuming you saved the above script to the filename samba_username_update.sh):

```
# crontab -e
0 1 * * *            samba_username_update.sh > /usr/local/samba/lib/username.map
```

This is useful in an environment where every user has an NT name with the format Firstname Lastname, but at the same time each user also has an account on a UNIX system where he needs access to his home directories via Samba.

Samba and Encrypted Passwords

Unfortunately, Microsoft made a serious security blunder with the initial versions of Windows NT and Windows 95. By default, when connected to SMB servers, it negotiated the lowest security level of authentication both systems had in common. This meant that if they connected with older-style LAN Manager servers that did not support password encryption, SMB connections were negotiated with plaintext passwords, which is an obvious security problem. Microsoft since remedied this problem with file updates for Windows 95 (for more information, see http://support.microsoft.com/support/kb/articles/Q165/4/03.ASP) and Service Pack 3 or greater for Windows NT. Windows 98, luckily, negotiates encrypted passwords by default. Back in Chapter 3, you learned a registry setting that turned plaintext passwords back on if you are running Windows 98 or Windows NT SP3+. That's fine for a quick test environment, but for a full corporate environment, having cleartext passwords flying around your network is not a good idea! What you can do is configure Samba to accept encrypted passwords, which solves the cleartext problem. The following steps outline the basic procedure to follow for enabling NT encrypted password support.

First of all, make sure encrypted passwords are turned on in smb.conf:

```
encrypt passwords = yes
```

Samba uses a file called smbpasswd to store Windows NT-compatible encrypted passwords. If you compiled Samba with default options, Samba looks in /usr/local/samba/private for this file. If you have used a precompiled package, this file could be anywhere! An easy way to find out where your smbpasswd is located is to run this command:

```
# testparm -s | grep smbpasswd
smb passwd file = /etc/smbpasswd
```

The command testparm is a utility distributed with Samba that processes your smb.conf file and gives you a definitive answer as to what each Samba variable is set to, as well as checking your smb.conf file for errors. Here, smbpasswd will be found in /etc.

Assuming you want all your currently registered UNIX users to be able to log into Samba, log in as root and create an initial smbpasswd file with this command: (replacing the destination path with the path you found from the testparm command):

```
# cat /etc/passwd | mksmbpasswd.sh >/usr/local/samba/private/smbpasswd
```

Alternatively, if your site uses NIS:

```
# ypcat /etc/passwd | mksmbpasswd.sh >/usr/local/samba/private/smbpasswd
```

The smbpasswd file should be treated as carefully as a shadow password file, so check that it has the correct restricted permissions. If you are using the path in the example, make sure the private directory has permissions:

```
# chmod 500 /usr/local/samba/private
```

This changes the permissions to look like this:

```
dr-x------   2 root     root           1024 Oct  4 11:40 /usr/local/samba/private/
```

Then you need to make sure that the smbpasswd file has the correct permissions:

```
# chmod 600 /usr/local/samba/private/smbpasswd
```

The permissions on the file should now look like this:

```
-rw-------   1 root     root            230 Oct  4 10:49 /usr/
➥local/samba/private/smbpasswd
```

In Red Hat Linux, the smbpasswd file is by default located in /etc. Do *not* change the permissions on the directory /etc to be 500! This will break many things—UNIX systems require world read access to /etc! However, do be sure that the actual smbpasswd file has permissions 600 as described earlier.

Each entry in this file will look something like this:

```
matt:500:XXXXXXXXXXXXXXXXXXXXXXXXXXXXXXXX:XXXXXXXXXXXXXXXXXXXXXXXXXXXXXXXX:
➥[U      ]:LCT-00000000:Matthew Gillard,,,,
```

There are two rows of 32 bytes of Xes. Windows NT uses two methods of storing a user's password hash. One is LAN Manager-compatible, and the other is the much stronger Windows NT LAN Manager version. For Samba to be compatible with any LAN Manager client, it must also store both versions of the password. With all passwords stored as Xes, this disallows any connections as any user. You will need to set all users' passwords to a default. You can do this with the command `smbpasswd`.

smbpasswd

The `smbpasswd` command is very similar to the regular UNIX `passwd` command. There are two formats of this command. When you run this command as root, you get these options:

```
smbpasswd [options] [username] [password]
options:
  -s                use stdin for password prompt
  -D LEVEL          debug level
  -U USER           remote username
  -r MACHINE        remote machine
  -R ORDER          name resolve order
  -j DOMAIN         join domain name
  -a                add user
  -d                disable user
  -e                enable user
  -n                set no password
  -m                machine trust account
```

When you run this command as an unprivileged user, there is a subset of the commands available:

```
smbpasswd [options] [password]
options:
  -s                use stdin for password prompt
  -D LEVEL          debug level
  -U USER           remote username
  -r MACHINE        remote machine
```

Several tasks can be accomplished quite easily with `smbpasswd`, as described in the following sections.

Adding a Large Number of Passwords at Once

When running `smbpasswd` as root, you can change any user's password without knowing the original one, just as with the `passwd` command. One nice feature is easy bulk password changing. For example, if you have 100 UNIX users and a newly created `smbpasswd` file, you can write a script to automatically change all their SMB passwords to a default one by specifying the username and new password on the command line:

```
smbpasswd matt newpassword
```

Using `smbpasswd` in conjunction with a program that allocates random passwords, like the `mkpasswd` utility with Red Hat Linux, you can quickly set a large number of passwords relatively securely.

Adding New UNIX Users to smbpasswd

As `root`, when you add a new UNIX user, you need to be able to add him to `smbpasswd` as well. This process is made simple with the `-a` option:

```
# smbpasswd -a newuser newuserpasswd
```

This will add *newuser* to the `smbpasswd` file with the initial password *newuserpasswd*.

Users Changing Their Own Passwords

Any user can change her own password by simply typing at a UNIX shell prompt:

```
$ smbpasswd
Old SMB password:
New SMB password:
Retype new SMB password:
Password changed for user matt
```

She is asked for her old password, then asked for her new password, and then asked again for verification.

Changing the Password on a Remote SMB Server

Support is included in `smbpasswd` for changing the passwords on remote SMB servers, such as Windows NT. Anyone can issue a command like this:

```
$ smbpasswd -r <remote machine>
```

This command by default uses the current UNIX username as the remote username that the user is changing the password for. If you don't want this, you can specify a remote username with the following command:

```
$ smbpasswd -r <remote machine> -U <remote username>
```

The parameter `<remote machine>` can be any Windows NT Server, Samba server, or other SMB-style server that supports remote password changing.

Keeping smbpasswd Entries and passwd Entries in Sync

Consider the consequences of using both an `smbpasswd` file and a regular UNIX `passwd` file. Most of your users would appreciate having one password for both logging on to the UNIX server, and making an SMB connection to a share on the same UNIX box. When they change their SMB password with `smbpasswd`, they need to change their UNIX password with `passwd` at the same time to keep everything up-to-date. Samba can be configured to automatically change a UNIX password at the same time as the SMB password change. Because this functionality is disabled by default, you need to switch it on:

```
unix password sync = True
```

The other parameters that are used in conjunction with **unix password sync** are **passwd program** and **passwd chat**. **passwd program** defines the program that Samba calls as `root` to allow the new password to be set when the **smbpasswd** entry is changed. Set **passwd program** like this:

```
passwd program = /bin/passwd %u
```

As usual, %u will be replaced with the username doing the password change. The `passwd chat` parameter is what controls the password changing conversation with the `passwd program` and might need a little tweaking depending on what environment you are in. The default setting is

```
passwd chat = *old*password* %o\n *new*password* %n\n *new*password* %n\n *changed*
```

Full details on how you can tweak this parameter are in the `smb.conf` online manual page.

Migrating Existing Windows NT Encrypted Passwords to a Samba Server

The initial set of steps to produce an `smbpasswd` file was most appropriate for just using encrypted passwords on a single UNIX server with existing user accounts. This is for an environment that is predominantly UNIX-based, but with Windows clients and a small number of Samba servers dotted around the place. You also want to be able to use Samba in a secure manner without cleartext authentication for your SMB connections. Many sites use plaintext authentication when turning on support for NT-encrypted passwords is very trivial (as you have seen) and provides that added level of security.

There is one other way of creating an `smbpasswd` file. This method is used in environments where you have an existing Windows NT server and are migrating all users to a Samba UNIX server, and then removing the Windows NT machines when you are done.

This magical program is called `pwdump`. It was written by the Samba team and is freely available from your closest Samba mirror in `/pub/samba/pwdump`. There are three files in this directory, a `README` file, the source code file `pwdump.c`, and a Win32 x86 executable `pwdump.exe`. If you are interested in Win32 programming, go ahead and look at the source, but if you change anything, you will need a Win32 compiler such as Microsoft Visual C++ as well as a DES library such as the freely available `ftp://ftp.psy.uq.oz.au/pub/Crypto/DES/libdes-4.01.tar.gz`.

Using pwdump

Actually using `pwdump` is relatively painless. It works by following the registry key `HKEY_LOCAL_MACHINE\SECURITY\SAM\Domains\Account\Users` and dumping the associated Windows NT logon names and hashed passwords in a file in the `smbpasswd` required format (see the preceding section). To do this, you must execute `pwdump` as Administrator, and to be able to access the registry keys it requires, it needs to modify the registry permissions on each key it needs to access. The permissions are returned to normal after each user is dumped. Although to date there are no known problems with this program, the Samba team assumes no responsibility if for some reason it breaks your system!

If you have multiple Windows NT servers, you first of all have to decide which server to run `pwdump` on. If the users who are being migrated to Samba are on a Windows NT domain, you can execute `pwdump` on any domain controller that is a member of the domain. If the users you want to migrate are only on a Windows NT server, you just need to run it on that server.

If they are registered on multiple Windows NT servers, you can run it on all of them, and then concatenate the resulting `pwdump` files. If you are joining multiple `pwdump` files, make sure that in the final file, each user has a unique id (second field in the file).

Use Caution with the Output File Created by pwdump

Unlike the UNIX password file, the file that is created with `pwdump`, although not containing plaintext passwords, contains the actual hashes that are used in the CIFS authentication process. This means that if someone with enough know-how gets a copy of this file, he has enough information to compromise your environment. Always treat the `smbpasswd` file with care, and securely copy it from your Windows NT system to your Samba system, either by using SSH, or floppy disk! And check and double-check that the permissions on the `smbpasswd` file on your Samba system are set to owner root and no access to anyone else (`rw-------`).

Unless you have to for other reasons, you do not want to use this method in conjunction with continuing to use a Windows NT server. The main reason is that the `smbpasswd` file will *not* keep in sync with your current domain SAM—effectively your users need to keep two passwords in sync, and this is not fun! You can use `pwdump` periodically and securely copy the resulting dump file to the Samba server as some form of primitive password-syncing process, but if you are doing this, you may as well use the SAM on the NT machine for password authentication in the first place by setting the `security = server` option.

User Home Directories

When you had Windows NT servers only, it is more than likely each user had a specified home directory, with an accompanying share. Remember that Windows NT home directories are specified in `User Manager`. Samba provides an easy way of managing user home directories. There is a special section in the configuration file called `[homes]`. This section causes shares for the home directories of the users registered on your Samba server to be automatically generated on the fly using the directories specified in either `/etc/passwd` or the `smbpasswd` file as the home directories. This is very useful because it means that you do not have to go and create home shares for each individual user. This `[homes]` section is effectively cloned with each connection and `[homes]` is renamed to the service name being connected to. An example of a `[homes]` section is as follows:

```
[homes]
        comment = Home Directories
        read only = No
        create mask = 0750
        browseable = No
```

The `comment` makes for easy identification in a share list, of which `share` is a home directory. The `read only` parameter allows all home directories to be writable. An alternative is to put `writable = Yes`. Both achieve the same end result! The `create mask` variable specifies the default permissions of files that are created on the share, and `browseable` indicates that each home share is hidden from the sharelist, seen from a `net view` command or in Network Neighborhood.

Some sites use different home directories for PC users than UNIX users. If your site would like to do this, you need to add a parameter like this to the [homes] section:

```
path = /home/pcdata/%S
```

The %S will be substituted for the name of the current service being connected to. For example, if you connected to \\goofey\matt, %S would substitute to matt.

Restricting Home Directory Users

There may be times where you do not want users to be able to access their home directory shares. This can be tackled in one of two ways. You can deny everyone by default and have a list of valid users with these people the only ones who can access the service:

```
valid users = matt, mikec, djk, @pcusers
```

The "@" specifies that a UNIX group follows. This example assumes that a UNIX group called pcusers exists with a list of users in it.

The other way is to allow everyone by default, and only deny some users:

```
invalid users = baduser, fred
```

This also works for regular shares as well.

Samba as a Print Server

Another popular task that Windows NT servers perform is print serving, and of course, Samba can do that as well! Samba actually does not do any of the printing grunt work. It acts as the interface between your Windows machines and the UNIX printing subsystem. Today, Samba can print to almost any UNIX printing system, be it BSD-based (Linux, SunOS, FreeBSD, and others), HP-UX System VR4 (SVR4), Solaris SVR4, or AIX.

UNIX Side Configuration

Two requirements must exist before Samba printing will work:

- You must have some existing UNIX printer queues.
- You must have either a valid /etc/printcap (if the printing is BSD-based), or you must have a supported lpstat command (for System VR4-based printing).

The first is pretty self-explanatory. You must have some UNIX printer queues that work before Samba will be able to print to them! Test them by printing some text from the UNIX command line. For BSD systems, try

```
$ echo "This is a test" | lpr -Pmyprinter
```

For SVR4-based systems, try

```
$ echo "This is a test" | lp -dmyprinter
```

Replace *myprinter* in both cases with the name of your printer queues. If the test prints work, you're well on your way! If they don't work, troubleshoot the problem until you get some output.

The second requirement is to let Samba know which print queues exist on the system. This is so that Samba can automatically create a printer share for each configured printer. If you use BSD-style printing (such as Linux), you will have a file called `/etc/printcap`. This is the central printer control file that stores the printer names, spool directories, and other printer-specific options. Each entry in the `/etc/printcap` file will look something like this:

```
lp|EpsonStylus600|epson:\
        :sd=/var/spool/lpd/lp:\
        :mx#0:\
        :sh:\
        :lp=/dev/lp1:\
        :if=/var/spool/lpd/lp/filter:
```

Note that in this example, the printer is known by three names: `lp` (the default printer name), `EpsonStylus600`, and `epson`. If this were defined on a system where Samba is used, Samba would create three specific shares for each alias. This is handy, especially if you have many aliases throughout your `/etc/printcap` file.

SVR4-based systems do not use a printcap file, so you have one of two options. You can create a fake one that contains all the printers on your system that you want to be accessible by Samba, like this:

```
printer1|printer2|printer3|printer4
```

It is effectively just a list of printer aliases, but because Samba only uses the `printcap` file to get the names of all the valid print queues, this is enough.

Alternatively, if your flavor of UNIX has the `lpstat` command, you can tell Samba to use this to get the list of available printers dynamically. This is the preferred method—if you use the `printcap` file, you need to make sure it is continually updated as new printers are added and deleted. The `lpstat` command always returns an up-to-date printer list.

Samba Printing Configuration

This consists of two parts, the global printer configuration and a printer share-level specification.

Global Printer Configuration

Global printer configuration involves only three global parameters to do with printers, and it is more than likely that the default values will not need changing:

- `printcap name` (default: `/etc/printcap`)—Here you can define the name of your printcap file. The default is most likely okay. However, if you use SVR4 printing, you must either create a fake printcap file (see the previous section) or specify `lpstat` like this: `printcap name = lpstat`.

- `load printers` (default: `yes`)—Here you control whether or not all the printers are loaded for browsing. By default they are, but you can turn it off by specifying `no`.

- `lpq cache time` (default `10`)—This option is to minimize the amount of times the command specified in the parameter `lpq command` (see the next section, "Share-Level Printer Configuration," for information on the parameter `lpq command`) is called (`lpq` is called when getting a list of jobs in a particular queue). When the `lpq` command is executed, the results are put in a file called `/tmp/lpq.xxxx` on a per-user basis where `xxxx` is a hash of the `lpq` command in use. The default is to cache the time for 10 seconds. If you have a slow `lpq` command (many jobs being spooled continuously or many printer queues), it is recommended to increase this number.

Where Is the Printcap File Under AIX?

Note that under AIX, the printcap file is called `qconfig`. Samba automatically assumes that the printcap file is in AIX format if the string `/qconfig` appears in the printcap filename.

Share-Level Printer Configuration

Share-level printer configuration can work in one of two ways. The most common minimal configuration is to create a section called `[printers]` (similar in concept to `[homes]`) in your `smb.conf` like this:

```
[printers]
        comment = All Printers
        path = /var/spool/samba
        create mask = 0700
        print ok = Yes
```

When Samba starts up and it finds a section like this, all the options in this section are used as the default options for each printer share that is created.

The other way is to create printer shares individually on a per-printer basis like this:

```
[hpljet]
    comment      = HP Printer @ Level 2
    path = /var/spool/samba
    print ok = Yes
    guest ok = Yes
```

This would be useful if you only require a few printers for access from Samba.

The most common method is to create a `[printers]` share. The different options used are as follows:

- `comment` (default: none)—This is just a text string that appears when browsing the printer shares. This comment will appear next to the name for the share `printers`.

- `path` (default: none)—This is the default directory that is used to store the spooled print jobs directly after they arrive from Windows. Make sure that the permissions are set to `drwxrwxrwt` for this directory. You can do this with the command: `chmod 1777 /var/spool/samba`. This ensures that print jobs can be spooled to that directory. The 't' ensures that users can delete only their own print jobs.

- `print ok` (default: `no`)—This is a mandatory parameter for printers that tells the system print jobs may be spooled to the `path` previously specified.

- `guest ok` (default: `no`)—If this is set, shares can be mapped to the printer share (or any printer share if in the global `[printers]` section) without specifying a username or password. The connection will be made as the user defined in the `guest account` parameter, which is usually `nobody`.

The following optional share-level parameters may be useful in some circumstances:

- `printing` (default: `bsd`)—This controls how the underlying UNIX printing subsystem is manipulated. This includes the way spooled jobs are printed to the actual UNIX printer, how the printer queues are paused and continued, how print jobs are removed from the queue, and how you get a list of the jobs in a queue. As you are probably aware, many of the different UNIX systems have decided their way is best to print, so as a consequence there are several different ways to control the printing, depending on which UNIX you are using at the time. This parameter can be one of: `bsd`, `aix`, `lpng`, `plp`, `sysv`, `hpux`, `qnx`, and `softq`. If you are using Solaris, you would set this to `sysv`. Setting this parameter causes the defaults for these commands to be changed accordingly: `print command`, `lpq command`, `lppause command`, `lpresume command`, and `lprm command`.

- `min print space` (default: `0`)—This controls the amount of free disk space in kilobytes that must be available before print jobs can be spooled. The default behavior is that print jobs can be spooled at any time.

- `print command` (default: depends on the setting, `printing`)—This setting is usually set to something like this: `lpr -r -P%p %s`. Normally you do not need to touch this setting unless you have a UNIX system that prints using a method that printing does not cover, or you are debugging printing problems. If you find that printing a certain type of job does not work correctly, you can set this command to something like this to try to debug the problem: `cp %s /tmp/printing.debug`. Instead of printing the job, it will be copied to the `/tmp` directory. From there, you can look at the file to try to find out what is going wrong.

- `postscript` (default: `false`)—This forces a `%!` to be prepended to the print job output. Sometimes PCs force a Control+D to be placed at the start of the print job, which will either cause any PostScript jobs to be printed as text, rather than the PostScript being interpreted by the printer, or make the jobs seem to disappear.

Broadcasting Messages to Your Windows Clients

Another thing that Windows systems provide is a NetBIOS messaging service. On Windows 95/98 systems, it is called WinPopUp. On Windows NT systems, you can send messages with the command `net send` at a command prompt. For those unfamiliar with Windows messaging, it is a method by which messages can be sent to users and computers. The messages are transported as NetBIOS datagrams. For example, if the author is logged into machine DAFFY as `matt`, among other things DAFFY will have the NetBIOS names `MATT<03>`, and `DAFFY<03>` registered. The NetBIOS resource `<03>` is used by the messenger service. Using `net send` from DAFFY or any other machine that can resolve NetBIOS names (for example, both machines being on the same subnet, or by the use of a WINS server), the author can send himself a message like this:

```
C:\>net send matt "This is a test message"
```

Windows Messenger will respond by popping up a message like that in Figure 5.4.

To be able to send messages to Windows 95/98 clients, they must be running the WinPopUp program. These machines by default do not register the Messenger NetBIOS resource.

Probably the most common application of Windows Messenger is for system administrators to send messages to users currently connected to the server warning them to save their work and log out, like this:

```
C:\> net send /users "Please log out and save your work.
➥The server is to be rebooted at 5pm."
```

The `/users` option on the command line sends the message to every user with a connection to the server.

Now that you have migrated all your services off Windows NT, how do you notify your users of system downtime? For interactive users, this is easy:

```
# wall "System will be down from 6pm tonight for maintenance"
```

This sends a message to all users' terminals. But for those Windows users using Samba, the message will not get through, and they will not know you are going to drag the server from under their feet!

The answer is to use the `smbclient` command as follows:

```
$ smbclient -M daffy
Added interface ip=192.168.66.4 bcast=192.168.66.15 nmask=255.255.255.240
Connected. Type your message, ending it with a Control-D
System will be down from 6pm tonight! Remember to save your files.
sent 68 bytes
```

The command **smbclient** is quite versatile, as you will see later in Chapter 8, "Using **smbclient**." The **-M** option tells **smbclient** to send a WinPopUp style message to a particular computer name. So with a bit of UNIX scripting, you can send a message to all users connected to your Samba server. A sample script could be as follows:

```
#! /bin/sh
for i in `smbstatus | egrep -ive "^Samba" -e "^Service" -e "^-" \
  -e "^No" -e "^Share" -e "total$" \
  | awk '{print $5}'`
do
  echo $1 | smbclient -M $i
done
```

If this script were called **windows_wall.sh**, you could call it like this:

```
$ windows_wall.sh "System will be down from 6pm tonight!
➥Remember to save your files."
```

Receiving Windows Messages on UNIX

Believe it or not, you can now set up Samba to receive Windows Messenger messages sent to it! The global variable **message command** controls this. An example might be

```
message command = /bin/sh -c "wall `cat %s`" &
```

This will send the contents of the **net send** command as a broadcast to all logged-in users. Make sure that whatever command you specify here, you put an ampersand (&) at the end. Samba expects the command here to return immediately. If there is any delay, Samba processing may stop and a performance hit might occur—for example, if hundreds of users are logged in at one time, it might take a while for **wall** to send out the message to everyone.

Summary

This chapter started by discussing the different requirements that a Windows NT server fulfills in your network, and then showing how Samba can achieve all these tasks.

The first task was NetBIOS name resolution. Samba supports **lmhosts** files as do Windows machines, and also has the capability of being a WINS client and server. One drawback is that Samba cannot replicate WINS data with another WINS server, but you will find that this capability should not be too far away.

Drawing on the browsing discussion from the previous chapter, the chapter then showed how Samba can fully participate in browser elections, including being a domain master browser if this capability is required. However, if there is already an existing Windows NT PDC, you have to be careful not to set Samba in this mode, or strange things will happen to the network!

Samba can either process authentication requests itself, or pass these on to an existing Windows NT server for authentication if you have an existing Windows NT infrastructure that you will not be replacing any time soon. This is handy if you are slowly bringing in Samba servers, but don't want to give the users the hassle of having separate passwords to access the Samba resources.

You went through the method that Samba uses to handle encrypted password authentication. Samba uses an `smbpasswd` file, which is similar to the UNIX `passwd` file. The main difference is that the `smbpasswd` file contains two different hashes for a user's password: the old LAN Manager version and the newer and more secure Windows NT LAN Manager version. You can easily create the `smbpasswd` file using an existing Windows NT SAM with the `pwdump` utility.

User home directories are easily managed under Samba. You just need one section, `[homes]`, and new home shares are cloned on the fly as connections are requested using this special section of the configuration file.

Samba can handle Windows printing quite easily. Samba is the recipient of the Windows print job, and Samba then sends it on to the UNIX printing subsystem to actually get the job to the printer. You must have a working UNIX printing system before printing via Samba will work, and if you do, it should be a painless exercise to get Samba printing to work. Similar to the `[homes]` section, there is a `[printers]` section to quickly and simply make available all printers defined on the system as printer shares. Doing this requires the use of either a `printcap` file or the `lpstat` command to get the list of printers depending on whether the printing is BSD- or SVR4-based.

Finally, you learned how Samba can participate in Windows messaging. You can send messages to all users who are logged in, as you can do with a normal Windows NT server. And also for whatever reason, you can set up Samba to deliver Windows messages sent to it, and in the example you saw how to set up Samba to send a broadcast message to all logged-in users.

Review Questions

1. What are the sorts of tasks that a Samba server can fulfill in your network?

2. What are the drawbacks of using only `lmhosts` files for NetBIOS name resolution?

3. You have noticed a problem with your Samba WINS server. How would you go about checking what entries are currently in the database?

4. What is the Domain Master Browser, and how do you configure Samba to not ever be one?

5. What are the different methods that Samba can use for authentication and how do you set them in `smb.conf`?

6. What is `smbpasswd` used for, and how would you use it to change the password for mikec on the Windows NT server `OYSTER`?

7. How do I configure my Samba server to make available only printers I explicitly define?

8. Describe how to send a Windows Message to a Windows NT machine called `BBQ` with both Windows NT and a UNIX system running Samba.

CHAPTER 6

USING SAMBA WITH
WINDOWS 95/98

You will learn about the following in this chapter:

- What Samba can do for you in a Windows 95 or Windows 98 network

- How to configure Samba as a domain login server for Windows 95/98 clients

- How to configure Windows 95/98 roaming user profiles

- An introduction to Windows system policies and how to implement them on your Samba domain login server

- How to go about troubleshooting your Samba domain login server if it fails to work for you the first time

*U*ntil recently, Samba supported only domain logins for Windows 95/98 clients. Due to the stringent security requirements of a Windows NT client authenticating to a domain controller, the implementation of this process in Samba required a lot of work—and reverse engineering of how Windows NT processes the login request—by the Samba development team. To fully implement Windows NT domain controller functionality required many hours of coding and testing to get it right. However, this chapter focuses on the domain authentication for the less secure Windows clients such as Windows For Workgroups, Windows 95, and Windows 98. This process is relatively straightforward and has been implemented in Samba for quite a while now—at least the last three years. This chapter discusses the issues involved in getting Samba to authenticate with these less secure Windows clients. If you want to get Windows NT clients using Samba as their domain login server, skip to the next chapter.

Samba's Role in a Windows 9x Network

Samba provides a number of features that are important or useful in a network of Windows 9x clients, other than the usual file-sharing services:

- Domain authentication for users as they log in, identical in functionality to a Windows NT domain controller

- Support for login scripts

- Support for user home directories

- Support for roaming profiles

- Support for Windows 95/98 policies

The first feature effectively emulates a Windows NT Domain Controller for Windows 9x clients. It means that you have all the valid users for your site defined on the Samba server, and all your Windows clients are configured to use the name of your Samba workgroup as the user authentication domain.

The second feature is support for the batch files that are configured to run when users log in. These batch files are called *login scripts*. They can be defined on a per-user basis, or by using a common login script for everyone.

There is also support for the special Windows 9x directive "`net use <drive>: /home`", which automatically maps a drive to the currently authenticated user.

The next feature is support for roaming profiles. An environment is created each time a user logs in to a Windows 9x system for the first time. Then as users change settings, these are remembered the next time they log in. This environment is called a "user profile," and normally each user has an individual profile. The term "normally" is used here because there are occasions when *mandatory* user profiles are put in place by administrators if they want consistent settings each time a user logs in, such as would be required for a shared account that is used by many different people. A "roaming profile" is a simple extension that allows users to have the same profile on whatever machine they log in to on the network. For this to occur, when a user logs out of a Windows client, the profile must be saved back to a central server, rather than the Windows client the user was working on.

Finally, system administrators can put restrictions on what users can do to their Windows 9x machines. These restrictions can include things like not allowing access to the registry, allowing only approved software to be executed, disabling access to the network settings, and so on. These restrictions are usually enabled in the registry using a tool called the System Policy Editor. This policy editor creates a file called `config.pol`, which is placed on a read-only share on a server. Then when a user logs in to the Windows client and this `config.pol` file is detected, the registry settings in this file are applied to the Windows system and the user is restricted to do only what the system administrator has allowed him to do.

Workgroups and Domains Revisited

Let's briefly return to the earlier discussion related to the differences between domains and workgroups that was explained to you in Chapter 4. Consider Figure 6.1.

FIGURE 6.1

A Windows 95/98 client participating in a workgroup.

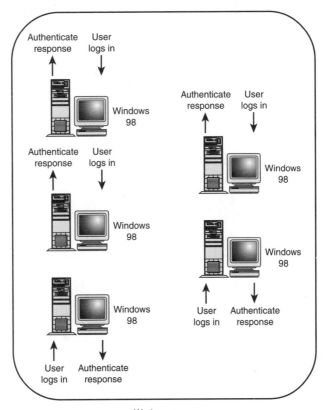

Workgroup

Remember, in a workgroup, there is no such thing as centralized user management. In the less secure Windows clients like Windows For Workgroups and Windows 9x systems, if a user has not logged in before, he will be asked to verify his password and an "account" will be created for him. Unfortunately, this is not a real account. The only "user account" information stored is the username and password, and optionally passwords to other resources that the user uses so he does not have to type his password in all the time. For each user, a file called *username*.pwl is created in the Windows directory that stores these passwords. As you can see, this method is archaic in that it results in numerous .pwl files being created on the system for each different user that logs in. Not only that, but it is trivial to break the simple encryption used in these .pwl files, which means that passwords for users can be recovered by using tools that are very easy to find on the Internet. This might seem like not much of a problem because any one can log in to the Windows clients anyway. But users generally have one or two passwords that they use for everything. So, after this password is recovered, it will more than likely get the cracker into other accounts the user holds, including Internet access accounts with the local ISP!

Luckily there is a better way, as shown in Figure 6.2.

FIGURE 6.2
A Windows 95/98 client participating in a Windows NT domain.

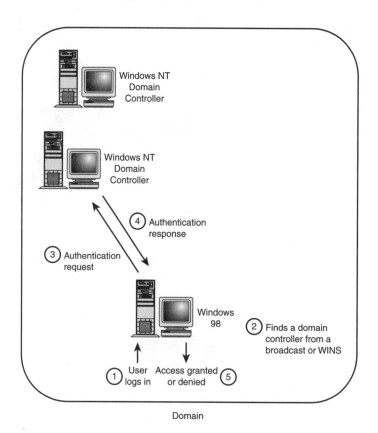

With the Windows NT domain model, all valid accounts in the domain are defined on the primary domain controller (PDC), which is replicated to all backup domain controllers (BDCs). In simple terms, when a Windows client is a member of the domain and it needs to authenticate a user to a particular domain, it first has to choose a domain controller to which to authenticate. This is done by requesting authentication to an NT server, or a Samba server that has registered the domain controller NetBIOS resource type <1c>, which indicates that it provides domain controller services (see Chapter 4, "Understanding Windows NT Networks"). The Windows client then encrypts a challenge that is sent to it from the selected Domain Controller using the username/password combination that the user initially entered, and sends this encrypted string to the Domain Controller. The Domain Controller also encrypts the same challenge with what it knows as the password. The Domain Controller next compares these encrypted strings, and if they are the same, the Domain Controller responds by providing access to the domain; if they are different, the Domain Controller denies the user access to the domain.

Unfortunately, by default, `pwl` files are still created that contain a user's username and password. This time, it is a user's domain password that is stored in this file! This means that if these files were cracked, an intruder would have a correct username and password and have a head start on gaining unauthorized access to the entire domain, not only on the PC he stole it from, but any PC that is a member of the Windows NT domain! If he gains access to the domain, he has access to all file shares that the user he stole it from has access to. Luckily, you can turn off the creation of these `pwl` files by setting a registry key that disables password caching on all your Windows 95 and Windows 98 clients. Start `regedit.exe` and follow the registry tree:

`HKEY_LOCAL_MACHINE\SOFTWARE\Microsoft\Windows\CurrentVersion\Policies\Network`

And add a value with the following parameters:

`"DisablePwdCaching"=dword:00000001`

With that key set, and all `pwl` files deleted from each system, you can be sure you have done your best to secure the unsecurable! You can execute this command to see if there are any `pwl` files on your system:

`C:\>dir \windows\*.pwl`

If your installation of Windows is in an alternative directory, substitute that directory name instead of *windows*.

There is one other problem with the less secure Windows clients (any other Windows operating system other than Windows NT). To join a domain, all that has to be done is to tell the Microsoft Windows client network layer on the system to authenticate to a particular domain name (this is described in "Configuring Samba as a Domain Login Server," which follows). Of course anyone who can install Windows can do that. With Windows NT, not only each user has an account on the PDC, but also each computer has an account. A computer account name is always the NetBIOS name with a dollar sign at the end; for example, if your machine is called `daffy`, the account on the PDC will be called `daffy$`. The good thing about adding a Windows NT client to a domain is that the person adding the computer needs to be in the Domain Administrator group. Until a Windows NT client has an account on a domain, it may not authenticate any users from the initial login dialog box to that domain. This process will be explained in more detail in the next chapter.

Configuring Samba as a Domain Login Server

Setting up Samba as a domain login server is a relatively simple and painless process. You first have to configure the Samba server, and then configure each Windows client. To configure your Samba server, follow these steps:

1. Samba must be configured as a master browser. If you do this, make sure that there are no NT domain controllers around, or a browser election war could start. To do this, set `local master` in `smb.conf` to `yes`:

   `local master = yes`

2. If your network is distributed over a number of different subnets, you should configure Samba as a WINS server as well:

```
wins support = yes
```

If you decide to do this, remember to configure your Windows machines as WINS clients.

3. When a Windows client uses a login server to authenticate users, a special read-only share is also accessed called `netlogon`. On this share you can put programs that are accessed during login or other files you want any host to be able to access during the logon process. This is where the logon scripts (see step 5) and system policy files are located. You will need to create this share on your Samba server by adding something like this to your `smb.conf` file:

```
[netlogon]

    path = /samba/netlogon
    read-only = yes
    guest ok = no
```

4. Finally, you need to tell Samba to register the special domain controller NetBIOS type `<1C>`. This is the special NetBIOS name that allows Samba to be used as a domain controller. Set this parameter in `smb.conf`:

```
domain logons = yes
```

If the workgroup name of your Samba server is HOME, the output of `nbtstat -a sambaserver`, run from Windows, will contain this NetBIOS name:

```
HOME            <1C>  GROUP       Registered
```

This indicates that your Samba server is ready to process user authentications for the HOME domain.

5. Decide whether or not you want to create logon scripts for your users. Most likely you will want to, even if they will only be simple (for example, providing access to two resources: a home directory and a shared group directory). You will need to decide whether you want to use common logon scripts for everyone:

```
logon script = logon.bat
```

Or if you want to have individual scripts for each user:

```
logon script = %U.bat
```

You can of course use any of the standard Samba variables. In this case `%U` is the name of the user accessing the logon script. Whichever your choice, put the relevant entry in your `smb.conf`.

6. Now you will need to actually create the logon script(s). The example assumes that you have chosen to have one global logon script. If you create this script file under UNIX, you need to make the text file in DOS format. If you are using `vi`, this is just a simple matter of pressing Ctrl+V and then Ctrl+M to add a ^M at the end of each line. The file in `vi` might look like this:

```
net use h: \\sambaserver\%U^M
net use g: \\sambaserver\group^M
pause^M
```

It's helpful when creating a logon script for the first time to add a pause at the end so that you can see what worked, and what didn't. Then when everything works as you expect, you can delete the line with the pause in it. Notice also that the variable %U expands to the name of the user logging in. Alternatively, a better way to do it is as follows:

```
net use h: /home^M
net use g: \\sambaserver\group^M
pause^M
```

If the Windows clients were using Windows NT as a domain controller, in User Manager on Windows NT you can specify a home directory for each user. Then, when you do the following command, this is a signal for Windows 95/98 to map the h: drive letter to this directory:

C:>net use h: /home

There is a similar value in your **smb.conf** file. The parameter is **logon home**, which, by default is "\\%N\%U". This value expands to the name of your Samba server and the username of the current user. If you have the **[homes]** section in your configuration file, this should be valid. Now when you perform that special **net use** command, Samba knows where the user's home directory is located. Of course, you can change **logon home** to wherever your home directories are located. They might not even be on the Samba logon server; it could be another Samba server or even a Windows NT server!

7. When you have finished configuring Samba for domain logons, you will need to stop and start the Samba daemons. Under Red Hat Linux you would do this:

   /etc/rc.d/init.d/smb restart

   Other flavors of UNIX have a similar way of restarting **smbd** and **nmbd**. Note that doing a **kill -HUP <pid of smbd> <pid of nmbd>** will not be enough. You will actually need to stop all the Samba daemons and restart them again. Now on to configuring your Windows 9x machine.

8. If you are not using encrypted passwords, which were described in the previous chapter, and you are using Windows 98 or Windows 95 service release 2, you will need to disable encrypted passwords. Follow the registry tree using **regedit**:

   HKEY_LOCAL_MACHINE\System\CurrentControlSet\Services\VxD\VNETSUP

   And add the following value:

   "EnablePlainTextPassword"=dword:00000001

   However, do *not* reboot yet.

9. You then need to configure your Windows client to use domain logons by going to Start, Settings, Control Panel, Network Client for Microsoft Networks, Properties. Select the check box next to Log on to NT Domain and click OK, but do not reboot yet. See Figure 6.3.

FIGURE 6.3

Configuring Windows 98 for NT domain logons.

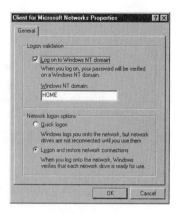

10. Now, configure all your Windows clients to use your Samba server as the WINS server by clicking Start, Settings, Control Panel, Network, TCP/IP, Properties, WINS Configuration, and filling in your Samba server's IP address as shown in Figure 6.4.

FIGURE 6.4

Configuring a Windows 98 WINS client.

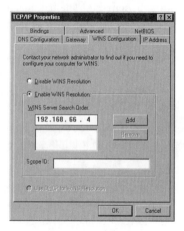

Configuring things this way allows all your Windows clients to be able to find your Samba logon server no matter which subnet it is located on. Of course, the alternative is to turn on NetBIOS broadcasts through your routers, but this is not recommended!

11. You can reboot now! When your Windows system has rebooted, you will get a login screen that looks like that in Figure 6.5.

If you log in with a valid username and password, the logon script you set up previously should execute as shown in Figure 6.6.

FIGURE 6.5

Windows 98 ready to log
in to the domain HOME.

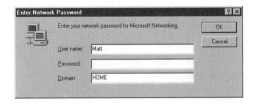

FIGURE 6.6

The Windows NT logon
script after it has finishing
executing.

12. When you press any key, your normal Windows desktop should appear. Then when you
go to Explorer, the two network drives that were connected via the logon script should
be there and accessible.

Congratulations—that's all there is to it! The following section discusses how to get roaming
user profiles working.

Configuring Roaming User Profiles

You are probably aware of or have heard about the concept of roaming user profiles. It was
briefly talked about in the beginning of this chapter, but here is some more information for
you. In a nutshell, roaming profiles means that you can theoretically log in to one Windows
machine and set it up the way you personally like it. You may like a particular color scheme,
prefer a particular screensaver and want a particular background style. Then when you log off
that machine and go to another one somewhere else in the same company, you will get all your
same preferences back again. Enabling roaming profiles is a way of personalizing your
machine. You configure your machine the way you like it the first time, and it will stay like
that no matter where you log in.

Configuring roaming user profiles for Windows 9x clients is easy. Just follow these steps:

1. Start up Windows, log in, go to Start, Settings, Control Panel, Passwords, and click the
User Profiles tab. Check the check box Users Can Customize Their Preferences and
Desktop Settings, and then select either of the two check boxes underneath, depending
on what you want included in your roaming profiles. See Figure 6.7.

FIGURE 6.7

Enabling individual user profiles.

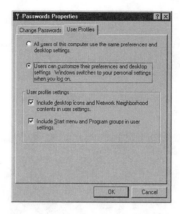

2. Click OK, and then click Yes to reboot your computer.

3. By default when individual user profiles are enabled, Samba saves each user's profile to her home directory under a profile subdirectory. This setting is controlled via the `logon path` parameter in `smb.conf`. By default it is set to `\\%N\%U\profile`, but it is recommended that you change it to a separate share (which could even be on another server) specifically for user profiles, like this: `\\%N\profiles\%U`. Wherever you put each user's profile, make sure the directories have the correct permissions. It is suggested that you test with a few users first to make sure you have the permissions right, or the user profiles will not save correctly.

Security Problems with Windows 9x Clients and Profile Directories

Sometimes Windows 9x clients maintain a connection to the Samba [homes] share even when no one is logged in, so never set `logon path` to `\\%N\homes\profile`. If you do, the next person to log in may find that he has access to the home directory of the previous person who was logged in. Try to have a specific profile share to store profiles in, and do not use home directories.

---

4. When your Windows 95/98 machine has finished rebooting, you can log in. If all goes well, after the logon script has executed, a dialog box will appear asking whether you want your user preferences saved. Say Yes, and your initial user profile will be created. See Figures 6.8 and 6.9.

FIGURE 6.8

Initializing a user profile for the first time.

FIGURE 6.9

The creation of a new
user profile.

5. Your Windows desktop will come up soon after. Your user profile is not saved to the server just yet. For it to be saved, you need to log off. When you are logging off, all your preferences and other profile information should be saved to the location specified in the `logon path` parameter. You will see this process happen via a dialog box appearing on logout.

6. When you have logged out, check the directory on your user profile save location. It should look similar to this:

```
$ ls -l
total 133
drwxr-xr-x  4 matt     matt          1024 Oct 30 10:43 Application Data
drwxr-xr-x  2 matt     matt          1024 Oct 30 10:45 Cookies
drwxr-xr-x  3 matt     matt          1024 Oct 30 10:45 Desktop
drwxr-xr-x  3 matt     matt          1024 Oct 30 10:45 History
drwxr-xr-x  2 matt     matt          1024 Oct 30 10:43 NetHood
drwxr-xr-x  2 matt     matt          1024 Oct 30 10:45 Recent
drwxr-xr-x  3 matt     matt          1024 Oct 30 10:45 Start Menu
-rw-r-----  1 matt     matt        127008 Oct 30 10:51 USER.DAT
$
```

The file `USER.DAT` is the preferences file (individual registry settings), and the rest are self-explanatory. If you want all users to be unable to change their profiles, rename `USER.DAT` to `USER.MAN`. This makes their profile mandatory.

7. There are three other settings that you need to make sure are set correctly:

```
preserve case = yes
short case preserve = yes
case sensitive = no
```

The first, `preserve case`, specifies that long filenames should have their display name's case preserved. The second, `short case preserve`, specifies that filenames in 8.3 format should also have case preserved. The last, `case sensitive`, determines whether or not filenames are case sensitive. The default settings of Samba 2.0 are set to these settings, which also replicates the behavior of Windows NT Server.

Now, you have Samba acting as a Domain Logon server for your Windows 95/98 clients, as well as having roaming user profiles working!

System Policies

Many sites choose to implement system policies on their Windows clients. They choose their policies with the special System Policy Editor tool available on the Windows 95 and Windows 98 CD-ROM under `tools\reskit\netadmin\poledit`. `poledit` is a graphical user interface with which it is easy to restrict what can be done on a Windows client machine. When the administrator is finished, she saves the settings to a file called `config.pol`. This file is then put onto the domain controller's `netlogon` share, which is accessed when users get authenticated. Now that you are using Samba as a domain login server for your Windows clients, you can put this `config.pol` file on the Samba `netlogon` share, and then your system policies will continue to restrict what can be done on each Windows 95 or 98 workstation.

Because discussion of this very detailed topic is out of the scope of this book, you can search for more information on system policies at `http://support.microsoft.com` and `http://technet.microsoft.com`. If you have a subscription to Microsoft's Technet CD, look on that as well for system policy information. Microsoft has many white papers on how to set up and use system policies to create a consistent environment for your users.

Troubleshooting Samba as a Domain Login Server

You may come across some problems in the process of working through this chapter. This section discusses a couple of the most common issues here that are fairly easy to remedy.

If you see the screen in Figure 6.10, you have either entered the wrong password/username combination, or you are using a Windows 9x system with encrypted passwords and are not using encrypted passwords on the Samba side. If this is the case, either enable Samba encrypted passwords, or enable plaintext passwords in Windows (see "Configuring Samba as a Domain Login Server," earlier in this chapter).

FIGURE 6.10

Logon incorrect.

You may get the message shown in Figure 6.11. This error means what it says: Windows cannot find a domain server to authenticate you. This can happen for a number of reasons:

- You may not have configured the Windows WINS client correctly, either by putting an invalid IP address in, or none at all.

- You may have put the right address in the Windows WINS client, but your Samba server may not be configured for WINS support.

- Your Samba server might be on a different subnet to your Windows machine and you expected them to be on the same subnet. If this is the case, configure WINS or use an `lmhosts` file.

FIGURE 6.11

Unable to find a Domain
Controller to authenticate
the logon request.

If you are still having problems, you can erase Windows 9x's knowledge of any user profiles in existence, and effectively start again. Follow these steps:

1. First check with all users who use this computer to find out whether they have any programs or data located in their profiles that they want to keep. If they do, tell them to copy it elsewhere, perhaps to a network drive where it will get backed up.

2. Go back to the Windows 9x login screen, and instead of logging in, press Esc. This puts you in the default system user profile.

3. Go to Start, Run and type `regedit`. Follow the tree `HKEY_LOCAL_MACHINE\Software\Microsoft\Windows\CurrentVersion\ProfileList`. There should be a subkey for each user who has logged in to this machine. Go to one of them and note the value of `ProfileImagePath`. Now delete all the subkeys of the users that have profiles you want deleted.

4. Go to Explorer and delete the profile directories of all the users. The location of these profile directories was what you noted in the value `ProfileImagePath`. It is usually in the directory `C:\win98\profiles\<username>` or `C:\windows\profiles\<username>`.

5. Log off.

6. Now, when you log in, the profile creation process should begin again.

If you had outstanding problems, this might have fixed them. If you still have a problem, turn to Chapter 12, "Debugging Samba," and utilize some of the tips there.

Summary

This chapter covered the steps for configuring Samba as a domain login server for Windows 95/98 clients. The chapter was split into four sections. In the first section, you learned how to set up Samba by using the `smb.conf` file to accept domain logins. You saw how to use login scripts to give each of your users a consistent environment, including being able to use the following command to automatically map a drive to the user's home directory:

```
net use h: /home
```

Then you learned how to set up your Windows client to use domain logins. If you have a multisubnetted network, it was also suggested that you set up Samba as a WINS server and your Windows machines as WINS clients, so they will all be able to see the Samba server during logon.

The next section covered roaming profiles. You learned how easy it is to set these up, so your users will have their same preferred environment, including Start menu and all preferences including wallpaper, screen saver, and color scheme. It was also recommended that you use a separate share as a profile share rather than each user's home directory. Users tend to delete things they don't know about, so if the profiles are stored in home directories, users might tend to delete the profile without knowing what it is!

Next was a short section on system policies. There is a system policy editor called `poledit.exe` on the Windows CD-ROM, and this is used to create a policy file called `config.pol`, which is placed on the netlogon share on your logon server. If you want more information on system policies, you can go to Microsoft's Web site, or if you subscribe to Technet, look there. The topic of system policies is a large one and out of scope for this book.

Finally, the last section covered some basic troubleshooting techniques. These are the things that most system administrators have problems with, and you learned how to best rectify the problems to get everything working.

The next chapter will cover using Samba as a logon server for Windows NT clients.

Review Questions

1. What are the main features of Windows NT domains that are supported with Samba being a domain controller for Windows 95/98 clients?

2. What is the difference between a Windows 98 client logging in to a workgroup versus a Windows 98 client logging in to a Windows NT domain?

3. What are the main configuration statements that must be included in `smb.conf` for Samba to operate as a domain login server? Assume that a Windows NT WINS server already exists and logon scripts are being used on a per-user basis and are located in the directory `\\sambaserver\netlogon\logonscripts`.

4. What are roaming profiles?

5. Suppose that your roaming profile server is called `ronald` and the share is called `profiles`. How do you configure Samba to save all users' profiles to this location?

6. You have set up Samba to be a login server, but when you log in to Windows 98, you get the error `Login Incorrect`. What might be wrong?

7. What are System Policies and why are they useful?

## CHAPTER 7

SAMBA IN A WINDOWS NT/2000 DOMAIN ENVIRONMENT

You will learn about the following in this chapter:

- How to add a Samba server in your NT domain as a member server

- The different tasks Samba can perform when in a PDC role

- How to set Samba up as a PDC for Windows NT clients

- How to use Windows NT ACLs on your Samba server

- How to use Server Manager with Samba

- How to use User Manager for Domains with Samba

- How to set up roaming profiles for Windows NT clients using a Samba PDC

S amba can do many more things in the Windows NT environment than it used to. Until the last year or so, all you could do with Samba in an NT environment was use it purely as a file and print server. And of course, Samba could be configured to pass the authenticating username/password to an NT domain controller for authentication. This was very useful. It meant that Samba's potential users did not need a second account on the Samba server; they would still get authenticated by the NT environment for access to the Samba resources. Now, however, Samba users can go one step further.

This chapter gives you an introduction to using Samba in an existing domain environment in two new roles. First, you will learn how to set up Samba as a member server in a domain. Second, you will learn how to use Samba as a Primary Domain Controller (PDC). Keep in mind, though, that most of the PDC functionality is still experimental, and full functionality will not be available until Samba 2.1. Also, as it stands currently, if you use Samba as your PDC, you cannot have Backup Domain Controllers (BDCs) because System Account Manager (SAM) replication is not working in the current Samba production code; however, it should be working with Samba 2.1. Other miscellaneous issues will also be covered, such as using the standard Windows NT administration tools like User Manager for Domains and Server Manager with Samba servers and the information you can glean using those tools. Finally, you will learn how to set up Windows NT roaming profiles when you have Samba as your PDC.

One thing that should be mentioned is that you can also safely use Windows 2000 instead of Windows NT unless otherwise noted.

Adding a Samba Server as a Domain Member

In Chapter 5, "Integrating Samba into an Existing Windows Network," you learned that you could direct Samba to send authentication request packets to an existing Windows NT domain controller. However, there is a drawback to that method. Suppose that you have the following setting in your `smb.conf` file:

```
security = server
password server = NTDC1 NTDC2 NTDC3
```

Remember that when a user tries to connect to a share on a Samba server, a new `smbd` daemon is spawned for the life of that connection. This means that when an instance of `smbd` starts up, Samba will try each domain controller until it finds a domain controller that is available. That `smbd` then stays connected to this chosen domain controller for the life of that particular Samba thread. This is bad for two reasons. First, if it stays connected to the one NT server for a lengthy period of time, the resources of that NT server will get strained, especially if more than one Samba server is doing the same thing. Second, if that NT server goes down, authentications will fail for that Samba session because it cannot change NT domain controllers. That Samba session will have to be killed before authentications will work again.

Now that Samba can participate in a Windows NT domain as a member server, communications can become more reliable—because Samba basically acts like an NT server in that there is a secure communication channel between the Samba server and an authenticating domain controller. This is the same behavior that a regular NT server displays. The new configuration is this:

```
security = domain
password server = NTDC1 NTDC2 NTDC3
```

This time there is a new security mode that this book has not discussed before. It is called "domain security." In this mode, the Samba server makes a secure RPC connection to one of the password servers each time a user needs authenticating, and then closes the connection. No connections are left open for the life of the Samba process. Not only that, but more information is brought back with the authentication reply. This information includes but is not limited to the users' Windows NT security identifier (SID), groups they are members of, and the times they are allowed to log in to the network. This information is obviously very useful and provides a good framework for extending Samba in the future.

Configuration Details to Make Samba a Member Server

Recall that each user who needs access to a domain must have an account in that domain. Similarly, each computer in a domain also needs an account in the domain. This computer account is called a *trust account*. Each computer that has a trust account and is a member of the domain can authenticate to that domain. Trust accounts are a fundamental aspect of the

Windows NT domain security model. Any computer that does not have a trust account in a particular domain cannot access that domain at all from the login prompt. This means that only trusted Windows NT clients are given accounts (usually those managed by the IT department of a particular organization). The trust accounts are represented in the PDC's SAM by *<computername>*$, which is each machine's NetBIOS name followed by a dollar sign. Each computer has its own password as well, which is initially just the computer's NetBIOS name. This password is automatically changed every seven days for security reasons, and is initially changed when the computer joins the domain for the first time. For your Samba server to be able to participate as a member server, a trust account must be created. To do this, open Server Manager on your Windows NT PDC. Server Manager is located under Start, Programs, Administrative Tools. Click Computer, Add to Domain as shown in Figure 7.1.

FIGURE 7.1

Adding your Samba server to your Windows NT domain.

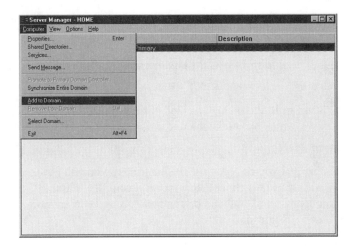

Keep the default computer type (Windows NT Workstation or Server) selected, enter the name of your Samba server, and click Add. The new server should be added to the list of servers in the domain.

Next, stop all the Samba daemons. In most distributions of Linux, you would do as follows:

```
# /etc/rc.d/init.d/smbd stop
```

Now, as root, you need to tell your Samba server it is now a part of the domain. If your Windows NT domain is called HOME and your Windows NT PDC is called DAFFY, you would type the following command:

```
# smbpasswd -j HOME -r DAFFY
1999/11/08 22:34:56 : change_trust_account_password: Changed
➥password for domain HOME.
Joined domain HOME.
```

Notice that when you added the server to the domain, it immediately changed its password. This is done for obvious security reasons because the initial password is just the name of the server. The new password for this machine's account on the domain is stored in a file of the format *DOMAIN.SambaServer*.`mac` (for the preceding example, the file is called `HOME.DAFFY.mac`) in the same directory that the `smbpasswd` file is located in. This is usually `/usr/local/samba/private`, but could be anywhere. In Red Hat Linux it is in `/etc`. This file should be read/write only to root and no access to any other user. If this file were compromised, the integrity of your entire system would come into question.

Now you just need to set up your Samba configuration. You need domain-level security:

`security = domain`

Because of the way domain authentication is implemented in NT, plaintext passwords are not accepted—you need to turn encrypted passwords on if you have not already:

`encrypt passwords = yes`

You need your workgroup set to the domain that your NT servers are in:

`workgroup = HOME`

You either need to specify your password servers as some selected domain controllers:

`password server = NTPDC NTDC1 NTDC2 NTDC3`

Or, new in Samba 2.0.6, you can make Samba behave as a normal NT server and specify an asterisk (*), which makes Samba find a domain controller to authenticate against:

`password server = "*"`

Remember that you can only use the latter method if you have Samba 2.0.6 or later; otherwise, you need to manually choose some domain controllers. Using the asterisk is the recommended method because it allows load balancing to occur. Different domain controllers may be chosen each time authentication occurs.

Now, you just need to start your Samba daemons and you will be in business. In Red Hat Linux, use the following command:

`# /etc/rc.d/init.d/smb start`

Your Samba server is now ready to participate securely using the Windows NT domain security model! Choose this method of user authentication rather than `security=server`, the method discussed in Chapter 5. It gives you more security and load balances the requests against different domain controllers, rather than using "server" security and staying with one domain controller only.

Samba as a Primary Domain Controller

People have been asking for PDC functionality from Samba for a long time. The problem with providing it, though, is that Microsoft has not publicly documented the many protocols that are used in the Windows NT domain model. The Samba development team had to reverse engineer as best they could the different protocols so that they could implement them all in Samba. A common misconception is that domain controller functionality for Windows NT clients is included in Samba 2.0. Strictly speaking, this is true, but it is very buggy, and not supported! To be able to use domain controller functionality with any success and reliability, you must grab the HEAD branch source code from the read-only Samba CVS repository. Instructions on how to do this are detailed in the laer section, "Samba as a Login Server for Windows NT Clients (PDC Role)."

With the development code, Samba can act, for all intents and purposes, as a Primary Domain Controller for both Windows 9x clients (see the previous chapter) and Windows NT clients. This means that for machines that have joined the domain controlled by a Samba PDC, users can be authenticated to the domain to access resources, execute login scripts, and have roaming profiles.

There are some Windows NT capabilities that are not yet implemented in the development code at the time of this writing:

- Samba cannot participate in trust relationships with another Windows NT or Samba domain. Although this is partially implemented, it should be finished for the production release of Samba 2.1.

- Currently, Samba forces printer connections to an NT server to use a lower level of the SMB protocol, rather than NTLMv2. Again, code for this should be complete for Samba 2.1.

- Remember that in a pure Windows NT domain environment there are BDCs as well as PDCs. The BDC's role is to store up-to-date backup copies of the main SAM for disaster recovery as well as for load balancing purposes. This BDC functionality is still in a developmental phase and should be complete for Samba 2.1.

- Windows NT servers allow you to put ACLs on a share level as well as a file-system level. When connecting, NT gives the connecting user the most restrictive combination of permissions. This share-level ACL manipulation is not yet implemented in Samba.

Understanding Trust Relationships

Trust relationships are an integral part of the Windows NT domain model. Trusts come in two forms: one-way trusts and two-way trusts. A one-way trust is useful when you have two independent Windows NT domains and you want to provide users in one particular domain access to the resources of both domains but restrict the users in the other domain to their own resources. For example, consider the computer retail outlet Acme Inc. Acme has a Windows NT domain called ACME. Acme's goods supplier is called ComputerBits Inc., and has a Windows NT domain called BITS that is separate from its corporate network for the use of customers only. ComputerBits allows its customers to dial in to its Windows NT domain and download drivers, look at its warehouse databases, and various other things. Here a one-way trust would be useful to allow Acme to access the resources available on the ComputerBits domain with its own SAM. A one-way trust is illustrated in Figure 7.2. ComputerBits is set up to trust ACME. The Administrator of the ACME domain adds the BITS domain to its list of trusting domains, and then the Administrator of the BITS domain adds ACME to its list of trusted domains. The facility to do this is in User Manager for Domains under Policies, Trust Relationships.

FIGURE 7.2
A one-way trust in which
BITS trusts ACME.

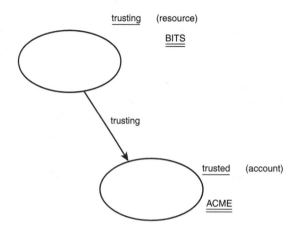

Note that the reverse does not hold true in this case. ACME does not trust BITS, so there is no way that user accounts in the BITS domain can access resources in the ACME domain, which in this case is what should happen. There are a few terms you have to come to grips with here. The "trusted" domain is known as the *accounts domain*. The "trusting" domain is known as the *resource domain*. In the diagram you see that the arrow points to the domain that holds the SAM database you want to trust.

A *two-way trust* is effectively two one-way trusts. In a two-way trust, there are two separate domains that trust each other, which means that users in both domains can access resources in both domains. This situation is pictured in Figure 7.3. In this case the domains involved are the United States division of ACME, whose domain is called ACME-US, and the Australian division of ACME, called ACME-AUS. ACME-US trusts ACME-AUS and ACME-AUS trusts ACME-US. This means that employees of each division of the company can access each others' resources freely without requiring extra accounts on either domain.

FIGURE 7.3
A two-way trust in which
ACME-US and ACME-
AUS trust one another.

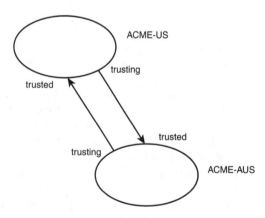

Samba as a Login Server for Windows NT Clients (PDC Role)

As mentioned earlier, as of this writing, the latest version of Samba released was 2.0.6. The domain controller code is broken, so do not use it! You will need to download the latest HEAD code using the **cvs** utility. If you are using a Linux distribution such as Red Hat, cvs will be available as a package you can install from your distribution CD if it isn't already installed. Just type **cvs**, and you should get output like this:

```
$ cvs
Usage: cvs [cvs-options] command [command-options-and-arguments]
  where cvs-options are -q, -n, etc.
    (specify --help-options for a list of options)
  where command is add, admin, etc.
    (specify --help-commands for a list of commands
     or --help-synonyms for a list of command synonyms)
  where command-options-and-arguments depend on the specific command
    (specify -H followed by a command name for command-specific help)
  Specify --help to receive this message

The Concurrent Versions System (CVS) is a tool for version control.
For CVS updates and additional information, see
    Cyclic Software at http://www.cyclic.com/ or
    Pascal Molli's CVS site at http://www.loria.fr/~molli/cvs-index.html
```

As the help says, go to `http://www.cyclic.com/` for more information on this useful tool, including the source code if you need it.

Assuming you have a working **cvs** and an Internet connection up and running, the following two commands will do the job of pulling down the latest Samba code for you:

```
$ cvs -d :pserver:cvs@cvs.samba.org:/cvsroot login
```

When you are prompted for a password, enter **cvs**. Next, enter

```
$ cvs -d :pserver:cvs@cvs.samba.org:/cvsroot co samba
```

The first command logs you into the cvs server anonymously, and the second actually checks out a copy of the Samba source code. A directory called **samba** will be created, and the entire tree will be created under this directory automatically.

When Samba has finished downloading, type

```
$ cd samba
$ ./configure --prefix=/usr/local/samba-dev
```

You will probably want to install a separate copy of this development Samba code so that you still have your original one if this version does not work correctly.

Then when **configure** has finished, build it with this command:

```
$ make
```

Finally, install it (as root of course!):

```
# make install
```

Now you need to build up your `smb.conf` file to allow domain logins by Windows NT clients.

Note that at some point you may want to update the HEAD branch you downloaded with current code. You can do this with the following command:

```
$ cvs update -d -P
```

The `-d` option removes files that have been deleted, and the `-P` option prunes any directories that have been emptied after the updating process. Make sure you run this `cvs update` command when your current working directory is the one above the Samba directory.

Creating a PDC `smb.conf`

You need two major options turned on in your `smb.conf` file.

First, you must have encrypted passwords switched on:

```
encrypt passwords = yes
```

You also need to use user-level security (this is the default security level, but it never hurts to explicitly define it):

```
security = user
```

You need to set domain logons:

```
domain logons = yes
```

Of course, you need to tell Samba which domain you want it to be in:

```
workgroup = TESTDOM
```

A regular Windows NT PDC acts as domain master browser. You should set Samba up the same way, or you may find your browselists are incomplete:

```
domain master = yes
```

Creating Machine Trust Accounts

You now know enough about the Windows NT domain model to know that each Windows NT client that is a member of the domain must have a machine trust account on the Primary Domain Controller. Remember that a machine trust account name is the NetBIOS name with a dollar sign on the end. You will need to create these accounts on your Samba PDC in two places. First, add them to `/etc/passwd` using your favorite editor:

```
daffy$:*:1001:1000:Windows NT machine 1:/dev/null:/bin/false
mickey$:*:1002:1000:Windows NT machine 2:/dev/null:/bin/false
```

For security reasons, set the home directory and shell to `/dev/null` and `/bin/false` respectively. If your UNIX system has shadow passwords, create an appropriate shadow password entry as well. I usually start user accounts with UIDs at around 5000, and reserve the UIDs less than 5000 for the various system accounts and administrator accounts required on the system. So these Windows NT accounts would be placed in this area.

Next you need to add these NT accounts into the smbpasswd file:

```
# smbpasswd -a -m daffy
# smbpasswd -a -m mickey
```

This will create entries in your smbpasswd file that look like this:

```
daffy$:1001:6B3EF92A0680AC8BAAD3B435B51404EE:
FA5852C4BE0FE0842A21CFE8DF04E380:[W            ]:LCT-382FF24C:
mickey$:1002:807CDA06AD520210AAD3B435B51404EE:
F09AB1733A528F430353834152C8A90E:[W            ]:LCT-382FF252:
```

Remember that in the smbpasswd file, there are two hashes: the LAN Manager (LM) hash and the NT LAN Manager (NTLM) hash. The initial password values for machine names are their NetBIOS name. These passwords will automatically get changed when the actual Windows NT machines join the domain.

What Is a Hash?

A hash is basically the result of a one way cryptographic function. It cannot be reversed. A hash can go by one of many names: compressions function, message digest, fingerprint, or cryptographic checksum, just to mention a few. Windows NT stores two different hashes of the one password, both using separate crytographic algorithms. There is the less secure LAN Manager hash (LM) and the more secure NT LAN Manager hash (NTLM). The only reason the LM hash is still stored is for backward compatibility reasons—older LAN manager clients do not understand the NTLM hash. When a password is being checked, it is hashed and the resulting hash value is compared to that stored. If they are identical, the password is correct; if they differ, the password is incorrect.

You will also need to create a test account to use when trying to log in to the domain for the first time. Create one as follows:

```
$ smbpasswd -a matt
```

Make sure the user you add has a current entry in /etc/passwd as well, or your smbpasswd command will fail. You will be prompted for a password when you add the account.

After all that is done, you can start the Samba daemons. But make sure that if you have a previous version of Samba installed, you turn off its daemons first; otherwise, the new daemons will not start.

```
# /usr/local/samba-dev/bin/smbd
# /usr/local/samba-dev/bin/nmbd
```

When you start smbd for the first time, a file is created called TESTDOM.SID, under the directory <sambapath>/private/. This file contains the domain SID for the Samba PDC. You must make sure this never changes or is accidentally deleted. If either of these things happen, Samba will get totally confused until you recover this file from a backup!

Setting Up Your Windows NT Clients

Now you just need to set up your Windows NT client machines. Go to Control Panel, Network. Click the Change button, and in the Domain box, enter the domain name that you specified in the workgroup parameter in `smb.conf`. This is shown in Figure 7.4. Do not try to create the machine account using the lower part of the dialog—it will not work. That is what you did earlier using the `smbpasswd` commands. If all goes well, you should get a message like that shown in Figure 7.5.

FIGURE 7.4

Adding a Windows NT client to your Samba domain.

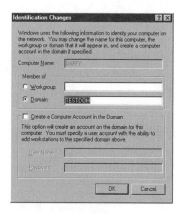

FIGURE 7.5

A message welcoming you to the domain.

As with many system changes, after you click OK, you will be asked to reboot the system. Windows NT should be rebooted now to make the changes to the system take effect.

After you reboot, press Ctrl+Alt+Delete, and you should get a screen similar to that in Figure 7.6.

FIGURE 7.6

Logging in to the domain.

Your domain should be listed in the drop-down list box. Select it and proceed to log in. You will need a valid user account in your `smbpasswd` file to be able to log in here. Log in with the account you created earlier. If all is well, Windows NT has accepted your password, and your NT desktop should appear.

> ### You May Not Be Able to Log In Immediately on a Windows NT Server
>
> If you are using Windows NT Server rather than Workstation, there is a small gotcha you have to look out for. You will not be able to log in straight away with your Samba user account. You will probably get a message telling you that the local policy does not permit you to log in interactively. If this happens, log in to the local machine as administrator (by selecting the machine name in the domain list drop-down box). Open up User Manager for Domains, go down to the groups section, and open up the Users group. Add all the Samba users that you want to allow to log in interactively to this group from your Samba domain, and click OK. Then log out, log back in, and you should be let in this time.

If Your Domain Controller Cannot Be Found

If the NT machine you are logging in to and the Samba server are located in different subnets, it is quite possible that they will have a hard time finding each other. When you log in, you may get a message saying that Windows NT is unable to find a domain controller. If this is the case, there are two solutions.

The first is to create a file in the directory `%SYSTEMROOT%\system32\drivers\etc\lmhosts`. In this file put these two entries:

```
192.168.66.4     goofey     #DOM:TESTDOM
192.168.66.4     TESTDOM
```

Replace `goofey` with the name of your Samba PDC, and `TESTDOM` with the name of your Samba domain. Now, when NT tries to resolve the NetBIOS domain name, TESTDOM, it can.

The second method is to use WINS. This is probably the more scalable solution. Make sure this is set in your `smbd.conf`:

```
wins support = yes
```

Then point all your Windows NT machines WINS IP address entries to your Samba server.

Windows NT Functionality Available on Your Samba PDC

Now that you have Samba acting as your Domain Controller, you are probably wondering what other Windows NT functionality is available from your Samba server. The 2.1 Samba development code has implemented a few features, such as being able to look at and partially manipulate file permissions, view Samba server details in Server Manager, and look at your Samba SAM equivalent (`smbpasswd` file) in User Manager for Domains. To use the utilities mentioned in this section, you will need to have a copy of the Windows NT Server tools. You need a copy of Windows NT Server where these tools are built in, or access to the Internet,

where you can download the server tools from `ftp://ftp.microsoft.com/Softlib/`
`MSLFILES/SRVTOOLS.EXE`. The Windows 9x version is at the same location but the filename is
called NEXUS.EXE.

File Permissions

One of the cool things you can do with Samba now is manipulate file and directory permissions on your active share connections to a Samba server via the Security tab, just as you can
with regular Windows NT machines.

NT ACLs on Samba

With Samba 2.0.4 and higher, the parameter `nt acl support` is set by default to `true`. To be able to
manipulate file permissions on your Samba server from within NT, either make sure that this parameter
is not in your configuration file (which means it is on by default), or if it is there but is set to `false`,
change it or remove it altogether to get the default value. If it is set to `false`, the only Access Control
Entry (ACE) in the Access Control List (ACL) will come up as Everyone (Full Control). If `nt acl support`
is turned on (the default), you will generally see two parts to an Access Control Entry, a name in the format SERVER\Name (Long Name), and a permission. The SERVER will be the NetBIOS name of your
Samba server, the Name will be the name of the user or group the entry is describing, and if the ACE is
describing a user, the Long Name will be the Gecos Entry in the `passwd` file on the Samba server for that
user.

If you are reading this and wondering what this mystical Security tab is, check out Figure 7.7.

FIGURE 7.7

The Security tab under
Windows NT.

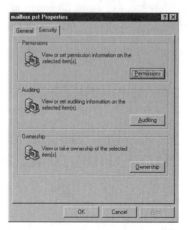

When you right-click a file or directory that is located in a Samba share and go to Properties,
you get a General properties tab, as well as a Security properties tab. If you click the Security
tab, you will see three sections: Permissions, Auditing, and Ownership. The most useful of
these at the moment is Permissions, but the other two are described briefly first.

At the time of this writing, Auditing is totally unimplemented in Samba. If you click it, you will get no entries. In a Windows NT environment, you can audit the success or failure of different types of file accesses such as read, write, and change of ownership, to name a few. This can be very useful in an environment in which you have some files that have open permissions, but you would like to know who accesses the files. Another example could be that you want to remove some files but you are not sure if anyone still uses them. You can turn auditing on and see who accesses them, and then find out why they are still being accessed. The applications of file auditing are endless, and in some secure environments it is a requirement. This will come in Samba, but might be a little way off yet.

The Ownership button tells you who owns the file. If you click Ownership, you get a dialog that looks like the one in Figure 7.8.

FIGURE 7.8

Viewing file ownership.

Because in UNIX you need to have root privilege to be able to change the ownership of files or directories, there is no support of the Take Ownership button yet. But again, when details are worked out as to how this functionality is to be implemented with Samba, the Take Ownership feature will certainly be implemented.

Now, back to the Permissions button. This button allows you to look at and change permissions on a file or directory (with limitations). The limitations are due to the differences in the way NT and UNIX implement file permissions.

Modifying File Permissions

Samba now allows you to modify the file permissions that are located on the UNIX filesystem. This means that when you are connected to a resource, assuming that you have authority to modify file permissions, you can now do so from your Windows client, in a limited way. It is best to illustrate how this works with an example, so look at Figure 7.9.

FIGURE 7.9

Changing file permissions on files located in a Samba share.

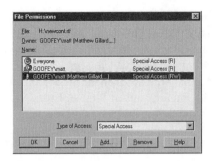

If you think about how UNIX handles file permissions for a second, you will understand how this maps to what you see in the File Permissions dialog box. UNIX has three components of a permission bit: user, group and world. These each have three subcomponents, (r)ead, (w)rite, and e(x)ecute. Here's an example:

```
-rw-r--r--  1 matt     matt          596 Aug 20  1997 newconf.rtf
```

Here, the user part has both read and write permissions and the group and world parts have only the read bit set. The user in this case is `matt`, and the UNIX group is also called `matt`. Some UNIX variants such as Red Hat Linux set up each user with a personal group because sometimes it makes administration easier.

The world UNIX read permission for this file maps to the Windows NT **Everyone** global group. Because anyone can access this file in UNIX, anyone in NT should be able to access it as well. You will notice the first permission in the File Permissions dialog in Figure 7.9 is Everyone Read only. Note that Windows NT has three more permission bits in addition to the standard UNIX RWX. The additional permissions are (d)elete, change (p)ermissions, and Take (o)wnership. The Special Access (R) you notice in the figure designates that the combination of permissions (read in this case) do not map to one of the Windows NT special names such as List, Read, Add & Read, Change, or Full Control. You will find that all UNIX permissions will probably map to Special Access because of the differences between the two systems.

The UNIX group permission, `matt,` is the next entry. Now, because the group `matt` is located on the Samba server only, it is classed as a local group. Because the UNIX permission is read-only for the `matt` group, it is also read-only for the Windows NT equivalent local group.

Finally, the UNIX user permission is mapped. In this case, `matt` is the user, so this permission is mapped as a Windows NT user permission also. You can tell it is a user permission because of the face next to the username. Because the UNIX user permission is read and write, the Windows NT user permission is set accordingly.

A small note about Windows NT groups: You can distinguish between global groups and local groups by the icon that sits to the left of the group name. If the icon contains a picture of the earth, it is a global group; alternatively, if the icon contains a picture of a person and a computer screen, it is a local group.

Windows NT Global and Local Groups

You are probably wondering what global and local groups are in Windows NT, especially if you are coming from the UNIX world, where there is no concept of such a thing. In very brief terms, a *global group* is a group that is available throughout the domain, and therefore in the domainwide SAM. A *local group* is a group that is available only on a per-machine basis. Microsoft's recommendation is that Windows NT local groups should *never* be applied to resources. local groups should be put in only as members of global groups, and users are put into local groups. These global groups then are applied to shared resources throughout the domain. This in fact makes a lot of sense.

Say you have a global group called `Marketing`. You also have local groups called `north-mrktg`, `south-mrktg`, `east-mrktg`, and `west-marktg`. You have four different servers that are located in the north, south, east, and west regions. All users in the northern region use the machine with the local group `north-mrktg` and so their user accounts are placed in this local group, and the same procedure is used for all the three other regions. The four marketing local groups are applied as members of the global (domain-wide) group `Marketing`. Now the global `Marketing` group is applied to any shared resources that all the members of the marketing group need to have access to. Because all the members of the local marketing groups are also members of the global marketing group, they all have the correct access. So when a new person arrives in the southern region, for example, he or she just needs to be added to the southern region local marketing group, `south-mrktg`. This implies that the new person has access to all the resources that all the other marketing people have access to. See Figure 7.10 for a diagrammatical look at how users, local groups, and global groups fit together. In the figure, the emphasis is on users being put in their marketing local groups which are named depending on whether they are in the north, south, east or west regions. These groups are then put into the global `Marketing` group, which is applied as a permission on the resource. The obvious advantage here is that when a new user arrives in the western marketing region, he has to be added to the local `west-mrktg` group once, and he automatically has access to all the marketing resources.

FIGURE 7.10

How users, local groups, and global groups fit together.

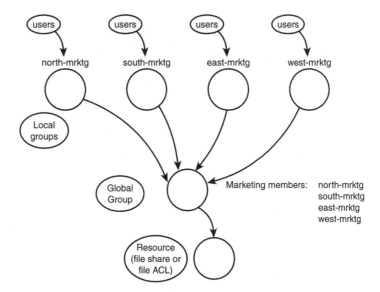

Now you can see the permissions, but can you change them? The answer is yes, you can. If you decide to give members of the local group `matt` write as well as read access, you can click the group and then click the drop-down box and select Special Access. Then, click the Write check box and click OK, as shown in Figure 7.11.

FIGURE 7.11
Modifying the group permission `matt` to add write access.

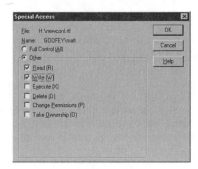

After you click OK, Samba changes the UNIX filesystem permission bit. When you go back to the File Permissions dialog box, you will notice that group `matt` now has write permission as well as read. This is illustrated in Figure 7.12.

FIGURE 7.12
The changed group permission with the addition of the write bit on the file.

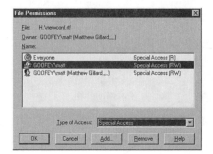

If you try to change permissions that do not map to UNIX permissions, such as one of the D, P, or O permissions, the change you made will be ignored, as these other permissions mean nothing on a UNIX system.

When connected to a Windows NT server, if you click the Add button, you will get a list of users and groups in the domain from which you can select and add to the ACL. Because Samba does not support ACLs, this function is unimplemented currently. There are plans to provide support for this in the future. Now, however, if you click the Add button, you will get an RPC Protocol error as shown in Figure 7.13.

FIGURE 7.13

Samba produces an error when attempting to add a new Access Control Entry to an ACL.

If you click the Remove button for a particular ACE, the ACE will seem to disappear from the list. In fact, Samba just removes all file permissions on the UNIX side, and on the Windows NT side, the permission "O" signifies that No Access is available to that file. Of course the change occurs only to the particular class of user that was removed, be it world, group, or user permission. So if you come back in after clicking OK and look at the permissions after you have removed an ACE, the ACE will appear with the Special Access (O) permission. This is illustrated in Figure 7.14. This is so that you can add back permissions later if you need to because you cannot add a new ACE yet with the Add button.

FIGURE 7.14

The group `matt` now has no access.

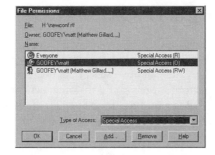

Modifying Directory Permissions

Directory permissions work in a similar manner to File permissions, but they are different in that each ACE has two sets of permissions. Consider Figure 7.15.

FIGURE 7.15

The directory permissions on a Samba share.

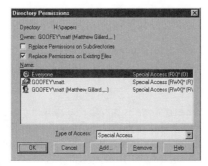

There are still the three ACEs, one each for user, group, and world sets of permissions, but there are two sets of permissions for each. Why? The first is the set of permissions for the directory itself, and the second is called the inherited permissions. Each file created in a subdirectory has its default permission set to the inherited permission of its parent directory.

In the figure, the directory that's being used is called **papers**. The local group **matt** (second ACE) has actual permissions of RWX, but the inherited permission is only R. So any file created under this directory, **papers**, is created with only the R permission set for the local group **matt**. Because there is no such thing as inherited permissions in UNIX, Samba fakes it by showing what permissions a file would have if it was created in this directory.

If you do decide to change the permissions for a directory, by default the file permissions (inherited permissions) are applied to all files in the directory below. If you do not want this, be sure to uncheck the box Replace Permissions on Existing Files before you click OK.

Also, you can apply all your changes down a whole directory tree by checking the Replace Permissions on Subdirectories box.

Controlling the Changing of File and Directory Permissions Within smb.conf

You can control how permissions are applied to files and directories by using configuration directives in your **smb.conf** file. There are two sets of parameters. The first set controls what permissions new files and directories receive, and the other set controls what parts of the ACEs in the Windows NT security dialog a user can modify when they change the file permissions. The values for all the parameters are specified in octal format, which is what the **chmod** and **umask** UNIX commands use.

The four parameters that control what permissions a file and directory receive when they are created for the first time are

- create mask
- force create mode
- directory mask
- force directory mode

The parameters **create mask** and **force create mode** are applied on newly created files. The default value for **create mask** is 0744, which maps to the UNIX permissions:

-rwxr--r--

The default value for **force create mode** is **0**. When a new file is created, Samba first maps any DOS attributes to UNIX equivalent permissions. As an example, if the DOS attribute read-only is set, the user write bit is not set (effectively making the file read-only for the user). After the DOS-UNIX mapping, the resultant UNIX permission is bitwise ANDed with the value of **create mask**. This effectively means any bits that are not set in **create mask** are removed from the UNIX permission at this stage. Finally, the permission that Samba is now left with is bitwise ORed with the `force create mode` parameter. This allows the administrator to force certain bits to be on in the final UNIX file permission. This is especially handy in shared group Samba resources. In that case, you probably want the group part of the UNIX permission to be `rw-` to allow other members of the group to access and modify the file. To do so, you would set `force create mode` to be `060`.

The other parameters, `directory mask` and `force directory mode`, work exactly the same way as `create mask` and `force create mode`, but for directories rather than files. The default for directory mask is `0755`, which maps to the UNIX permissions:

`-rwxr-xr-x`

And the default for force directory mode is `0`, which means no extra permissions are forced to be on.

The other four parameters that control which ACEs a user can change are

- `security mask`

- `force security mode`

- `directory security mask`

- `force directory security mode`

These work in the same manner as the four parameters just described, but their purpose is slightly different. They were added to allow support for changing of the ACE entries in the NT security dialog and how that relates to UNIX permissions. The first two, `security mask` and `force security mode`, have default values of `create mask` and `force create mode` respectively. With `security mask`, when a user changes an ACE in the security dialog, any bits not set, or zero bits, are bits the user is not allowed to modify. To achieve this, the `security mask` parameter is ANDed with the changed bits, which are then ORed with `force security mode` parameter. This means that any permission bits set to be on in `force security mode` are set to be on in the final ACE entry after the user clicks OK. By default, `force security mode` is set to `0`, which means no additional permissions are added.

`directory security mask` and `force directory security` mode are similar, but apply to directories rather than files.

If you want your users to have full control in setting their permissions and you don't want any particular bits to be set on, set the security parameters to these values:

```
security mode      = 0777
force security mode = 0
directory security mask = 0777
force directory security mode = 0
```

Adding Samba Users and Groups to ACLs on NTFS File Systems

One of the other interesting things you can do now with Samba as your PDC is to apply your Samba users and groups to your Windows NT ACL lists for files and directories.

As administrator, create a directory on your NTFS partition on your Windows NT machine called **Marketing**. Create a group on your Samba server (in /etc/group) called **markting**. Add as a member of this group one of the users in your **smbpasswd** file. Modify the ACL on this directory you created and click Add. You will get a list of groups and users from your Samba domain that you can add to the ACL for this directory. Choose the group you created, **markting**, as shown in Figure 7.16.

FIGURE 7.16
Modifying the permissions of a directory on an NTFS permission.

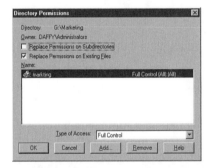

Click OK. Now log out, and log back in as the user you added to the **markting** group. You should be able to put files in there. If you log in again as a user who is not in the group, that user should not have any access to the directory whatsoever.

Server Manager

In a Windows NT environment, Server Manager provides a means to tell at a glance who is connected to the server, what resources each user is using, whether or not the connected users have files open, the resources that are available, and more. Server Manager in a Samba environment does exactly the same thing. There are some functions that are not implemented at the time of this writing. These unimplemented functions include the ability to disconnect users and close resources, and the Replication and Alerts buttons in Server Manager. The best way to explain how Server Manager can be of use to you is by running through an example.

The Samba server in this example is called **GOOFEY**, and is a PDC in the domain **TESTDOM**. First, on your Windows NT machine, go to Start, Programs, Administrative Tools, Server Manager. Server Manager will start up and a list of all the servers and workstations in your current domain will show up. Click Computer, Select Domain and type the name of your Samba server preceded by two backslashes, like \\GOOFEY in the example in Figure 7.17.

FIGURE 7.17

Selecting a server name in
Server Manager.

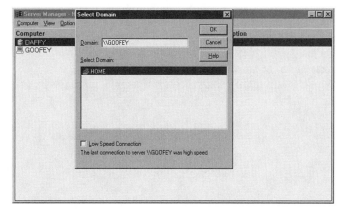

Click OK, and all servers in the domain that your Samba server is a primary domain controller
for will appear, as shown in Figure 7.18. In this example there is only one server in the
domain, which is the Samba server itself. If your Samba server is a PDC, it will be specified as
a Primary in the Type field. You will also notice that Server Manager thinks Samba is Windows
NT 4.2. Believe it or not, this version number can be changed! In `smb.conf` you can add a
variable, `announce version`. By default it is 4.2. The `smb.conf` man page recommends against
changing this parameter.

FIGURE 7.18

Browsing a Samba PDC in
Server Manager.

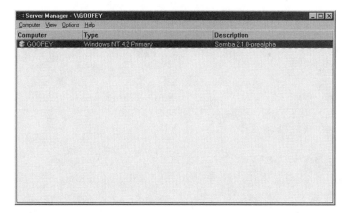

As with Windows NT servers, you can use Server Manager to perform quite a number of useful administrative functions on your Samba server. You can do things such as send Windows
messages to connected users, see SMB server statistics, get a list of currently connected users to
the Samba server, see the number of connections to each share, and see what files `smbd` has
open.

Sending a Message to Connected Users

Messaging can be a very useful tool. In Chapter 5, you learned a method of sending a message to all users with a connection to your Samba server. This is a way of doing the same thing, but doing it in Server Manager. All you need to do is make sure the server to which you want to send messages is highlighted, click Computer, Send Message, and you will see a text box like in Figure 7.19.

FIGURE 7.19
Sending a Windows pop-up message in Server Manager.

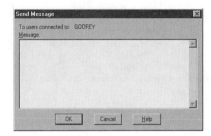

Type some text and click OK. All users connected will get a message like that shown in Figure 7.20. You may find this especially handy if the server needs to go down for emergency maintenance. Using Server Manager for this task is a simple way to send a message to all users.

FIGURE 7.20
All users who are connected to the server will receive the message.

Remember that Windows 9x clients will need to have WinPopUp running to receive any of these Windows messages. This is because Windows 9x has no message listening process like Windows NT systems.

See the SMB Server Statistics

You can see a number of useful smb-related statistics of your Samba SMB server at a glance using Server Manager. If you double-click your Samba server, you will get a screen titled, "Properties for GOOFEY." Obviously yours will have a different name. The author's statistics screen is shown in Figure 7.21.

FIGURE 7.21
SMB statistics for Samba—the PDC named GOOFEY.

You will see the number of NetBIOS sessions connected, the total number of currently open files, file locks, and open named pipes. This is useful if you want to know exactly how many users are connected at a point in time, or if you need to track down a performance problem. The statistics may help you see the cause of a problem. For example, a high Sessions parameter number could indicate that Samba is not closing connections properly.

Get a List of Currently Connected Users

When you have the properties for a server displayed and you click the Users button at the bottom, you will get a list of who is connected and which computer they are connected from. If you click a user at the top of the screen, all the resources that user has open will be displayed in the bottom half of the screen as shown in Figure 7.22.

FIGURE 7.22

Getting a list of users connected to the Samba server.

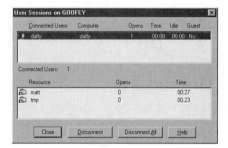

Many of the features of Server Manager when being used with Samba servers are not fully implemented yet. For example, if you click the Disconnect button at the bottom you will get a message, "The remote procedure call failed."

See How Many Connections Are Open to Each Share

Click Close if you are still in the Users screen, and click Shares. Here you will see the full list of all shares on your Samba server. The author's Samba server displayed what is shown in Figure 7.23. Again, the Disconnect buttons do not work at the time of this writing. If you have network problems, you can bring up this list to help pinpoint the cause of the problem.

FIGURE 7.23

Checking the list of shares and connected users in Server Manager.

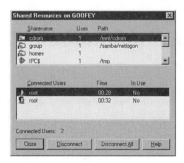

See Which Files smbd Has Open

Finally, you can use the In Use button to see which files are currently open on the Samba server as well as to show which files are open with a lock on them (see Figure 7.24). Being able to see currently open files is extremely useful when you have a problem removing a file and cannot figure out why. Bringing up the list of open files can help you see in an instant if someone on the network has the file open.

FIGURE 7.24

Checking the files that are open using Server Manager.

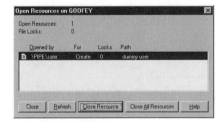

User Manager for Domains

User Manager for Domains is not very functional now, but it is well on the way. You can point User Manager for Domains at your Samba PDC and it will list all the groups on your system and all username entries in your smbpasswd file. If you are logged on to the domain that your Samba PDC controls currently, go to Start, Programs, Administrative Tools, User Manager for Domains. A list of all users in your smbpasswd file and all your entries in /etc/group will be displayed as in Figure 7.25. It is the Samba equivalent of the Windows NT SAM.

FIGURE 7.25

The entries in your Samba SAM.

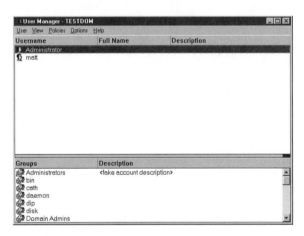

Notice in the figure that Administrator is specified! You are probably wondering how that happened. There is no Administrator account in UNIX! Well, it is quite simple. Samba provides a facility to map UNIX accounts to Windows NT account names. For this example, this variable was set as follows:

```
domain user map = /usr/local/samba/lib/domain_user.map
```

The contents of this file are currently:

```
root        "Administrator"
```

This maps the UNIX root account to the Administrator name. Next, add the root account to `smbpasswd`:

 # smbpasswd -a root

Now, you can log in as Administrator in your Samba-controlled domain! However, Administrator does not yet have the normal administrator privileges. Two other map files are needed. They are

```
domain group map = /usr/local/samba/lib/domain_group.map
local group map = /usr/local/samba/lib/local_group.map
```

The first maps UNIX group names to Windows NT global group names. The second maps UNIX group names to Windows NT local group names. There are two important groups on regular Windows NT Domain Controllers: the global group **Domain Admins** and the local group **Administrators**. To give your administrator account administrative privileges on your Samba server, you need these groups and Administrator as a member of these groups. So put this into your **domain group map** file:

```
adm     "Domain Admins"
```

And this into your local group map file:

```
Wheel   "Administrators"
```

When you open up User Manager, you will see Domain Admins and Administrators in the group listing instead of **adm** and **wheel**. You should see these groups at the bottom of Figure 7.25. Now all you need to do for all your administrative accounts is to put their usernames into the UNIX group **adm** and **wheel** by editing the **/etc/group** file. When you have done that, open up User Manager again and double-click the Domain Admins group (see Figure 7.26). You should see the user account you added to the group as well as Administrator.

FIGURE 7.26

Looking at the contents of the Domain Admins group in User Manager.

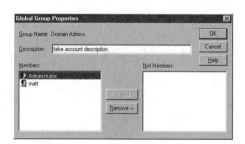

While logged in as this user to whom you just gave administrative privileges, open up User Manager for Domains. Double-click one of your Samba users, and you should see something like Figure 7.27.

FIGURE 7.27
Viewing an entry in the
Samba SAM in User
Manager.

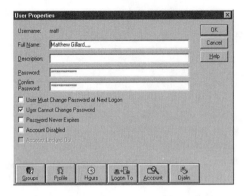

The full name entry is whatever is specified as the real name in /etc/passwd. If you click the
Profile button, you will see the profile settings and home directory setting that you set up in
smb.conf. For an example, see Figure 7.28.

FIGURE 7.28
Looking at the user pro-
file and home directory
settings in User Manager.

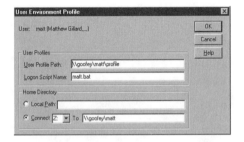

You should now be confident doing administrative tasks on your Samba server using Server
Manager and User Manager for Domains. In the next year or so it will be interesting to see the
new developments in the Samba code to deal with the remaining administrative functions that
are currently unimplemented or partially implemented, as well as all the new functionality that
Microsoft is placing with Windows 2000.

Roaming Profiles Under Windows NT

Setting up roaming profiles in Windows NT is almost the same as doing it for Windows 9x
clients; however, you need to be a little more careful regarding file permissions. This section
first goes through the login process for a Windows NT workstation, and then moves on to
how you can have roaming profiles for all your users.

When you log in to a Windows NT machine for the first time, a subdirectory is created under
the %SYSTEMROOT%\Profiles directory. The name of this directory is the username you use to
log in with, and this is the directory where the local copy of your personal profile is stored.
This profile is initially copied from the %SYSTEMROOT%\Profiles\Default User directory.

It consists of a set of subdirectories as well as a file called `NTuser.DAT`. The `NTuser.DAT` file contains the data for the registry key known as `HKEY_CURRENT_USER`. This registry key contains a user's personal preferences for applications and the Windows NT system such as wallpaper, screen saver, fonts, and colors. If you want to make a change to the default system for all new users who log in, you make the change to the Default User profile, which then gets read when new users log in to the system.

One method you can use to create a standard environment for all users who use the system is to utilize the Windows NT feature so that it looks for the Default User profile on the `netlogon` share first, before it goes looking in `%SYSTEMROOT%\Profiles\Default User`. Create a user-name called `profile`. Log in as this user and set up the environment the way you want it to look. You might put a corporate logo as the wallpaper, change any colors as appropriate, create shortcuts on the desktop for any corporate applications such as a phone directory, and then log out. If your PDC runs Samba, temporarily modify the Samba config file with the following line:

```
admin users = matt
```

Of course, replace `matt` with the username you use to connect with. Otherwise, if it is an NT PDC, modify the ACLs on the `netlogon` share so you have write permissions. Log back in as Administrator and open up a command prompt. Map a temporary drive to your PDC's netlogon share (Samba or NT; this works with either) like this:

```
C:\>net use * \\goofey\netlogon /user:matt
The password is invalid for \\goofey\netlogon.

Type the password for \\goofey\netlogon:
Drive E: is now connected to \\goofey\netlogon.

The command completed successfully.
```

Open up Start, Settings, Control Panel and click System. Then click the User Profiles tab and you should see an entry for the user profile you logged in as before. Click the Copy To button and enter the drive letter to which the netlogon drive was connected. Then enter the text "Default User", as shown in Figure 7.29.

FIGURE 7.29

Copying a user profile to be the default.

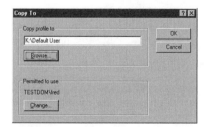

After you've completed those steps, click OK and the profile will be copied to the server. Check on the server so that it will be accessible to everyone, and then log in as a new user and try it out. The user you log in as should have all the preferences that you selected when you were logged in as the profile user.

Using this method, all users log in with your initial preferences you set using the user account profile. If you don't want users to be able to change their own profiles, rename `NTuser.DAT` to `NTuser.MAN` under the Default User directory. This creates a mandatory profile that cannot be changed by the users, even if they try!

Now that you have your standard environment set up, you want all your users to have their environment follow them whenever they log in to a different NT machine. Nowadays with Samba, this all happens by default. After you set up Samba to be a domain login server, by default, all user profiles get saved to a directory called `profile` under the user's home directory. Even though it is already set up for you, this section goes through the different parameters in case you want to change their default values. First, the global parameter `logon path` in `smb.conf` should be set to something appropriate like this:

```
logon path = \\sambaserver\profiles\%U
```

By default, it is set to:

```
logon path = \\%N\%U\profile
```

It is generally good practice to allocate a share on a server (either NT- or Samba-based) dedicated for user profiles. Because by default the user profiles are saved to a user's home directory, users tend to say, "Oh, what's this? I don't need that; I think I'll delete it!" Then they wonder why all their preferences have disappeared next time they log in! The logon path that is specified must be a directory.

If you have set the logon path per the preceding example, a subdirectory will be created for each user when they log in. Make sure that the top level, that is, `\\sambaserver\profiles`, has permissions to allow subdirectories to be created for everyone; otherwise, the roaming profiles can't be created. After each individual user's profile is created, check that the permissions on each user's profile directory are set so that only the user who owns the profile can access it (this should be the case by default).

You might also want to set the `logon home` global parameter to specify where a user's home directory is if it is different than the user's UNIX home directory:

```
logon home = \\othermachine\%U
```

This defaults to `\\%N\%U`, which is probably okay in most environments. You will probably want to also set the global parameter logon drive to the drive letter you want the user's home directory mapped to; by default it is set to Z:, but it is more commonly set like this:

```
logon drive = h:
```

If you had not guessed, H: is for home. Only Windows NT clients use this logon drive parameter. See the previous chapter for how to map a home directory with Windows 9x.

Although this point is not directly related to profiles, just as with Windows 9x clients, you can create system policies using the system policy editor (POLEDIT.EXE). Although the procedure for how to do this is out of the scope of this book, the policy file you will eventually create using POLEDIT.EXE should be put on the `\\pdc\netlogon` share. The file that Windows NT clients look for is `NTconfig.pol`. This is in contrast to what Windows 9x clients expect to see, which is `config.pol`. This means that both files can be on your PDC if you have a mixed network consisting of Windows 9x and Windows NT clients. The system policy editor comes on the Windows NT server CD, or if you don't have that, it is available with the download version of Windows NT server tools I mentioned at the beginning of this chapter.

rpcclient

Remember the tool `smbclient`? It was originally designed by the Samba team primarily as a testing tool for Samba for when they didn't have a Windows-based machine nearby. The `rpcclient` program is used for a similar purpose. It too was designed for the Samba team to use in development, but this time it is used as an MS RPC client. You can connect to all the different MS RPC services on Windows-based machines (the most interesting information, of course, is found when you connect to a Microsoft Windows NT machine) and get all kinds of useful information and opportunities, including being able to browse the registry tree!

You start up `rpcclient` in a similar manner to `smbclient`:

```
$ rpcclient -S daffy -U matt
Added interface ip=192.168.66.4 bcast=192.168.66.15 nmask=255.255.255.240
session setup ok
Domain=[HOME] OS=[Windows NT 4.0] Server=[NT LAN Manager 4.0]
smb: \>
```

You can then get a list of all the currently supported commands by typing "**?**":

```
smb: \> ?
?

eventlog        svcenum         svcinfo         svcstart        svcstop
at              regenum         regdeletekey    regcreatekey    shutdown
regqueryval     regquerykey     regdeleteval    regcreateval    reggetsec
regtestsec      spoolenum       spooljobs       spoolopen       time
brsinfo         wksinfo         srvinfo         srvsessions     srvshares
srvtransports   srvconnections  srvfiles        lsaquery        lsaenumdomains
lookupsids      lookupnames     querysecret     ntlogin         domtrust
lookupdomain    enumusers       addgroupmem     addaliasmem     delgroupmem
delaliasmem     creategroup     createalias     createuser      delgroup
delalias        ntpass          samuserset2     samuserset      samuser
samgroup        samalias        samaliasmem     samgroupmem     samtest
enumaliases     enumdomains     enumgroups      dominfo         dispinfo
samsync         quit            q               exit            bye
help            ?               !
smb: \>
```

You can get information about the NT box you are connected to:

```
smb: \> srvinfo
srvinfo

Server Info Level 101:
        DAFFY           Wk Sv PDC NT LMB
        platform_id     :       500
        os version      :       4.0
```

You can stop services:

```
smb: \> svcstop alerter
svcstop alerter

Stopped Service alerter
```

And you can start them again:

```
smb: \> svcstart alerter
svcstart alerter

Started Service alerter
```

You can also get the time:

```
smb: \> time
time

        Remote Time:    Sat, 27 Nov 1999 20:04:35 GMT
```

You can pretty much do anything like add and delete users and groups, change passwords, query the registry, set values in the registry—and there are no checks for invalid operations! You could quickly cause the machine you are connected to to crash and burn if you are not careful. Any of the commands can be prefixed by the keyword `help,` which may give you information on what arguments can be supplied and what the command actually does.

> ### rpcclient Could Be Hazardous to Your Health!
>
> Using `rpcclient` is dangerous if you do not know what you are doing. Because `rpcclient` bypasses the standard Windows NT error-checking interfaces, you could very easily fry any of the machines you connect to with it. Be careful!

Summary

This chapter began with an explanation of machine trust accounts, and how to add Samba to an existing NT domain. You learned that for this to happen, the Samba server must have a trust account in the domain, and then the Samba server must be joined to the domain using the following command:

```
smbpasswd -j DOMAIN -r PDC
```

The chapter then discussed the functionality that is implemented in the Samba PDC code currently, and you learned how to make Samba a PDC for its own domain that any number of Windows servers/workstations or other Samba servers can join. At the time of this writing, you must download the HEAD code from the Samba CVS site for Samba PDC code. It works fairly well, and the full production release is slated for Samba 2.1.

File-system permissions came next and you learned what you can currently do with the permissions on your Samba shares. The user/group/world UNIX permissions map to similar ACEs in the File Permissions dialog box when viewing them on an NT machine. Eventually you will be able to manipulate them the same way as you can with pure NT machines currently.

You then learned how you can add groups defined on your Samba PDC to regular NTFS partition ACL lists. This is quite handy for environments that have file shares on NT servers, but the domain is controlled by a Samba machine.

We then went on to talk about how you can use the Windows NT Server tools such as Server Manager and User Manager for Domains to see SMB statistics, and look through all the users and groups defined on your Samba server.

The last major section in this chapter involved looking at how roaming profiles work when using Samba as a PDC. You have seen that roaming profiles are enabled by default and get saved in the user's home directory under the directory profile. You have also learned that that should really be changed to a share someplace that is dedicated to the storage profiles.

The `rpcclient` utility was quickly reviewed and you learned how useful it can be to gain information about your NT machines from UNIX systems. Until now, if you needed such information as details on registry entry keys, currently connected users, and general server information, you needed a Windows machine—but not any more!

This chapter has given you the information you need to be able to set up Samba as a domain member server or primary domain controller in a Windows NT/2000 domain environment. You also learned that you can do many of the administrative tasks that you can do to a Windows NT server, but with the security and scalability of a UNIX server running Samba.

Review Questions

1. What is a machine trust account?

2. How do you set up Samba as a member server in an already existing domain?

3. How do you set up your Samba server as a PDC?

4. You want to create a group on my Samba PDC called Manufacturing. You have another Windows NT server that is a part of the Samba domain that has a share on it that you only want accessed by users in the Manufacturing group. How do you implement this?

5. Can you use all the normal Windows NT domain tools to manage your Samba server?

6. Can you implement system policies using your Samba server?

7. You want to give each user in your company a standard corporate profile incorporating the company logo as a background. How do you go about this?

8. What is the significance of the file `NTuser.DAT`?

9. What is `rpcclient`?

CHAPTER 8

USING SMBCLIENT

You will learn about the following in this chapter:

- What smbclient is and what it is used for

- Some common smbclient options

- How to use smbclient to print to a Windows print server

- How to use smbclient to back up Windows machines

T he smbclient program is probably one of the most useful utilities available in the Samba distribution. It is convenient for debugging when you don't have a Windows machine handy, or even if you do and don't wish to use it! Also, it can provide extra SMB-type services that don't fit anywhere else. These extra services include being able to send Windows Messaging messages to Windows-based machines and sending print jobs from UNIX machines to printer shares on Windows machines.

The Purpose of smbclient

smbclient was developed by the Samba team primarily for testing the Samba code. It has since developed into a full-fledged smbclient that has an easy-to-use interface. If you are familiar with using FTP, you will be right at home using smbclient. You can effectively connect to any shared resource on any SMB-compliant server and perform a number of commands that do different things such as get a directory listing, traverse the directories in the share, send and receive files to and from the share, and even print to shared printer resources.

Common smbclient Options

smbclient has quite a few different options. When you execute smbclient with no options, you should get output similar to this:

```
$ smbclient
Added interface ip=192.168.66.4 bcast=192.168.66.15 nmask=255.255.255.240
Usage: smbclient service <password> [options]
```

```
Version 2.0.5a
        -s smb.conf            pathname to smb.conf file
        -B IP addr             broadcast IP address to use
        -O socket_options      socket options to use
        -R name resolve order  use these name resolution services only
        -M host                send a winpopup message to the host
        -i scope               use this NetBIOS scope
        -N                     don't ask for a password
        -n netbios name.       Use this name as my netbios name
        -d debuglevel          set the debuglevel
        -P                     connect to service as a printer
        -p port                connect to the specified port
        -l log basename.       Basename for log/debug files
        -h                     Print this help message.
        -I dest IP             use this IP to connect to
        -E                     write messages to stderr instead of stdout
        -U username            set the network username
        -L host                get a list of shares available on a host
        -t terminal code       terminal i/o code {sjis|euc|jis7|jis8|junet|hex}
        -m max protocol        set the max protocol level
        -W workgroup           set the workgroup name
        -T<c|x>IXFqgbNan       command line tar
        -D directory           start from directory
        -c command string      execute semicolon separated commands
        -b xmit/send buffer    changes the transmit/send buffer (default: 65520)
```

As with most commands, if you do not supply valid arguments, a usage reminder or help output is displayed. This is effectively smbclient's way of telling you to give it some options to tell it what you want to do. At the top of the output is the primary interface that smbclient finds on the system, as well as broadcast address and subnet mask. This provides an easy check for you if there are any network configuration problems. Get in the habit of checking that information when you see it to make sure that it is correct. It will save you heartache later if you check this information as you go—otherwise, you could spend hours debugging problems that are simply network configuration problems. I will be discussing some of the most useful arguments in this help screen later on in the chapter.

The following sections first go through an example of an smbclient session, and then go through some of the more useful options that are available to you with smbclient.

An Example of an smbclient Session

Suppose that the UNIX machine running smbclient is called GOOFEY, and the Windows NT machine smbclient will be interacting with is called DAFFY. DAFFY has a share called \\DAFFY\NTSHARE. If you are not sure what shares are available on an SMB-compliant server such as Windows NT, from UNIX you can execute smbclient like this:

```
$ smbclient -L //daffy -U username
Added interface ip=192.168.66.4 bcast=192.168.66.15 nmask=255.255.255.240
Password:
Domain=[HOME] OS=[Windows NT 4.0] Server=[NT LAN Manager 4.0]
```

```
Sharename      Type        Comment
---------      ----        -------
NETLOGON       Disk        Logon server share
ADMIN$         Disk        Remote Admin
IPC$           IPC         Remote IPC
C$             Disk        Default share
ntshare        Disk        NT Share for smbclient test purposes
F$             Disk        Default share
X$             Disk        Default share
Y$             Disk        Default share


Server                     Comment
---------                  -------
DAFFY
GOOFEY                     Samba 2.0.5a


Workgroup                  Master
---------                  -------
HOME                       DAFFY
```

For the *username*, make sure you specify a username that exists on the server.

Notice two things here. The first is that normally, you do not have to specify a username with the -U option. smbclient defaults the value of this option to the environment variables LOGNAME or USER, if they exist. But for reasons known only to the Samba development team, they force the user to provide a username when getting a list of resources. The other interesting thing to note is that you generally specify resources using forward slashes (/) rather than backslashes (\) as you do in the Windows world. The main reason for this is that the backslash has a special meaning in the UNIX world—to escape out characters. You can specify backslashes if you want; smbclient just converts them to forward slashes when processing command arguments.

You also had to stop and specify a password. If you enter an incorrect password or specify an invalid username, you will get an error message like this:

```
session setup failed: ERRDOS - ERRnoaccess (Access denied.)
```

You can specify both the username and password on the command line if you want:

```
$ smbclient -L //daffy -U matt%mypass
```

In this example, the password is specified as part of the username preceded with a % sign. This can be very useful when using smbclient as part of scripts. However, be sure to carefully protect any files with passwords in them with 700 permissions (chmod **700** *filename*) so that no prying eyes can get to any sensitive passwords.

Notice that in the preceding share listing there is a share called ntshare. You can connect to it with smbclient:

```
$ smbclient //daffy/ntshare -U matt
Added interface ip=192.168.66.4 bcast=192.168.66.15 nmask=255.255.255.240
```

```
Password:
Domain=[HOME] OS=[Windows NT 4.0] Server=[NT LAN Manager 4.0]
smb: \>
```

You are now at the `smbclient` command prompt. You have the current directory relative to the root of the share you just connected to so that you can easily see where you are. You can type any valid `smbclient` command here, such as getting a directory listing:

```
smb: \> dir
  .                                D        0   Thu Oct 14 23:01:22 1999
  ..                               D        0   Thu Oct 14 23:01:22 1999

              65514 blocks of size 32768. 49865 blocks available
smb: \>
```

You can get help any time:

```
smb: \> help
ls            dir           du            lcd           cd
pwd           get           mget          put           mput
rename        more          mask          del           open
rm            mkdir         md            rmdir         rd
prompt        recurse       translate     lowercase     print
printmode     queue         cancel        quit          q
exit          newer         archive       tar           blocksize
tarmode       setmode       help          ?             !
smb: \>
```

If you are familiar with ftp, you will notice that a lot of the commands are similar, and others might seem new to you. Don't be afraid! Experiment—try things out! This is a pretty boring directory listing at the moment, so make some directories:

```
smb: \> mkdir apps
smb: \> mkdir "important files"
smb: \> dir
  .                                D        0   Tue Oct 19 17:44:42 1999
  ..                               D        0   Tue Oct 19 17:44:42 1999
  apps                             D        0   Tue Oct 19 17:43:02 1999
  important files                  D        0   Tue Oct 19 17:44:16 1999

              65514 blocks of size 32768. 49865 blocks available
smb: \>
```

If you look at this directory structure from the Windows NT system, it looks like Figure 8.1.

You can change directories using `cd`:

```
smb: \> cd apps
smb: \apps\>
```

Notice that the current directory is in your prompt for easy reference. This section does not go through all the interactive `smbclient` commands. They are documented in the man page for `smbclient`, which you should be able to bring up with this command:

```
$ man smbclient
```

FIGURE 8.1

Looking at the
\\daffy\ntshare direc-
tory through Windows
Explorer.

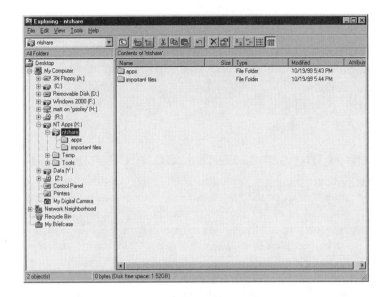

Connecting to a Share as Another User in Another Domain or Workgroup (-W)

Remember in the previous section, you learned to specify the username you want to connect as with the -U option. Sometimes this will not be enough. Suppose your Samba server is a member of the workgroup HOME. You also have a Windows NT server in the domain called TEST. To log in to the server in the TEST domain, you can simply type

```
$ smbclient -U matt -W TEST //daffy/ntshare
```

You are effectively telling smbclient to send the login credential TEST\matt as the username. This of course is only necessary if you need to log in to a server in another domain.

Sending WinPopUp Messages (-M)

The previous chapter briefly touched on sending WinPopUp messages. The -M option allows you to send a Windows Messaging-compliant message to any resolvable NetBIOS hostname on your Windows network. An example of using the -M option is this:

```
$ smbclient -M daffy
Added interface ip=192.168.66.4 bcast=192.168.66.15 nmask=255.255.255.240
Connected. Type your message, ending it with a Control-D
This is a test Windows Messaging message sent to Daffy!
sent 57 bytes
```

And on the host DAFFY, you will see a dialog box like that in Figure 8.2.

FIGURE 8.2
Windows NT's Messenger
Service displaying a mes-
sage to the user on Daffy
initiated from the
`smbclient` command on
a UNIX server.

Debugging `smbclient` Connections (`-d`)

If you have problems using `smbclient`, there is a debug option you can use to help track
down problems you might have. This debug option is `-d <debug level>`. You would normally use debug level 3 to debug most connection problems because it provides the most user-
friendly output. Anything higher is meant for the Samba developers, as you will soon find out.
For now, start `smbclient` and connect to an SMB server with the debug level set to 3:

```
$ smbclient //daffy/ntshare -d 3
Added interface ip=192.168.66.4 bcast=192.168.66.15 nmask=255.255.255.240
Client started (version 2.0.5a).
resolve_name: Attempting lmhosts lookup for name daffy<0x20>
resolve_name: Attempting host lookup for name daffy<0x20>
Connecting to 203.37.66.6 at port 139
Password:
Domain=[HOME] OS=[Windows NT 4.0] Server=[NT LAN Manager 4.0]
smb: \>
```

Notice that in the example, you can deduce a couple of things. `smbclient` first attempted to
use an `lmhosts` file on the Samba server looking for the server DAFFY. It failed, then tried the
local `hosts` file. `smbclient` found the name in the `hosts` file so it used the resulting IP address
to connect a NetBIOS session to port 139 (the NetBIOS session port).

As an example of why you would generally not use debug levels greater than 3, see Listing 8.1.
Note that you see what we had before, but so much more! There are many important variables
and values that are critical to see what is going on when debugging:

LISTING 8.1   Output Generated from a Debug Level of 5

```
[matt@goofey matt]$ smbclient //daffy/ntshare -d 5
Added interface ip=192.168.66.4 bcast=192.168.66.15 nmask=255.255.255.240
Added interface ip=203.37.66.4 bcast=203.37.66.15 nmask=255.255.255.240
Client started (version 2.0.5a).
resolve_name: Attempting lmhosts lookup for name daffy<0x20>
getlmhostsent: lmhost entry: 127.0.0.1 localhost
resolve_name: Attempting host lookup for name daffy<0x20>
Connecting to 203.37.66.6 at port 139
Sent session request
size=0
smb_com=0x0
smb_rcls=0
smb_reh=0
```

```
smb_err=0
smb_flg=0
smb_flg2=0
smb_tid=0
smb_pid=0
smb_uid=0
smb_mid=0
smt_wct=0
smb_bcc=0
 session request ok
size=87
smb_com=0x72
smb_rcls=0
smb_reh=0
smb_err=0
smb_flg=136
smb_flg2=1
smb_tid=0
smb_pid=7117
smb_uid=0
smb_mid=1
smt_wct=17
smb_vwv[0]=7 (0x7)
smb_vwv[1]=12803 (0x3203)
smb_vwv[2]=256 (0x100)
smb_vwv[3]=1024 (0x400)
smb_vwv[4]=17 (0x11)
smb_vwv[5]=0 (0x0)
smb_vwv[6]=256 (0x100)
smb_vwv[7]=0 (0x0)
smb_vwv[8]=0 (0x0)
smb_vwv[9]=64768 (0xFD00)
smb_vwv[10]=67 (0x43)
smb_vwv[11]=57856 (0xE200)
smb_vwv[12]=32968 (0x80C8)
smb_vwv[13]=56744 (0xDDA8)
smb_vwv[14]=48926 (0xBF1E)
smb_vwv[15]=43009 (0xA801)
smb_vwv[16]=2301 (0x8FD)
smb_bcc=18
Password:
size=80
smb_com=0x73
smb_rcls=0
smb_reh=0
smb_err=0
smb_flg=136
smb_flg2=1
smb_tid=0
smb_pid=7117
smb_uid=2051
smb_mid=1
smt_wct=3
smb_vwv[0]=255 (0xFF)
```

continued on next page

continued from previous page

```
smb_vwv[1]=80 (0x50)
smb_vwv[2]=0 (0x0)
smb: \>
```

Normally this level of debug information is useful only to the members of the Samba development team. However, occasionally it may be useful for a power user to glean that extra piece of information that is needed to solve her problem.

Specifying the IP Address of the SMB Server (-I)

Normally when connecting to a resource, the NetBIOS name is resolved to an IP address for the NetBIOS session-level connection to kick in. For example:

```
$ smbclient //daffy/ntshare
```

In this example, `daffy` is the NetBIOS name and it is resolved using the normal name resolution methods to an IP address. Sometimes, however, this is not possible. An example of when you may need to use the `-I` argument is when the DNS name of a server does not match the NetBIOS name. If this is the case and you use the `-I` option, then the TCP/IP session is connected to the IP address specified, and from then on the normal NetBIOS name is used to finish making the connection. Here is an example of specifying an IP address on the command line, which will cause `smbclient` to skip the name resolution process:

```
$ smbclient //daffy/ntshare -I 192.168.66.6
```

Here, `smbclient` will connect directly to port 139 on the host with IP address `192.168.66.6`. Then after the TCP connection is made, the NetBIOS session will be made using the name DAFFY as usual.

Specifying a NetBIOS name (-n)

If you need to change the name of the host that `smbclient` is running on, you can do this easily with the `-n` command-line parameter:

```
[matt@donald]$ smbclient //daffy/ntshare -n pluto
```

Without the `-n` option, this command line would be seen to come from a host with the NetBIOS name `donald`, but as written, the request to connect will instead be seen to come from a host that goes by the NetBIOS name `pluto`. This parameter is rarely necessary, but on those infrequent occasions, it is helpful to know that you can use it if you need to.

Default Directory to Change to (-D)

This option is used to change the working directory that you will be dropped into when `smbclient` connects you to the server. The argument is simply a valid directory path that will exist in the share. An example where you will be changed into the directory apps follows:

```
$ smbclient //daffy/ntshare -D apps
Added interface ip=192.168.66.4 bcast=192.168.66.15 nmask=255.255.255.240
Password:
Domain=[HOME] OS=[Windows NT 4.0] Server=[NT LAN Manager 4.0]
smb: \apps\>
```

Using the -D option allows you to specify the directory you will land in after starting a connection to the server. It is the same as doing a cd once you have connected. A longer way of achieving the same end result as the previous command is the following:

```
$ smbclient //daffy/ntshare
Added interface ip=192.168.66.4 bcast=192.168.66.15 nmask=255.255.255.240
Password:
Domain=[HOME] OS=[Windows NT 4.0] Server=[NT LAN Manager 4.0]
smb: \> cd apps
smb: \apps\>
```

Commands to Run (-c)

The -c option allows you to chain several SMB commands together. When they have finished executing, smbclient exits. It is useful to run smbclient this way as part of a cron job. Here's an example:

```
$ smbclient //daffy/ntshare -c "cd apps;dir" -U matt%password
Added interface ip=192.168.66.4 bcast=192.168.66.15 nmask=255.255.255.240
Domain=[HOME] OS=[Windows NT 4.0] Server=[NT LAN Manager 4.0]
     .                          D      0  Mon Oct 25 22:03:10 1999
     ..                         D      0  Mon Oct 25 22:03:10 1999
  text.txt                      A     22  Mon Oct 25 22:03:18 1999

           65514 blocks of size 32768. 49874 blocks available
$
```

The only limitation to using -c is that you need to specify the username and password as part of the command line, or optionally as environment variables (see later). If you have any passwords in any files on your UNIX system, make sure they are protected so that only the appropriate people can see them!

Tar Options (-T)

The -T option is probably one of the most useful options of smbclient. You can create a standard UNIX tar archive of an entire share or part of a share. This is very useful for backing up Windows machines from a UNIX server (see the later section "A Common Use of smbclient—Backing Up Windows Machines"). An example could be

```
$ smbclient //daffy/ntshare -Tc files.tar
Added interface ip=192.168.66.4 bcast=192.168.66.15 nmask=255.255.255.240
Password:
Domain=[HOME] OS=[Windows NT 4.0] Server=[NT LAN Manager 4.0]
                directory \apps\
       22 (    1.0 kb/s) \apps\text.txt
                directory \important files\
tar: dumped 3 tar files
Total bytes written: 512
$
```

This puts everything in the share //daffy/ntshare into the tar archive files.tar which will be created in the current UNIX working directory by default. If, instead, you want only selected directories, you can use this:

```
$ smbclient //daffy/ntshare -Tc files.tar apps/*
```

This time, everything under the **apps** directory will get put into the tarfile. There are quite a few additional options to the -T option that you can specify, and they are fairly well documented in the **smbclient** manual page.

Environment Variables

smbclient knows to check whether certain environment variables are set, and if they are, **smbclient** behaves in a particular manner. There are two variables that are checked for a default username, **LOGNAME** and **USER**. If either of them is set, the default username for the **smbclient** session is whatever name was in these variables. If neither of these variables is set, the default username will be **guest**. Similarly, if the **PASSWD** environment variable is set, instead of a password prompt, the contents of this environment variable are used as the passwd.

Using the smbclient Interface

The purpose of this section is to familarize you with the user interface of **smbclient**. You should have noticed by now that **smbclient**'s interface is not unlike that of command-line ftp if you have used that before. Most commands, when executed, send an SMB over the NetBIOS connection to the server to achieve a particular task.

Once you have an **smbclient** session connected, there are a number of different commands you can use to navigate around the resource. There are the usual FTP or DOS-like commands such as

- dir—To get a directory listing. An alias is **ls**.
- del—To delete a file.
- get—To transfer a file from the shared resource to the local UNIX file system.
- mget—To transfer multiple files from the shared resource to the local UNIX file system.
- put—To transfer a file to the shared resource from the local UNIX file system.
- mput—To transfer multiple files to the shared resource from the local UNIX file system.
- help—Get a listing of valid commands. You can also get help on a particular command by typing: **help** dir.
- rename—Rename a file to a new name.
- mkdir—Create a directory. An alias is **md**.

Some more unusual commands are as follows:

- recurse—Turn directory recursion mode on. This means that the next time the command **dir** is executed, the entire directory structure of the resource is recursed. This command is similar to typing **dir** /s on a Windows system, or **ls** -**lR** on a UNIX system.
- tar—Exactly like the command-line option, -T, but in interactive mode.

- newer—Only `mget` files newer than the specified local file.

- setmode—Sets the remote file's modes.

The best way to show the **smbclient** interface in use would be through an example.

In the following example, the user matt is connecting to the SMB server (in this case Windows NT 4.0) DAFFY. The share being connected to is called NTSHARE. The first command entered is **dir** to get a directory listing at the share entry point:

```
[matt@goofey]$ smbclient //daffy/ntshare
Added interface ip=192.168.66.4 bcast=192.168.66.15 nmask=255.255.255.240
Password:
Domain=[HOME] OS=[Windows NT 4.0] Server=[NT LAN Manager 4.0]
smb: \> dir
  .                                 D        0  Tue Oct 19 18:44:42 1999
  ..                                D        0  Tue Oct 19 18:44:42 1999
  apps                              D        0  Mon Oct 25 23:03:10 1999
  important files                   D        0  Tue Oct 19 18:44:16 1999

          65514 blocks of size 32768. 48073 blocks available
smb: \>
```

Suppose the user wants to go into the important files subdirectory and place a file there. First he uses the **cd** command:

```
smb: \> cd "important files"
smb: \important files\>
```

Note that because there is a space in the directory name, he needs to put double quotes around the entire name. Next he creates a directory, using the **mkdir** command, to put the file in. He calls this directory **documents**:

```
smb: \important files\> mkdir documents
smb: \important files\> cd documents
smb: \important files\documents\> dir
  .                                 D        0  Mon Dec 20 23:31:23 1999
  ..                                D        0  Mon Dec 20 23:31:23 1999

          65514 blocks of size 32768. 48073 blocks available
smb: \important files\documents\>
```

Finally, he puts the file there using the **put** command:

```
smb: \important files\documents\> put pp_guide.doc
putting file pp_guide.doc as \important files\documents\pp_guide.doc (245.856 kb
/s) (average 245.856 kb/s)
smb: \important files\documents\>
```

After awhile, he decides to make a backup of this directory on his UNIX system. He can do this with the **tar** command:

```
smb: \important files\documents\> tar c archive.tar
    45568 (  380.3 kb/s) \important files\documents\pp_guide.doc
tar: dumped 1 tar files
```

```
Total bytes written: 46080
smb: \important files\documents\>
```

This creates a file called `archive.tar` in the current working directory on the UNIX host that `smbclient` is running on. `archive.tar` contains all the files that were in the directory \important files\documents on the NT server.

More detailed information on the `smbclient` commands are in the `smbclient` online manual page. Hopefully, this section has given you an idea of how easy it is to use `smbclient` to access SMB servers.

Using `smbclient` to Print to a Windows Print Server

A very useful feature of `smbclient` is that you can connect to printer shares, as well as normal fileshares. There might be a situation where the only way you can print to a particular printer is through a fileshare. This printer could be attached to the parallel port on a Windows 95/98 or even a Windows NT box. This printer also would be shared out, such as \\`windows95`\ `hplaser`, so that any Windows user can access it. Of course, this makes it slightly difficult for a UNIX system to print to it without using a standard UNIX remote printing method such as SYSV `lp` or BSD `lpd`. Samba saves you here by providing the functionality to print to remote SMB print shares. A script called `smbprint` that comes in the Samba distribution is very useful for this purpose. It is known as an *input filter*. `smbprint` takes a print job as input, and then sends it to a remote SMB printer share using `smbclient`.

To set up a Linux system (or any BSD-based UNIX system) to use this filter for printing to an SMB resource on a Windows 95/98 machine, you need to first set up your printcap entry, and then set up a configuration file on a per printer basis, which contains sharename and password information. You need a printcap entry that looks something like this:

```
cdcolour:\
        :cm=HP Laserjet 4si:\
        :sd=/var/spool/lpd/hplaser4si:\
        :af=/var/spool/lpd/hplaser4si/acct:\
        :if=/usr/bin/smbprint:\
        :mx=0:\
        :lp=/dev/null:
```

There are two lines of particular significance here. You need to specify the input filter to use. The entire print job is passed through this input filter, and this is specified with the `if` keyword. Make sure you specify the entire full pathname to the `smbprint` script on your particular system. Make sure also that you specify an accounting file with the `af` keyword. `smbprint` requires this to determine the spool directory, which in turn contains the configuration file for `smbprint`.

Now, you need to set up a special configuration file called `.config`, and it is stored in the spool directory of the printer. In the preceding example, the file `.config` will be found at

/var/spool/lpd/hplaser4si/.config. This file contains three things: a server name, a service name, and a password for the service. For example:

```
server=windows95
service=hplaser
password="googley"
```

Make sure the permissions are locked down on this file so prying eyes cannot find out the password.

Of course, if you just want to send a single print job to a printer and do not want to go to all the effort of creating a queue for it, you can do that simply by typing something like this:

cat file.ps | smbclient //windows95/hplaser -U windows95%googley

The -N option will cause the password prompt to not be printed, and the -U option causes the computer name to be used as the username—which is needed if you are printing to a Windows 95/98 host in share-level mode. If, however, you are printing to a Windows NT server in user-level mode, something like this will suffice:

cat file.ps | smbclient //windowsnt/hplaser-U matt%googley

In Samba versions prior to 2.0, you needed to explicitly use the -P option to smbclient when connecting to an SMB print share, but now smbclient can autodetect whether the share you are connecting to is a fileshare or printer share.

A Common Use of smbclient—Backing Up Windows Machines

As mentioned earlier, a very cool feature of smbclient is that it can tar up the contents of a fileshare. Think about this for a second. This in effect makes it possible to back up Windows machines from UNIX servers. This can be very useful, considering that UNIX systems are more likely to have a tape device than a Windows box. There is a small gotcha that might turn some of you off, however. If you are archiving a directory with tar on a Windows NT system that uses NTFS, the permissions will not be saved. This may not be a problem to many people; most people would probably care that the data is backed up, rather than the permissions are lost. It depends on your situation. Of course, if you are backing up Windows 95/98 machines, they do not have permissions, so you do not lose anything. There is a nifty script that comes in the Samba distribution called smbtar. smbtar is a wrapper to smbclient in much the same way as smbprint, which was discussed in the previous section.

Using smbtar is very easy. If you run smbtar with no arguments, a help screen is displayed:

```
$ smbtar
Usage: smbtar [<options>] [<include/exclude files>]
Function: backup/restore a Windows PC directories to a local tape file
Options:        (Description)               (Default)
  -r            Restore from tape file to PC Save from PC to tapefile
  -i            Incremental mode            Full backup mode
```

```
-a              Reset archive bit mode      Don't reset archive bit
-v              Verbose mode: echo command  Don't echo anything
-s <server>     Specify PC Server
-p <password>   Specify PC Password
-x <share>      Specify PC Share            backup
-X              Exclude mode                Include
-N <newer>      File for date comparison
-b <blocksize>  Specify tape's blocksize
-d <dir>        Specify a directory in share \
-l <log>        Specify a Samba Log Level   2
-u <user>       Specify User Name           matt
-t <tape>       Specify Tape device         tar.out

Please enter a command line parameter!
```

For easy reference, the last column contains the default value for each of the switches. If the default value is blank, there is no default value for that switch. Here's a simple example:

```
$ smbtar -s daffy -p password -x ntshare -t ntshare.tar
```

This example archives the entire contents of **ntshare** on the server DAFFY to the file **ntshare.tar**. Instead, you can send the contents directly to a tape device like this on a BSD UNIX, such as Linux:

```
$ smbtar -s daffy -p password -x ntshare -t /dev/st0
```

Or, like this on a System V UNIX, such as Solaris or HP-UX:

```
$ smbtar -s daffy -p password -x ntshare -t /dev/rmt/0m
```

Alternatively, you can select a subset of the share like this:

```
$ smbtar -s daffy -p password -x ntshare -t /dev/rmt/0m apps/*
```

If you have problems and want to find out exactly what is going on, use verbose mode:

```
$ smbtar -s daffy -p password -x ntshare -t /dev/rmt/0m -v
```

By default, **smbtar** provides no output, which is very useful especially because **smbtar** would normally be used as a **cronjob** entry when output would be a nuisance anyway.

If you have a small network, a good way to use this functionality of **smbclient** would be to create a share on all your Windows machines that points to the root directory. Then when you connect with **smbtar**, you will back up the entire system in one go, and then either store it compressed on a UNIX disk farm somewhere, or archive it to tape.

Summary

This chapter introduced you to the Samba tool, **smbclient**. You learned what this tool is for, and why you would want to use it. It, of course, is used to connect to SMB shares, whether they reside on a Windows NT server, or another Samba server—it does not matter.

You also learned the most common and useful options to the `smbclient` command. And you went through using the `smbclient` interactive interface. If you are familiar with a command-line `ftp` client, you will be right at home with `smbclient`. You can transfer files to and from SMB shares, as well as the usual tasks like changing directories, making directories, removing files, and so on.

The chapter went on to discuss two useful tasks that `smbclient` can perform. The first was being able to print to an SMB print share. A script is provided in the Samba distribution that makes this easy. It is called `smbprint` and is used as an input filter for the print queue. You learned how to set this up for BSD-based printing systems, like that used in Linux.

The second task is being able to archive an entire fileshare into a `tar` file. This is very useful for backup purposes. Imagine all those Windows 95 or 98 machines that you would have liked to back up, but there was no easy way to do it. Now you can not only back them up, but `tar` them directly to a tape device on a UNIX machine. Of course, restoring the files is as easy as backing them up!

The next chapter will discuss Samba's SSL support.

Review Questions

1. What is the command line to `smbclient` to connect to a fileshare called `apps` on a server called `alfred`?

2. Modify the previous command to connect to the fileshare as a user different from the one you are logged in as.

3. How do you turn on debugging to level 3 with `smbclient`?

4. How do you list the shares available on a server called `rhino`?

5. Your Samba server is in the workgroup `OFFICE`. You need to be able to temporarily access some files on a machine called `INT60239` in a domain called `ACCOUNTS`. The resource is called `documents`. What is the `smbclient` command line to achieve this?

6. What is the `-P` option to `smbclient`, and why is it not used any more?

Exercises

1. System VR4 UNIX systems, such as Solaris and HP-UX, use a completely different printing method than do BSD-based variants of UNIX. They use an `lp` printing subsystem. Rather than a printcap file, each printer has a model file that tells it how to print to a particular printer. Create a model script to print to a Windows printer using the `smbprint` script. Then test it by creating a printer using this new model script.

2. Write a shell script and accompanying `crontab` entry to back up a single Windows NT server each weeknight at 2 a.m. to a tape device on a UNIX machine.

PART III

ADVANCED TOPICS

9   Samba with SSL

10   Additional Share Level Options

11   Tuning Samba for Better Performance

12   Debugging Samba

13   Samba Security

14   Third-Party Samba Tools

15   A Look at Samba's Future

CHAPTER 9

SAMBA WITH SSL

You will learn about the following in this chapter:

- What SSL is
- How the SSL protocol works
- What a certificate is
- The significance of a certificate authority
- How certificate signing works
- How to generate your own certificates

- How to compile Samba to include SSL support
- How to configure Samba to run as an SSL server
- How to enable client-side certificates

T his chapter discusses how to use the Secure Sockets Layer (SSL) functionality of Samba. It begins by discussing what SSL is and why you would want to use it. Some new terms are introduced that you will need to know in this section. Next is a short discussion on SSL certificates and what they are for. The chapter moves on to discuss how to go about compiling Samba with SSL support. Then there is a section on the Samba configuration options you can set when using SSL, including a sample Samba SSL configuration file. Toward the end, there is a discussion on which clients you can use to connect to an SSL-enabled Samba server.

What Is SSL and How Does It Work?

SSL stands for Secure Sockets Layer, and is a standard that Netscape put forward in the mid-nineties. It was originally intended for the secure transfer of Web pages between a Web server and client. Secure is defined in this case to mean that all data transferred over the Internet between the Web browser and Web server is encrypted, and an authentication protocol is provided so that you know for sure who you are talking to. The initial design (SSL v1.0) was completed in mid-1994. SSL v2.0 followed at the end of 1994. SSL v3.0 was released in mid-1995, and that is where the standard stayed for a few years. Then in January 1999, a proposed extension to SSL v3.0 was released as RFC 2246 (`ftp://ftp.isi.edu/in-notes/rfc2246.txt`). This extension is called the Transport Layer Security (TLS) protocol v1.0, and TLS will be used more and more until it succeeds SSL v3.0. Throughout the remainder of this chapter, the term SSL will be used to refer to both SSL v3.0 and TLS v1.0.

Since the inception of SSL, it has been extended to many applications. You can search through the RFC lists to find emerging standards for TLS working with other protocols, such as RFC 2487, "SMTP Service Extension for Secure SMTP over TLS," and RFC 2595, "Using TLS with IMAP, POP3, and ACAP." To give you an idea of how SSL fits into the standard host network model, look at Figure 9.1.

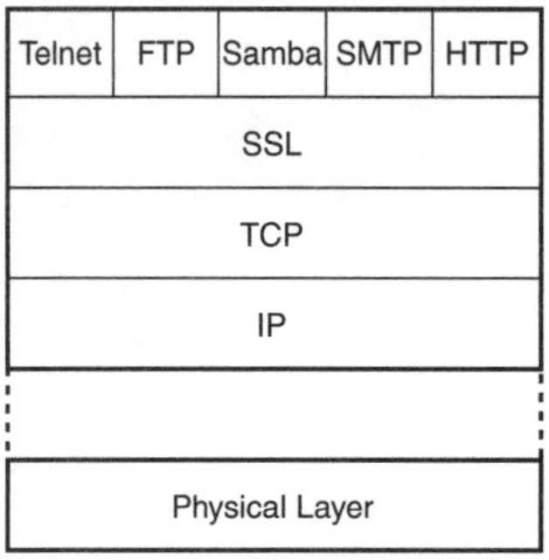

FIGURE 9.1
Where SSL fits into the standard host network model.

It sits above TCP, which means that after SSL is enabled for a given application, all data that passes through is encrypted.

Cryptography 101

There are two general types of cryptography, *symmetric* and *asymmetric*. Symmetric means that you have a single shared key between two people who want to communicate securely. It is usually very fast to process, but you have to share one (possibly different) key with everyone you want to communicate with. The more people you communicate with, the harder it gets to manage keys. Asymmetric cryptography is also known as public key cryptography. In public key cryptography, you have two keys, a public key and a private key. There is a complex mathematical relationship linking the two so that when you encrypt data with the public key, the only key that can decrypt that data is the private key, and vice versa. So if Alice wants to send some encrypted files to Bob, Alice gets Bob's public key, encrypts the data, and sends it to him. Bob then decrypts that data with his private key.

The great thing about public key cryptography is the relationship between the public and private keys. You can give out your public key to anyone you want, but the only key that can be used to decrypt data that was encrypted with the public key is your private one. This solves the key management problem with symmetric cryptosystems. For more information on cryptography in general, I highly recommend the book *Applied Cryptography* by Bruce Schneier (ISBN: 0471117099). It covers cryptography in great detail, and includes a lengthy discussion about public key cryptosystems.

Asymmetric cryptography is used for server and optionally for client authentication. After that is done, a key is selected by the client and encrypted with the server's public key. The server decrypts it with its private key. Then while application data is being transferred, it is encrypted using symmetric ciphers because they are many times faster than public key ciphers. To make this process easier to understand, the steps of the process are listed here:

1. The server is authenticated to the client and optionally the client is authenticated to the server.

2. The client selects a key for later use during the encrypted session.

3. The client encrypts the selected key with the server's public key, and then sends the resultant ciphercode to the server.

4. The server decrypts the ciphercode with its private key.

5. The data session can now proceed using a single shared key for encryption and decryption by means of a symmetric cipher. This relies on the fact that the shared key is kept private on both the server and client systems. As soon as the shared key is compromised, all encrypted communications are compromised.

6. The encrypted session is shut down when both sides have finished communications.

SSL has many uses. Two common examples are secure transactions such as banking and shopping applications where you don't want a third party snooping on credit card or other personal information. Of course, if you are doing such sensitive transactions, it is important that the session is encrypted—but you also want to be sure that the Web server you are connected to is actually who it says it is. For all you know, it could be someone else masquerading as your bank, ready to capture your personal banking details.

SSL solves this problem by introducing the concept of a *certificate*. A certificate effectively adds an identity to a public key. This identity is certified to be true by a *certification authority* (CA). After verifying an identity, a CA adds a *digital signature* to the certificate. When your browser connects to a secure Web site, the Web server supplies a certificate to the browser to prove it is who it says it is. This is called a *server-side certificate*. A server-side certificate authenticates the server to the client.

Anyone can set himself up to be a CA; however, the general public only trusts large, established CAs. It depends on the application whether you get your certificate signed by a well-known CA, or you create your own CA. For example, if a company has an SSL intranet Web site, it can be its own CA. If this is the case, the Web server's certificate will likely be signed by the company's own CA. This is in contrast to a bank's Web server site where the bank's customers will want a high level of confidence that the Web server's certificate has been signed by a publicly trusted CA.

An Alternative to SSL: IPsec

An alternative to using SSL is the new IPsec protocol. This allows secure IP communications end-to-end without requiring server and/or client support directly. This means that you will be able to have secure communications between `smbclient` and the Samba server without requiring special SSL versions of the software. All secure communication is done in the network layer by the operating system. There are a number of commercial implementations of IPsec for Windows 95/98/NT, and Windows 2000 supports it by default. Many UNIX variants have IPsec add-ons now. For a list of relevant Internet Drafts and Request For Comment standards see this Web site:

`http://www.ietf.org/html.charters/ipsec-charter.html`

Certificate Signing Explained

Many companies now sign certificates for a fee. An example of one of these public CAs is Verisign (`www.verisign.com`). Getting your certificate signed by one of these CAs is usually a costly and bureaucratic process, but it must be done if you want to be trusted throughout the Internet. You need to supply your selected CA with a *certificate signing request* (CSR). This CSR contains your public key and some information about your company, such as Country (C), State/Region (ST), Locality (L), Organization name (O), Organizational Unit (OU), and common name (CN). All these values combined create a Distinguished Name (DN). The L is usually the city, the O is the company name, and the OU is a group within the company (for example, Information Technology). By convention, the CN is the hostname of the server the software will be running on. In the case of a Web server, the CN will be the Web site address (for example, `www.cyber.com.au`). In the case of a Samba server, the CN will be the name of the server running Samba (for example, `sambaserver.cyber.com.au`).

The CA needs to be doubly sure that the company supplying the CSR is who it claims to be because it is the CA's reputation on the line if it is later found that the company was actually pretending to be someone else. After all details are verified, the CA sends back to the requesting organization its certificate, which contains not only all the information in the CSR, but also the name of the CA and the CA's digital signature. The digital signature is computed using the CA's private key, which means that it is using public/private key cryptography, and that anyone can verify it using the CA's public key, or certificate. The company, who now has its CSR digitally signed, is free to use this certificate with confidence that the company itself will be a trusted entity.

How Does the Client Verify a Server-Side Certificate?

If you think about this process, one small part of the equation is missing. If the company uses its certificate on a secure Web site, a browser (client) accessing this server begins the secure session and the server sends its certificate. How does the client know this certificate is real and the signature is valid? It needs to verify the signature on the certificate that was computed by the trusted CA. To do this, it needs the CA's certificate. All the major browsers these days have the certificates of the major players in the CA market already installed. So to verify a given certificate, all the client needs to do is compute its own digital signature from the details on the certificate and see if it matches the one that was put there by the CA. If there is a match, the client will continue to set up the encrypted session and all will be well. If there is a discrepancy, the client will no doubt sound some alarms to warn the user that there could be a problem.

The final step after the server has authenticated and, optionally, the client has authenticated to the server is that the encrypted session is set up. This encrypted session is where the data transfer between the client and server occurs. The session setup involves the client sending a key to the server that is encrypted with the server's public key. When that is done, all subsequent communications will be encrypted. The whole SSL establishment process is depicted in Figure 9.2.

FIGURE 9.2

The flow of messages during the SSL hand-shake process.

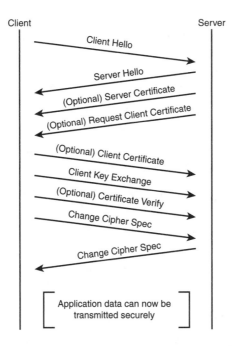

The very first messages sent are *client hello* and *server hello*. A number of initial parameters are exchanged: SSL protocol version, session ID, cipher suite, and compression method. The cipher suite is the cipher to be used when the application data starts to be transferred. You will also note that both the server certificate and client certificate are optional. If no certificates are involved, encryption still occurs, but you need to be able to trust the server you are connected to 100% as there are no authentication processes in place. For detailed information on the internals of the SSL protocol, see `http://home.netscape.com/eng/ssl3/ssl-toc.html`.

As you can probably imagine, the usefulness of SSL has meant that it has been used for many applications other than just Web servers; examples include telnet, ftp, and—you guessed it—Samba, just to name a few. In Samba, because SMB transactions between client and server are in plain text, anyone can snoop on the traffic and get an idea of what a user is doing, and in the process possibly see sensitive data. Consider this scenario: An organization has sensitive data located on a Samba server, and a particular user needs to be able to access this server from the Internet. This is a perfect example of how an SSL version of Samba could be useful. It also demonstrates that a digitally signed *client-side certificate* is also needed to verify that the client accessing the Samba server is really who it says it is.

A client-side certificate is the reverse of a server-side certificate: It authenticates the client to the server. You will generally not want just anyone connecting to your SSL Samba server—or even connecting to an SSL ftp or SSL telnet server for that matter. Each valid Samba server user can be issued a certificate that is signed by a CA. Most likely the CA in this situation will be the organization itself because it can readily identify its employees to be sure that they are who they say they are, and hand each employee his own unique certificate.

Creating SSL Certificates for Use with Samba

Before you can generate an SSL certificate that you can use with Samba, you need to check a few things. You need to make sure that OpenSSL is installed on your system. If you are running Red Hat Linux 6.1, there is a package on your CD called `openssl-0.9.3a-3.i386.rpm`. Install it with this command:

```
# rpm -i /mnt/cdrom/RedHat/RPMS/openssl-0.9.3a-3.i386.rpm
```

For other versions of UNIX, you can visit the OpenSSL Web site at `http://www.openssl.org` and download the source distribution. It is a simple matter of following the instructions to compile and install OpenSSL. It should compile on all the major UNIX platforms.

To work around a Red Hat distribution packaging bug with Red Hat Linux 6.1 (and possibly other versions), you need to create a link for the OpenSSL configuration file:

```
# ln -s /etc/openssl.cnf /etc/ssl/openssl.cnf
```

To be able to randomize the random number generator for generating the key pair, you need to put some random data into a file. Type this:

```
# cat > /tmp/random.txt
```

Then type some random text for about a minute to provide enough random data to create a strong public/private key pair. When you are done, press Ctrl+D.

You can now initialize the random number generator:

```
# openssl genrsa -rand /tmp/random.txt > /dev/null
# rm -f /tmp/random.txt
```

This creates a file called `.rnd` in the home directory of the user who ran it. The information in this file is used as the seed by the OpenSSL random number generator when choosing random numbers, for example, when generating your public/private key pairs. It is very important that you execute the `rm` command to remove the `random.txt` file. If a bad guy got his hands on this file, he would have a head start on cracking your encryption!

Next you need to create a key pair (public/private keys also known as the RSA algorithm). This is done using the `genrsa` command for an RSA key pair:

```
# openssl genrsa -des3 1024 > key.pem
```

The `-des3` indicates that OpenSSL is using the triple-DES encryption algorithm to protect your 1024-bit RSA key, and you are asked for a corresponding passphrase to use as the encryption key. This key protection you are specifying with a passphrase locks the private key. This means that if someone gets the file where the private key is stored, he cannot use it because it is encrypted and he would need to enter the passphrase to unlock it. You can generate the private key without encrypting it (by dropping the `-des3` option), but it is not recommended, because anyone with access to your files can copy your private key from you. You can choose any encryption algorithm that is supported—all supported encryption algorithms are listed in the OpenSSL man page, which you can find at `http://www.openssl.org/docs/openssl.html`. The OpenSSL distribution does not seem to come with manual pages just yet, so for documentation you should go to the OpenSSL Web site. Users today are opting for 1024-bit RSA keys. If you want information on why 512-bit RSA keys are not safe, read the Web article at the following address:

```
http://www.rsa.com/rsalabs/bulletins/twinkle.html
```

The resulting encrypted key in the `key.pem` file will look something like this:

```
-----BEGIN RSA PRIVATE KEY-----
Proc-Type: 4,ENCRYPTED
DEK-Info: DES-EDE3-CBC,07D6C438ECC95B49

/ueKI2FgKGjzVfZ+dYoydctIYAdmUWnmtM/XdGcn7KofRrv/qziHLWaxI8STSQkl
FJxgm8o38kTWSJ+rQ2FzoQ7jHTRmx6rij2HcbeG4FAdZbBD58AfD+1/U0Poehk+w
ruM6tAA4aT4ZmsASGM1m7eLkW2E1YTdlSKa3Ctet4t1CW9bju1mh/O16KT0NO47L
Vt6yER9FHj9m7PZhLrTm48c/Q2A5yw3rFIob9YJ2K5+NPdTbWBMgwewkiBkMaFz4
+94e9KSnj8zH9Pu1Zwvp4/aXCwRAMv6T0jlGtT+tzu0vbmfRHx47E00CO7taFqYG
fL0g/+iCrwOZ1vM2H1tEMXaB9ideZ0142zcuwfeykWkAs9P2KniDUjmkhHBQjaKL
jMqL99lgrdiguJagscscToLEeLZuZqyOmnbQJwgKFs4=
-----END RSA PRIVATE KEY-----
```

Note that at the top it says that the private key is encrypted using the DES3 cipher. You will need to enter the passphrase that you keyed in every time this file is read, including when **smbd** starts up (even at boot-time).

If you opted against using a passphrase, your `key.pem` looks like this:

```
-----BEGIN RSA PRIVATE KEY-----
MIIBOgIBAAJBAM9Fl8cia8WDzTEMPpAo6n0VNY/DMBZTW7EEVWhuSLzb1mBlZZLo
[...]
-----END RSA PRIVATE KEY-----
```

The advantage of having an unencrypted private key is that when **smbd** starts up, you will not be asked for a passphrase. But the big disadvantage is that the key plain text is ready for anyone to use if they get it. It is almost always better to encrypt the private key.

For testing purposes, you could now generate a self-signed dummy certificate. You can generate this certificate with the following command:

```
# openssl req -new -x509 -key key.pem -out cert.pem
```

For a real live production system where a number of people may be accessing your Samba server via SSL across the Internet, it is highly recommended that you get your key pair signed by a CA, which in your case will probably be yourself after you have set yourself up as a CA (see the following section, "Setting Yourself Up as a CA").

To do this, you need to be able to give your CA your public key. You should *never* give out your private key to anyone. You can generate a Certificate Signing Request (CSR) with this command:

```
# openssl req -new -key key.pem -out csr.pem
Using configuration from /etc/ssl/openssl.cnf
Enter PEM pass phrase:
You are about to be asked to enter information that will be incorporated
into your certificate request.
```

```
What you are about to enter is what is called a
➥ Distinguished Name or a DN.
There are quite a few fields but you can leave some blank
For some fields there will be a default value,
If you enter '.', the field will be left blank.
-----
Country Name (2 letter code) [AU]:
State or Province Name (full name) [Some-State]:
➥Australian Capital Territory
Locality Name (eg, city) []:Canberra
Organization Name (eg, company) [Internet Widgits Pty Ltd]:
➥MyCompany Pty Ltd
Organizational Unit Name (eg, section) []:Information Technology
Common Name (eg, YOUR name) []:samba.mycompany.com.au
Email Address []:matt@mycompany.com.au

Please enter the following 'extra' attributes
to be sent with your certificate request
A challenge password []:samba
An optional company name []:
```

You are first asked for your private key passphrase so that it can be read by OpenSSL. You are then asked for a number of details about your company. Enter information as appropriate. When you get to `Common Name` (CN), the convention is to enter the name of the server that this certificate will be used on. Web browsers check this sort of thing and sometimes do not let you go on if you enter a secure Web site and the CN does not match the Web server name. Currently Samba does not check this, but the capability to do so is planned for a future release. After you have entered all the required information, a public key is generated from your private key and it is put into the file `csr.pem`. This file is what you would give to your CA, who would sign it for you. Because in this case you will be using an SSL-ized version of Samba, most likely the only people who will be using it will be people in your organization. If this is the case, you can set yourself up to be the CA and sign the key pair yourself.

Setting Yourself Up as a CA

If, as a company, you will be using SSL frequently for internal use by your employees, you do not need to go to the expense of paying for a well-known commercial CA. You are probably better off being your own CA, signing your own certificates. However, as soon as you provide publicly accessible SSL Web sites, you will need to use one of the many commercial CAs so the Web browser (SSL client) can authenticate your certificate with the known CA's public key.

Setting yourself up as a CA is fairly easy to do. First, edit the `openssl` configuration file, `/etc/openssl.cnf`, and find this section:

```
[ CA_default ]
dir        = ./demoCA
certs      = $dir/certs
crl_dir    = $dir/crl
[ ... ]
```

Replace ./demoCA with the directory where you want to put your CA information. For example, enter /usr/local/ssl/CA. /etc/openssl.cnf should now look like this:

```
[ CA_default ]
dir          = /usr/local/ssl/CA
certs        = $dir/certs
crl_dir      = $dir/crl
[ ... ]
```

You now need to edit the script that sets you up as a CA, /usr/bin/CA.sh. Near the top of the script is something like this:

```
CATOP=./demoCA
CAKEY=./cakey.pem
CACERT=./cacert.pem
```

Change it to:

```
CATOP=/usr/local/ssl/CA
CAKEY=./cakey.pem
CACERT=./cacert.pem
```

Running CA.sh creates the directory structure under the CATOP root directory. So you need to make the root directory:

```
# mkdir /usr/local/ssl/CA
# chmod 700 /usr/local/ssl/CA
```

The chmod is to keep everything private from prying eyes. Change the ownership of this directory to whoever will be doing the CA tasks (which could be root), and then execute CA.sh as this user:

```
# /usr/bin/CA.sh -newca
```

Before the user does that, however, make sure she has initialized the random number generator as detailed at the beginning of the section "Creating SSL Certificates for Use with Samba." When this script is executed, you will be asked whether the CA should use an existing certificate or create a new one. Press Enter to create a new one. This new certificate will be self-signed and will be used later by clients when validating certificates that claim to be signed by this CA. You will also be asked for a passphrase to encrypt the CA's private key. You will need this passphrase when signing CSRs later on. Finally, fill in all the details as you have done before.

When you are done, you will see that the directory tree has been populated:

```
$ ls -l /usr/local/ssl/CA/
total 24
-rw-r--r--  1 root     root         1159 Jan 11 23:53 cacert.pem
drwxr-xr-x  2 root     root         4096 Jan 11 23:52 certs
drwxr-xr-x  2 root     root         4096 Jan 11 23:52 crl
-rw-r--r--  1 root     root            0 Jan 11 23:52 index.txt
drwxr-xr-x  2 root     root         4096 Jan 11 23:52 newcerts
drwxr-xr-x  2 root     root         4096 Jan 11 23:53 private
-rw-r--r--  1 root     root            3 Jan 11 23:52 serial
```

Now you can sign the `csr.pem` file you created earlier by entering this:

```
$ openssl ca -policy policy_anything -days 365 -config
➥/etc/openssl.cnf -infiles csr.pem > cert.pem
Using configuration from /etc/openssl.cnf
Enter PEM pass phrase:
Check that the request matches the signature
Signature ok
The Subjects Distinguished Name is as follows
countryName          :PRINTABLE:'AU'
stateOrProvinceName  :PRINTABLE:'Australian Capital Territory'
localityName         :PRINTABLE:'Canberra'
organizationName     :PRINTABLE:'MyCompany Pty Ltd'
organizationalUnitName:PRINTABLE:'Information Technology'
commonName           :PRINTABLE:'samba.mycompany.com.au'
emailAddress         :IA5STRING:'matt@mycompany.com.au'
Certificate is to be certified until Jan 11 13:57:18 2001 GMT (365 days)
Sign the certificate? [y/n]:y


1 out of 1 certificate requests certified, commit? [y/n]y
Write out database with 1 new entries
Data Base Updated
```

Note that you are asked for a passphrase. This is the passphrase you entered when you set up your CA. You may or may not need the `-config` parameter, but it does not hurt to include it. If you want the signed certificate to last a different amount of time than 365 days, feel free to put whatever expiry time you like. The `-policy` option allows you to make sure certain fields in the distinguished name are filled in and not blank. The policy "`policy_anything`" allows all fields to be optional. The resulting `cert.pem` file will look something like this:

```
issuer :/C=AU/ST=ACT/L=Canberra/CN=Matthew Gillard/Email=
➥matt@mycompnay.com.au
subject:/C=AU/ST=Australian Capital Territory/L=Canberra
➥/O=MyCompany Pty Ltd/OU=
Information Technology/CN=samba.mycompany.com.au
➥/Email=matt@mycompany.com.au
serial :02


Certificate:
    Data:
        Version: 3 (0x2)
        Serial Number: 2 (0x2)
        Signature Algorithm: md5WithRSAEncryption
        Issuer: C=AU, ST=ACT, L=Canberra, CN=Matthew Gillard
➥/Email=matt@mycompnay.com.au
        Validity
            Not Before: Jan 12 13:57:18 2000 GMT
            Not After : Jan 11 13:57:18 2001 GMT
        Subject: C=AU, ST=Australian Capital Territory,
➥ L=Canberra, O=MyCompany
Pty Ltd, OU=Information Technology, CN=samba.mycompany.com.au
➥/Email=matt@mycompany.com.au
```

```
        Subject Public Key Info:
            Public Key Algorithm: rsaEncryption
            RSA Public Key: (512 bit)
Modulus (512 bit):
                        00:c1:35:88:ed:80:29:cf:b7:93:84:32:a6:51:96:
                        8c:6b:d3:0f:5d:ff:0b:39:52:26:ad:66:ae:4e:32:
                        c3:58:3c:f4:64:84:e3:38:c7:fc:37:32:d1:0a:29:
                        37:79:41:69:86:03:cc:16:23:2c:2e:af:ff:43:fa:
                        e5:67:e4:7f:89
                    Exponent: 65537 (0x10001)
        X509v3 extensions:
            X509v3 Basic Constraints:
                CA:FALSE
            Netscape Comment:
                OpenSSL Generated Certificate
            X509v3 Subject Key Identifier:
                9F:DD:58:36:22:3A:69:66:64:68:85:44:8F:47:AD:E1:
➥23:B2:1A:B6
            X509v3 Authority Key Identifier:
                keyid:13:E2:25:E4:DA:64:14:8D:E7:3F:A7:88:42:5B:E1:
➥BF:0D:38:37:65
                DirName:/C=AU/ST=ACT/L=Canberra/CN=Matthew Gillard
➥/Email=matt@mycompnay.com.au
                serial:00

    Signature Algorithm: md5WithRSAEncryption
        9e:70:27:9d:be:2e:19:1f:91:40:05:4d:d2:8c:c3:5a:1d:0c:
        42:9f:a9:b7:04:89:58:d9:e7:14:1e:66:f1:88:63:7c:da:cb:
        18:a0:a0:1f:3b:08:98:23:17:d4:00:a2:eb:9d:87:44:87:cc:
        87:08:59:68:4b:8e:8d:8e:ab:35:09:40:59:63:c2:c2:1e:f8:
        ea:b7:9c:b3:dc:d5:55:ea:2f:2d:82:06:4b:00:21:98:1e:db:
        f7:df:e4:37:4d:f4:e9:dc:fa:50:7a:fa:4e:bc:bc:dc:49:0d:
        3d:7e:25:c8:13:87:93:06:bb:cc:88:84:00:59:4f:82:bc:9b:
        07:04

-----BEGIN CERTIFICATE-----
MIIDazCCAtSgAwIBAgIBAjANBgkqhkiG9w0BAQQFADByMQswCQYDVQQGEwJBVTEM
MAoGA1UECBMDQUNUMREwDwYDVQQHEwhDYW5iZXJyYTEYMBYGA1UEAxMPTWF0dGhl
[...]
-----END CERTIFICATE-----
```

The CA is the issuer ("Matthew Gillard" in this example). The subject is the certificate that was signed. You can also see information on when the certificate is valid. At the end is the actual certificate.

Installing the Certificates

Now you need to place the private key and certificate in place ready for Samba to use it. It is assumed that OpenSSL is set up to look for certificates in /etc/ssl/certs as is the default in Red Hat 6.x. To put your newly signed certificate in place, execute these commands:

```
# cp cert.pem /etc/ssl/certs/sambacert.pem
# cp key.pem /etc/ssl/certs/sambakey.pem
```

```
# cd /etc/ssl/certs
# ln -s sambacert.pem `openssl x509 -noout -hash < sambacert.pem`.0
# ls -l
total 24
lrwxrwxrwx   1 root      root           13 Jan 13 01:14 19577ab1.0
➥ -> sambacert.pem
-rw-r--r--   1 root      root         3544 Jan 13 01:12 sambacert.pem
-rw-r--r--   1 root      root          561 Jan 13 01:12 sambakey.pem
```

You may be wondering why there was a link created. The link is a hash of the certificate. When OpenSSL searches through the certificates in this directory, it is much faster to search for a hash than it is to search through the contents of each certificate. You also need to add the certificate and private key for the CA so that the Samba key can be verified:

```
# cd /usr/local/ssl/CA
# cp cacert.pem /etc/ssl/certs
# cp private/cakey.pem /etc/ssl/certs
# cd /etc/ssl/certs
# ln -s cacert.pem `openssl x509 -noout -hash < cacert.pem`.0
```

That is all there is to it. Now on to the main topic: how to get Samba to speak SSL.

Compiling Samba with SSL Support

Samba's SSL functionality was originally based on the freely available SSL implementation, SSLeay. SSLeay seems to have evolved into OpenSSL. You need to have OpenSSL installed before you go any further; see the section "Creating SSL Certificates for Use with Samba" for details on how to install it. There are no precompiled Samba packages that contain SSL support; due to the various cryptographic laws in different countries, it would make distributing Samba too complicated. If you want SSL support, you need to compile Samba yourself.

You need to download the Samba source. If you are not sure how to do this, return to Chapter 2, "Compiling and Installing Samba," to refresh your memory. After you have unpacked Samba, go to the source directory. You need to run the configure script like this:

```
# ./configure --with-ssl --with-sslinc=/usr/include/openssl
```

When it is done, execute make. When that has finished, run make install, which by default will install your new Samba configuration to /usr/local/samba. Next you need to configure Samba to enable SSL support.

Samba SSL Configuration

You need to put a Samba configuration file into /usr/local/samba/lib/smb.conf. When you have done this, you need to add three parameters to smb.conf. They are

```
ssl = yes
ssl server cert = /etc/ssl/certs/sambacert.pem
ssl server key = /etc/ssl/certs/sambakey.pem
```

The first indicates that you want to enable SSL for all connections. The second tells smbd where to find the certificate that it will give to connecting clients. The last tells smbd where to look for its private key.

When you have added these lines, you can start your smbd:

```
# /usr/local/samba/bin/smbd
Enter PEM pass phrase:
```

Enter the passphrase that was on your Samba certificate, and Samba should start up in the background. You can check whether it is running:

```
# ps -auwx | grep smbd
root    10648 0.0 1.5 3104 1488 ?    S  01:42  0:00
```

➥ /usr/local/samba/bin/smbd

You probably should start up nmbd as well to provide your computer browsing and name resolution services:

```
# /usr/local/samba/bin/nmbd
```

Your Samba server is now ready for SSL connections! Note that each time you start up Samba, you will be asked for this passphrase. This could be annoying, especially if a server reboots by itself (after a power failure, for example). If it does, the server startup will likely just sit there until the passphrase is entered at the console. A better option, especially if you have remote servers, is to not put Samba in your startup but instead start it up manually each time you restart a server. It is not an ideal solution, but at least you won't have the problem of a server hanging if it has an unscheduled reboot.

Using Samba with SSL

You can test that all is well by using smbclient to connect to a resource on your Samba server. You start up smbclient as you normally would:

```
# smbclient //daffy/tmp
Added interface ip=192.168.66.6 bcast=192.168.66.15 nmask=255.255.255.240
SSL: Certificate OK: /C=AU/ST=ACT/L=Canberra/CN=Matthew Gillard
➥/Email=matt@mycompany.com.au
SSL: Certificate OK: /C=AU/ST=ACT/L=Canberra/CN=Matthew Gillard
➥/Email=matt@mycompany.com.au
SSL: negotiated cipher: DES-CBC3-SHA
Password:
Domain=[MYGROUP] OS=[Unix] Server=[Samba 2.0.5a]
smb: \>
```

It tells you that the certificate it was sent by smbd was really signed by your CA. If you did not copy your CA certificate and private key to /etc/ssl/certs, you would have gotten this instead:

```
# smbclient //daffy/tmp
Added interface ip=192.168.66.6 bcast=192.168.66.15 nmask=255.255.255.240
```

```
SSL: Cert error: unknown error 20 in /C=AU/ST=ACT/L=Canberra
➥/CN=Matthew Gillard/Email=matt@mycompany.com.au
SSL: negotiated cipher: DES-CBC3-SHA
Password:
```

This error means that `smbclient` cannot verify whether the signature on the `sambacert.pem` is legitimate because it cannot find the CA certificate in `/etc/ssl/certs`. However, you will notice that Samba does not consider that a critical error, and continues with the encrypted session. Later versions of Samba could behave differently, so beware.

The final step is to enable client-side certificates. We will add this configuration to what we have already. Go through the process again to create another private key and certificate. Call the private key `smbclientkey.pem` and the certificate `smbclientcert.pem`. Copy them to your `certs` directory wherever that happens to be, and then set these SSL variables after the ones you added previously:

```
ssl require clientcert = yes
ssl client cert = /etc/ssl/certs/sambaclientcert.pem
ssl client key = /etc/ssl/certs/sambaclientkey.pem
ssl CA certDir = /etc/ssl/certs
```

The first parameter sets up Samba to require client certificates; otherwise, it will not let the client connect. The next two specify where the certificate and private key are kept. The final one is for the benefit of `smbclient`, so that smbclient can find the CA's certificate to verify the certificate that the SSL server sends during connection establishment. If you are setting up `smbclient` on a completely different machine than the Samba server, you would only need to add `ssl client cert`, `ssl client key`, and `ssl CA certDir` to the `smb.conf` file for `smbclient` to read. That also means you would need to install OpenSSL on all machines that would be running an SSL version of `smbclient`, as well as the `cacert.pem` and `cakey.pem` and the hash link.

Now you can start `smbclient`:

```
smbclient //daffy/tmp
Enter PEM pass phrase:
Added interface ip=192.168.66.6 bcast=192.168.66.15 nmask=255.255.255.240
SSL: Certificate OK: /C=AU/ST=ACT/L=Canberra/CN=Matthew Gillard
➥/Email=matt@mycompany.com.au
SSL: Certificate OK: /C=AU/ST=ACT/L=Canberra/CN=Matthew Gillard
➥/Email=matt@mycompany.com.au
SSL: negotiated cipher: DES-CBC3-SHA
Password:
Domain=[MYGROUP] OS=[Unix] Server=[Samba 2.0.5a]
smb: \>
```

Note that the first thing you are asked for is the passphrase for the private key you created for `smbclient`. This is so that `smbclient` can read its locked private key. The rest of the session continues as normal. The only difference is that you have client certificates enabled, so you need to generate certificates for all clients you want to be able to connect.

Other SSL `smb.conf` Parameters

There are many other SSL parameters that you can set in the Samba configuration file, all of which are outlined in the following sections. They have been included to serve as a reference for you. The following list is designed so you can read through all the parameters and decide which options you need and which are not required.

ssl CA certDir

The parameter `ssl CA certDir` is where Samba looks up the trusted CAs. It is only used when Samba is configured to verify client certificates. Each entry in the directory must be a hash value created from the distinguished name of the CA.

Here's an example:

```
ssl CA certDir = /etc/ssl/certs
```

ssl CA certFile

The parameter `ssl CA certFile` is an alternative to `ssl CA certDir`. This time a file is specified that contains all the trusted CA's certificates, one after the other.

Here's an example:

```
ssl CA certFile = /etc/ssl/certs/CAcollection.pem
```

ssl ciphers

The `ssl ciphers` parameter allows you to specify the different ciphers to be offered during the SSL handshaking process. It is recommended that you do not change this parameter. If you are interested in what values it could contain, see the OpenSSL source code or Web site (`http://www.openssl.org`).

Here's an example:

```
ssl ciphers = DEFAULT
```

ssl client cert

The `ssl client cert` variable is read by `smbclient`. The value of this parameter is required by `smbclient` if the server requires client certificates.

An example follows:

```
ssl client cert = /etc/ssl/certs/smbclientcert.pem
```

ssl client key

Again, the `ssl client key` parameter only needs to be used when the server requires client certificates. If set, this variable contains the client private key. If you are using `smbclient`, it will look here for its private key.

An example follows:

```
ssl client key = /etc/ssl/certs/smbclientkey.pem
```

ssl compatibility

The `ssl compatibility` parameter defines whether or not OpenSSL should be configured for bug compatibility with other SSL implementations. You should generally leave this variable alone.

This default value is

```
ssl compatibility = no
```

ssl hosts resign and ssl hosts

The parameters `ssl hosts resign` and `ssl hosts` control whether or not Samba will go into SSL mode. This is quite useful if you want SSL to kick in when clients connect from untrusted IP addresses. The syntax for these parameters is exactly the same as for the `hosts allow` and `hosts deny` parameters. If neither parameter is set, Samba will allow only SSL connections. If there are hosts listed in the `ssl hosts resign` parameter, these hosts will not be forced into SSL mode. However, if `ssl hosts` is set, the hosts in that parameter *will* be forced into SSL mode.

The following example forces hosts in the untrusted network (137.154) to connect via SSL, and the hosts in the trusted network (167.154) to connect via conventional methods:

```
ssl hosts = 137.154.
ssl hosts resign = 167.154.
```

ssl require clientcert

The `ssl require clientcert` variable forces clients to have a valid certificate before they will be able to connect. The previously mentioned variables `ssl CA certDir` or `ssl CA certFile` will be used by the server to verify the CAs who signed the client certificates.

The default value is

```
ssl require clientcert = no
```

ssl require servercert

If `ssl require servercert` is set, `smbclient` will request a certificate from the server.

The default value is

```
ssl require servercert = no
```

ssl version

The `ssl version` parameter is where you can define the version of the SSL protocol to be used. The value can be one of the following:

```
ssl2or3
ssl2
```

```
ssl3
tls1
```

The default is **ssl2or3**. You do not normally need to change this parameter.

Client Support for SSL-Configured Samba

It is important to be able to encrypt sessions using a Samba server, but you also need SSL-capable clients to be able to do this. Currently these are lacking in numbers. The only ones that seem to be around are **smbclient** and a package called Sharity created by a company called Objective Development. Sharity is a commercial SMB/CIFS implementation for UNIX systems. It functions similarly to Samba, and there is a demo version that can be downloaded that is limited to a directory hierarchy of three levels. Sharity is free for students and educational institutions and can be found at `http://www.obdev.at/Products/Sharity.html`. Objective Development also has an open source product called **sslproxy**. This allows two different functions: being able to tunnel practically any application over SSL for use by non–SSL-aware servers, and allowing access to SSL-aware servers from non–SSL-aware clients. Effectively you could install **sslproxy** in an environment where there is an SSL-enabled Samba server, and get access to that Samba server from a non–SSL-enabled client, such as Windows NT. Alternatively, you could tunnel Windows NT SMB file servers over SSL for access with Sharity or SSL-enabled **smbclient**. You can find **sslproxy** at `http://www.obdev.at/Products/sslproxy.html`. It is simple to compile and it comes with documentation.

Summary

This chapter went through the basics of SSL and how you can utilize this feature in Samba. We discussed in some depth what SSL is and how it works. SSL stands for Secure Sockets Layer and was developed by Netscape to create a secure environment in Web browsers to do sensitive transactions like banking and shopping.

You also learned the basics behind the SSL protocol. It uses public key cryptography to perform user authentication and regular symmetric ciphers for the application data channel. You learned that SSL relies heavily on certificates during the authentication phase of the connection.

You learned what a certificate is. Remember that it is just a public key with an identity attached. This identity is called a distinguished name.

You learned what a certification authority (CA) is. You now know that it is a trusted party who signs certificates. If the general public trusts a particular CA, they trust any certificates that that CA signs.

You saw how certificate signing works. You must generate a certificate signing request, which goes to the CA, who adds a digital signature to it so that you can prove you are who you say you are.

You learned the procedure to generate a private key and certificate. First, create your private key:

```
# openssl genrsa -des3 512 > key.pem
```

Next, generate your certificate signing request:

```
# openssl req -new -key key.pem -out csr.pem
```

Finally, sign your certificate:

```
# openssl ca -policy policy_anything -days 365
➥-config /etc/openssl.cnf -infiles csr.pem > cert.pem
```

You learned that you have to compile Samba yourself to include SSL support.

You also learned how to configure your Samba server to be SSL-enabled, generate a Samba certificate, and then add the certificate information to `smb.conf`:

```
ssl = yes
ssl server cert = /etc/ssl/certs/sambacert.pem
ssl server key = /etc/ssl/certs/sambakey.pem
```

Finally, you saw how to enable client-side certificates. You need to generate a certificate for each client that will access your Samba server, and then add these parameters to `smb.conf`:

```
ssl require clientcert = yes
ssl client cert = /etc/ssl/certs/sambaclientcert.pem
ssl client key = /etc/ssl/certs/sambaclientkey.pem
ssl CA certDir = /etc/ssl/certs
```

You will also need to add your CA certificates to each machine running an SSL client.

Review Questions

1. Why would you want to use SSL? Name a sample application that SSL could be used for.

2. What are CAs, and what is so important about them?

3. What is a certificate-signing request?

4. With Samba, are server-side certificates or client-side certificates important? Why?

5. What are the general steps you would follow when setting up your Samba server to use SSL?

Exercises

1. Choose a relevant Linux/UNIX server in your organization to use as a CA server. Secure it as much as possible by removing unneeded services. Implement this machine as your organization's CA using the steps outlined in this chapter.

2. Add SSL support to the SWAT utility that comes with Samba. (Hint: You might find the tools located at `ftp://ftp.obdev.at/pub/Products/sslproxy/` or `http://mike.daewoo.com.pl/computer/stunnel/` useful for this purpose.

## CHAPTER 10

ADDITIONAL SHARE LEVEL OPTIONS

You will learn about the following in this chapter:

- How to execute a script when a user connects and disconnects from a file service

- What "name mangling" is and which Samba parameters control how the name mangling process works

- How to hide files from the view of the user on a resource

- How to limit the number of connections to a share

- How to ensure connections to a particular share come from a particular user or group

- How to deny specific users access to a share

T his chapter explains some of the less frequently used options you can specify as part of a file share service. Although these options are not used as frequently, this does not mean they should be ignored—quite the contrary. This chapter covers Samba configuration parameters that allow you to execute commands on the server side before and after a user connects to a share. This chapter introduces the term *name mangling*, and includes parameters to control how the name mangling process works, parameters that relate to connecting users on a share (controlling what they can and cannot do), parameters that relate to files on a resource, and parameters that control share level options.

preexec, postexec

Probably the most useful of the advanced options are the **preexec** and **postexec** parameters. The **preexec** parameter allows a program to be executed on the Samba server when a user connects to a file share. Similarly, the command in the **postexec** parameter is executed when a client disconnects from the file share. These can have quite useful applications. Take, for instance, a share you are trying to decommission called **developers**. The share configuration is as follows:

```
[developers]
path = /export/developers
public = no
writable = no
```

Suppose that you want to know if anyone is connecting to this share any more to read data from it. You can change the configuration slightly and grab a log of connections made to it:

```
[developers]
path = /export/developers
public = no
writable = no
preexec = echo \"The share %S was connected to by %u\"
➥>> /var/tmp/samba-connections.log
```

Now, each time a user connects to the share **developers**, an entry will be made in the log file `/var/tmp/samba-connections.log`.

A slightly different version of the same parameters exists called **root preexec** and **root postexec**. These parameters function identically to the other two except for one important difference. The programs they execute are run as the root user. One obvious application for this is to mount a CD-ROM on connection to the share, and unmount it on disconnection:

```
[cdrom]
path = /mnt/cdrom
public = no
root preexec = mount /mnt/cdrom /dev/cdrom
root postexec = umount /mnt/cdrom
```

This example assumes that there is a link in /dev called cdrom that points to the correct device file for your CD-ROM.

What Is "Name Mangling"?

You have probably heard of the concept of *name mangling*. This was actually more relevant back when DOS and Windows 3.1 ruled the world. It came about because of the differences in the way filenames are stored in different operating systems. DOS filenames have an 8.3 format, whereas UNIX allows longer names. Name mangling is how Samba changes UNIX filenames to conform to the DOS 8.3 format. The options that control this behavior can be set on a per-service basis or globally.

The first parameter, **default case**, controls what the default case is for new files. By default it is set to **lower**. The alternative is **upper**.

The next parameter, **mangle case**, operates on filenames containing characters that are not of the default case, like "Mail." If this parameter is set to **yes**, a name like "Mail" is mangled. The default for this is **no**.

The **case sensitive** parameter determines whether Samba filenames are case sensitive. The default is **no**.

The **preserve case** parameter determines whether Samba creates new files with the case that the client passes, or causes the files to be created with the default case. The default for this parameter is **yes**.

The parameter `short preserve case` controls whether files that conform to 8.3 format are created uppercase (like all 8.3 filenames) or forced in the default case. The default for this parameter is `yes`.

The `mangled names` parameter controls whether non-DOS names that live in UNIX should be mangled to DOS format, or made invisible to the connecting DOS client. If you want to learn the process of mangling a name, see the `smb.conf` manual page in the section on `mangled names`. For example, a name like `great_train_robbery.txt` could turn into `GREAT~01.TXT`. The "~" character can be whatever character you specify in the `mangling char` option. Obviously, by default it is "~".

The `mangled stack` parameter is a global parameter that controls the number of mangled names that should be cached in the Samba server. This setting can dramatically increase performance in your Samba server because recently mangled names that are cached do not need to be mangled again if they are requested a number of times in a relatively short period of time. This mangled names cache consists of a stack of recently mangled original or base names. The larger this number, the more likely that mangled names can be successfully converted to correct long UNIX names. Each stack element costs 256 bytes, so the larger this value, the more memory required. The default value is `50`.

A very useful parameter called `mangled map` is used to cause certain files to be renamed in a user-definable way. HTML files are a good example of why this is useful. UNIX systems usually name HTML files with a .html extension, whereas on DOS systems they are named with a .htm extension. To map all the .html files on a UNIX Samba share to .htm so that you can see them properly under DOS, you would add this to your `smb.conf`:

```
mangled map = (*.html *.htm)
```

Parameters That Control User Access to Resources

The parameters in this section are for specifying groups and users in certain parameters for a shared resource. Described are `valid users` and `invalid users`, which specify users that are or are not allowed to connect to the resource; `write list` and `read list`, which allow you to explicitly set who is allowed to write to a resource or have read-only access to a resource; and `force group` and `force user`, which overrides a user's connection with that of another user.

valid users, invalid users

These parameters are pretty self-explanatory: `valid users` allows you to define users or groups that can access this particular share, and `invalid users` allows you to specify users that are not allowed to access the share. The latter option is useful when you know there are certain users or groups of users who should not be connecting to a share. Also note that if you have `valid users` set, any people not in the list are denied access implicitly. Similarly, if you have `invalid users` set, everyone not in this list is allowed access. In both parameters, groups are specified with a prepended "@." If you are running NIS, the NIS netgroup is looked at first, and then the local UNIX machine's /etc/group file. There are two additional special characters if you want to change this behavior. A "+" prepended to a string indicates that the group should be looked at on the local machine, and an "&" means to look at the NIS netgroup database. So &+group means the same as @group.

write list, read list

Using the write list parameter gives you a way to specifically list users or groups who can have write access to the share. Similarly, read list provides a method of giving specific users or groups who can have read-only access to the share. If a user is specified in both parameters, the write list takes precedence.

Here is an example:

```
write list = @operator, @techos, root
read list = matt, john, @mgmt
```

As usual with smb.conf, the "@" specifies a group rather than a user. The user root and the groups operator and techos are given write access, whereas matt, john, and the group mgmt are given read-only access. Note that if matt was in the write list as well as the read list, matt would actually have write access. This also applies if matt was in the group operator or techos.

force group, force user

The force parameters allow you to force connections to a particular share to become a certain group and/or user. As of Samba 2.0.5, if the force group parameter has a "+" prepended to it and the user is already a member of the group, this group is forced to be the user's primary group for this session. All other users retain their ordinary primary group.

Note that with force user, a user still needs to specify a valid username and password to connect to the resource. It is just that when he is connected, all operations are performed as the user specified in force user (which can be a different user). These force options can be used in an environment where not all users have a UNIX account and there is a common share available for software installations. In this case you might create an account called install. If you put this in smb.conf:

```
[install]
comment = "This share is for software installations"
path = /pc/install
read-only = yes
force user = install
```

Then all connections to the resource install will be done as the user install no matter who is connecting.

Parameters Related to Shares

These parameters change certain attributes of the particular share in which they are defined. The parameters covered include `max connections`, which specifies how many users will be allowed to connect simultaneously; `volume`, which allows you to have a volume name returned for the share; `locking`, which controls whether or not Samba is to grant locks requested by the client; `copy`, which allows you to implement template shares and copy them any number of times; and finally `blocking locks`, which controls whether Samba will grant locks on a part of a file rather than on the entire file.

max connections

The `max connections` parameter allows you to specify (and hence limit) the maximum number of simultaneous connections to a server. It defaults to `0`, which means that unlimited connections to a service are allowed. This may be useful in situations where you have a specific number of licenses to a particular software package that you make available over the network. When `max connections` is set, lock files are used to count the number of sessions to the share, and the location for these lock files is specified in the `lock directory` parameter. This defaults to `/tmp/samba`.

volume

The `volume` parameter allows you to specify the volume label returned for a share. This is displayed when you view the properties for a drive under Windows, as in Figure 10.1.

FIGURE 10.1
The volume label as returned by Windows NT.

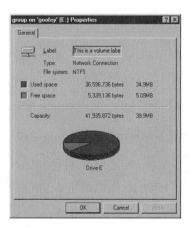

Some installation programs from CD-ROM expect a particular volume label or they will not run, so this is especially useful in those circumstances.

locking

Different connecting clients can specify lock requests for certain files. This parameter controls whether or not Samba will actually perform these lock requests. By default, `locking` is set to yes. If it is set to no, lock and unlock requests will appear to succeed to the client but will not actually be done. You will only need to change this parameter if you are having a particular problem that you think may be caused by locking.

copy

The `copy` parameter is very useful. It allows this service to be a copy of another service. This parameter is often used when you have different names for one share for backward compatibility purposes. It may also be used to create template services to simplify creating similar services. An example of its use follows:

```
[templ_mktg]
comment = "share used for marketing dept"
create mask = 0770
guest ok = no

[usa_mktg]
copy = templ_mktg
path = /groups/usa/marketing
```

This will copy all the parameters specified in the `templ_mktg` service to the `usa_mktg` service. You can put any other parameters you like in the new service—they override the template's service parameters. In the previous example, `usa_mktg` effectively looks like this:

```
[usa_mktg]
comment = "share used for marketing dept"
create mask = 0770
guest ok = no
copy = templ_mktg
path = /groups/usa/marketing
```

Being able to do this helps tremendously with administration, especially if you have many shares copied with similar options set.

blocking locks

SMB clients can specify a byte range lock on a region of an open file. This request has a time expiry with it, so if the lock cannot be granted immediately, it is queued and keeps trying until the time expires. In the Samba 2.x.x series, this setting defaults to true. If it is set to false, Samba will fail the lock request immediately, ignoring the request's time expiry parameter. You may need to do this if you have broken client applications that ask for this lock in an incorrect manner—this would cause noticeable delays that you might think are being caused by Samba. It is rare to use this parameter now because most applications behave correctly.

Parameters That Affect Files Located in Shared Resources

The next set of parameters affect how the files that are in a share display to the user. The parameters covered include the following: `delete readonly`, which allows a connecting user to override the read-only bit on a file to allow file deletions; `dont descend`, which causes certain directories to come up empty; `hide files` and `hide dot files`, which hide certain files from view in the share although they are still visible; and `veto`, which makes certain files inaccessible.

delete readonly

This parameter allows read-only files to be deleted. You would not normally need to set this. It defaults to `no`. You might find this useful if you have a particular directory tree that has the read-only parameter set on all the files and you have an administrator of that share (who does not know UNIX) who uses a different share for administrative purposes but points to the same place that has this parameter set. This allows the administrator to delete files that may not be required anymore.

dont descend

The `dont descend` parameter allows you to specify a comma-separated list of directories that Samba always displays as empty. This can be very useful if you have certain directory paths under a share that you do not want your SMB clients to access. There are also some areas on a UNIX box such as `/proc` and `/dev` that make no sense for a user to descend into. An example follows:

```
dont descend = /proc, /dev, /stand
```

hide files, hide dot files

The first `hide` parameter, `hide files`, specifies files that are still accessible, but hidden from view for this share. These files are separated by a "/" and may include spaces and the "*" and "?" DOS wildcards. The `hide dot files` parameter hides all files that begin with a dot. By default, `hide dot files` is set to `yes`, but no other files are hidden.

veto files, delete veto files, veto oplock files

The `veto files` option is similar to `hide files`, but instead of just hiding the specified files, it makes them inaccessible. The same rules for specifying files apply as with `hide files`. If you delete a directory with vetoed files in it, normally the vetoed files are kept and the directory deletion will fail. But there may be times when you want the directory to be deleted. If this is what you want, you set the `delete veto files` parameter to `true`. The directory deletion will be successful.

You may need to skip ahead to Chapter 11, "Tuning Samba for Better Performance," to read about oplocks to understand what the `veto oplock files` does. In a nutshell, setting this parameter allows certain files that you specify to be exempt from the granting of oplocks. Sometimes you may want to use this parameter if certain types of files cause your system performance difficulties.

Summary

In this chapter you have learned about some of the more interesting (and unusual) `smb.conf` parameters that you can use in your file services to achieve specific effects.

The chapter started with a discussion on the **preexec** and **postexec** parameters. These options allow you to execute a UNIX command or script when a client connects and disconnects from a share. It was mentioned that this has many uses; a common one is to mount a CD when a user connects and unmount it when the user disconnects.

The next section went through the name mangling process and showed how this allows DOS and Windows 3.1 clients access to long UNIX filenames. It was mentioned that Samba uses an algorithm to shorten the name so it fits into the 8.3 format required by DOS. You also learned which options you need to modify to tweak the name mangling process.

We then went through options that specifically affect the way users are handled when connecting to a share. You learned that you can force connections to occur as a user (`force user`) or group (`force group`) and also how to deny certain users from accessing a share (`invalid users`).

Next was a discussion on options that affect a share as a whole such as adding a volume label (`volume`) or limiting the number of allowable simultaneous connections (`max connections`).

Finally, you were taught options that apply to the files on a share. You learned some options that hide files but still keep them accessible (`hide files`) and others that hide files and make them inaccessible to the connecting user (`veto files`).

Review Questions

1. You want to make a file share on your UNIX system map to the CD-ROM. The directory where you mount your CD-ROM is at `/mnt`. What is the file share section you would add to your `smb.conf` file?

2. What is "name mangling"?

3. How do you hide, but still make accessible, all UNIX filenames beginning with "~" and "$" from file shares viewed by SMB clients?

4. Some software that the graphic design department uses is stored on a UNIX server running Samba. Users connect to a share to access this software. The license of the software states that it can be used with four concurrent users only. How would you comply with license requirements?

5. You have just installed a Samba server at an organization. All users need to be able to access this server to store temporary files; however, none of them currently have UNIX accounts. How could you go about giving them access with minimal effort?

6. You get a phone call from one of your users complaining that she has a lot of files with a dot as the first character of the filename on her home directory share. How could you resolve the problem?

CHAPTER 11

TUNING SAMBA FOR BETTER PERFORMANCE

You will learn about the following in this chapter:

- How to determine whether performance problems are Samba-related or due to some other factor

- What Samba configuration directives are the best to tweak to obtain better performance

- What opportunistic file locking is and how you can use it to speed up file operations

- What tuning you can do on a Samba client to improve performance

T he good thing about Samba is that it comes to you pretty well self-tuned. The options are tuned to the values that are appropriate to *most* server configurations; however, this does not mean they are appropriate for *all* configurations! This does mean that you can get Samba up and running with a minimum of fuss and without having to delve too deeply into the Samba configuration file. This chapter will give you some hints and tips on how to make your Samba server run faster by

- Pointing out obvious factors when choosing and configuring a server

- Showing you different Samba configuration parameters that may make things faster for you

- Showing you how to configure your client for better networking and SMB performance

Choosing a Machine to Run Samba on

Most people run Samba on a Linux machine running on a PC server. However, today Linux can also run on Sun hardware, Compaq Alpha hardware, and countless others. This section presents the information from a PC perspective, but many of the tips (such as operating system layout) apply equally to other systems such as SUNs or HPs as well.

The main factors to look at are as follows:

- CPU

- Memory

- Hard drive

- Network

- Tape drive

The obvious factor is a reasonably fast CPU. The simple rule here is: Purchase the fastest machine you can afford. For many companies, this will be a high-end Pentium III, and for others, the old Pentium 166MMX out the back will suffice. Also consider how many users will be connecting to your Samba server in this equation. There is no point in buying a high-end system if you will have only 10 users connecting at a time. However, if you will be using it for your corporate file server with many hundreds of connections during the day, you could probably do with a reasonably high-end system.

Regarding memory, a rule of thumb that may or may not work for you is to allow 128MB of memory for the base operating system, plus 1MB for every user who will be connecting. This may be an overestimation in many circumstances, but it is better to overspecify your system rather than underspecify it. Also allow some room for growth.

Your next decision is to choose the bus type that your hard drives will use, SCSI or IDE. With hard drives, remember that they are *cheap* these days! Even SCSI disks are only slightly more expensive than their IDE counterparts. For scalability you cannot go past SCSI. You can fit up to 15 disks per SCSI chain (the chain limit is virtually limited to your hardware)—this is in contrast to IDE, which has a maximum of four disks over two channels. Most likely you will have a SCSI port to connect the tape device to, so my recommendation for any serious system with many users is go SCSI. But for smaller systems (less than 100 users), you may not be able to afford the cost of SCSI, so IDE would be sufficient. In either case, buy as much disk as you can afford whether you need it or not, because you will use it! As soon as you buy more disk space, the applications quite quickly eat it up.

The next decision for the server is to choose your network card. If you already have a 100MB Ethernet infrastructure in place, get a good quality 100MB Ethernet card with your server. It will make a lot of difference, especially if you have many people trying to access the server. The 100MB card will allow it to serve more people at one time. Otherwise, the normal 10MB Ethernet would suffice, but make sure you get a 100MB/10MB combo card. Even if you are only using 10MB now, you might upgrade in the future to 100MB (it is getting cheaper), so then you can switch your server to 100MB immediately without buying new hardware.

Finally, I cannot emphasize enough: Buy a tape drive with your system! You will need to regularly back up your system and file services for your users. There is nothing worse than having a system with no backup regime. You would not believe the number of companies out there that don't bother to back up their servers! Do a test restore once every couple of weeks from a random tape to make sure backups are working as they should.

Checking Performance

The first question you may want to ask yourself is: How do I know I have bad performance? The next question you might want to ask is: Is it Samba that is providing the bad performance? Other factors that people often forget about are

- What else is my Samba server doing? Perhaps it is too overloaded with many interactive users using up all the CPU, and the SMB users are left with whatever CPU is left over. Check for processes using large amounts of CPU.

- Is my network the problem? Check that your network collisions are not too high:

```
# ifconfig eth0
eth0     Link encap:Ethernet  HWaddr 00:C0:A8:47:F1:1F
         inet addr:192.168.66.4  Bcast:192.168.66.15  Mask:255.255.255.240
         UP BROADCAST RUNNING MULTICAST  MTU:1500  Metric:1
         RX packets:66847898 errors:4 dropped:0 overruns:0 frame:211
         TX packets:114893973 errors:0 dropped:0 overruns:0 carrier:0
         collisions:7554
         Interrupt:10 Base address:0x300
```

If they are, your network is probably overloaded, or you have a faulty network card somewhere on the segment. One way to check network collisions is to check the value at one point in time. Transfer a large file over the network and check the value again. If it has changed significantly, you are likely to have a network problem.

- Compare your Samba performance with that of another TCP-based protocol such as the File Transfer Protocol (FTP). FTP should be slightly faster because it uses a less complex protocol than SMB, but it should give you an idea of what sort of maximum file transfer values you could expect in your environment.

Finally, an interesting Linux tuning tip that Jeremy Allison posted on the Samba mailing list is to increase the maximum open files from 1024 to 6000 (or however many files you expect to be open at once) and the maximum inodes in memory from 3072 to 12000 (tune this to match what you set file-max to). For the Linux 2.0.x series, you do it this way:

```
echo "6000" > /proc/sys/kernel/file-max
echo "12000" > /proc/sys/kernel/inode-max
```

For the 2.2.x series:

```
echo "6000" > /proc/sys/fs/file-max
echo "12000" > /proc/sys/fs/inode-max
```

Put these lines in your rc.local file so they get executed at boot time. He also suggested that you tell Linux to use most of main memory for file cache and to keep it in memory for a long time. Put this in your rc.local file:

```
echo "80 500 64 64 80 6000 6000 1884 2" > /proc/sys/vm/bdflush
```

Samba Configuration Options

There are many Samba configuration options or compile options that are performance-related. This section goes through some of them and comments on whether they are worth changing. Take note that with all the different performance options described here, it is up to you to try them out. Some may work, some may not. Some may even make things worse if you change them! There are so many different variables, such as what the hardware limitations are, and what other tasks the server is doing other than just file serving. There is no one way to make things magically faster. Experiment and see what works for you.

Compile Options

There is experimental code in the Samba source that opens files using memory mapping. This means that the file on disk is mapped to a region of memory, which in theory makes it faster to access. To enable memory mapping, you must recompile Samba. Run the configure program like this:

```
# ./configure --with-mmap
```

You may find that the memory mapping support makes no difference in your environment or could even make performance worse. The only way to know is to try it and see!

Socket Options

Quite a few TCP socket options are available that may improve performance. The various socket options currently supported by Samba are as follows:

- SO_KEEPALIVE
- SO_REUSEADDR
- SO_BROADCAST
- TCP_NODELAY
- IPTOS_LOWDELAY
- IPTOS_THROUGHPUT
- SO_SNDBUF (integer argument)
- SO_RCVBUF (integer argument)
- SO_SNDLOWAT (integer argument)
- SO_RCVLOWAT (integer argument)

Of all these options, the last four can take an integer argument (like =4096), and the rest can optionally take a 0 (to disable) or 1 (to enable). If no argument is specified, it is assumed you want to enable it.

By default `TCP_NODELAY` is turned on. In most environments it significantly speeds up Samba systems, but this is not to say that it does this for all systems. If you want to turn `TCP_NODELAY` off, you can put this line in `smb.conf`:

```
socket options = TCP_NODELAY=0
```

And you can also combine it with other options:

```
socket options = TCP_NODELAY=0 IPTOS_LOWDELAY
```

or:

```
socket options = TCP_NODELAY IPTOS_LOWDELAY
```

A configuration combination that many people have had success with in the past is

```
socket options = TCP_NODELAY IPTOS_LOWDELAY SO_SNDBUFF=8192 SO_RCVBUF=8192
```

But again, your mileage will vary.

These socket options are generally operating system–specific, so check out their behavior on your system before attempting to use them. Trying `man setsockopt` might help.

Opportunistic Locks (Oplocks)

Opportunistic locking (oplocks) is the Microsoft method of doing file locks and is supposed to speed up performance, but in reality it can cause serious performance problems in some cases, especially with older Paradox and Access databases. Sometimes, having oplocks turned on causes a performance increase, whereas sometimes it will cause serious performance problems. By default oplocks are turned on. You should turn them off only if you are having performance problems and you want to see whether turning them off will fix it.

There is also a parameter called `level2 oplocks`. This is turned off by default but will be changed to be on by default in a future release. Both parameters are share-based. For more information on how oplocks work, see the following sidebar.

Note that there is also a parameter called `fake oplocks`. Do not use it! It has been deprecated and will be removed in a future release of Samba. It was originally put in when real oplock support was not part of Samba.

Opportunistic Locking 101

Here's a brief description of how opportunistic file locking works, which may make things clearer and help you when you are tuning your server.

When a client opens a file in a nonexclusive mode, the redirector will request an exclusive opportunistic lock (oplock) of the entire file. As long as no other process has this file open, the oplock is granted. Currently, the oplock allows the client to perform read-ahead, write-behind, and lock caching for that file.

Now when another process requests access to the file, the original process is asked to either break oplock, or break to level II oplock. Level II oplocks allow multiple clients to cache their read data locally because they know that no other process is currently writing to the file. As soon as a client sends an SMB write frame that will modify the contents of the file, all clients with the file open with a level II oplock will be told to invalidate their cached data (because it may have now changed), flush any writes and locks they may have queued, and either release their oplock or close the file.

Level II opportunistic locks are great for data that gets opened read-only, like executables. It allows clients to cache the file locally without having to send SMB requests for parts of the file that are needed.

read size

The `read size` parameter is used to tune the way Samba tries to make efficient use of the time between the data leaving (or entering) the network to the time it hits a disk (or gets read from a disk). For example, when Samba does an SMB read operation of a file from disk and the amount of data being transferred is larger than the value of this parameter (default 16384), it begins writing the data to the network before it has completed reading from the disk. In general, this parameter will only be of use if the speeds of network access and disk access are similar. There is no one optimal value; try it and see what happens in your environment.

max xmit

This is the maximum packet size that Samba will be able to negotiate. The default is 65535. Sometimes, smaller values can make your Samba server faster.

strict sync

Windows applications and UNIX systems have two different understandings of what a "sync" means. In the Windows world, many applications want to do a sync to disk when they really mean they want to flush the buffer contents to disk. sync in the UNIX world means suspend all processing, and flush all kernel disk buffers to disk, which is slow! So, when a Windows client is connected to a Samba share and it tells it to sync to disk, Samba suspends and flushes all disk buffers to disk, which badly impacts performance on the UNIX server. The default value of strict sync is no, which causes Samba to ignore all requests to `sync`, which is usually what you would want.

sync always

The `sync always` parameter is similar to `strict sync`. This parameter controls whether writes will be written to disk before the `write` system call returns. For this parameter to have any effect, `strict sync` must be set to `yes`.

debug level

Amusingly enough, many people complain about Samba performance when their debug level is set to an unreasonably high number! The more logging you do, the less performance you should expect out of your Samba server. Set this to 0 (the default), unless of course you need to do some debugging.

read raw

The `read raw` parameter controls whether or not Samba will support raw read SMB requests when serving data to a client. These raw reads support packet sizes of up to 65535, which generally gives a big performance boost. However, there are some clients out there who are incapable of handling this much data at once, and for these clients you need to disable this parameter. `read raw` is set to `yes` by default.

getwd cache

`getwd cache` is used to control whether or not to use a caching algorithm to reduce the time taken to get the current working directory (`getwd()`). By default, it is turned off, but sometimes there is a large performance boost if you turn it on.

widelinks

If there are links in a directory tree being shared that point to some place in the file system that is not shared out, the `wide links` parameter controls whether these links should be followed. By default it is set to `yes`; however, when set to `yes`, it can impact your server's performance due to the extra system calls required for the checks. If you are running into performance problems, you may want to set this to `no`.

Client-Side Tuning

If you experience very slow network access to your Samba server, a lot of the time the problem will actually be with your client. My first suggestion is to check how many protocols you have bound to your network adapter. You should only have one, `TCP/IP Protocol`. If you have any others, remove them because having more than one protocol will affect performance. If that still does not fix your problem, try removing your TCP/IP protocol and then reinstalling it. Remember to reboot in between, and also reapply your current service pack after you reinstall the protocol. On Windows 9x systems, if you have the Novell client installed and you do not need it, remove it. It has been known to cause problems in the past as well.

If you still have problems, you may need to tune the TCP/IP parameters of your NT machine. See Q120642, "TCP/IP & NBT Configuration Parameters for Windows NT." If you have problems with NT on a 100MB Ethernet network, check out the article Q169789. If you have network connection problems with your Windows 9x clients, check out the article Q192534. If you have a problem with NT over a WAN link, this article might be of interest: Q140552. For a list of other TCP/IP parameters that might be worth changing on NT, see Q102973 and Q102974. Some LAN Manager tuning values can be found in article Q102630.

There does not seem to be much in the way of Windows 9x network tuning. You can try searching the Microsoft KnowledgeBase yourself at `http://support.microsoft.com` to see if there's anything new.

Summary

You have learned some useful tips and techniques for looking at Samba performance in this chapter.

The chapter first took you through choosing a server that should give you adequate performance. Remember to purchase the most high-end machine you can afford. When installing the operating system, try to put all your Samba data partitions on disks other than your operating system disk, and for those who can afford it, stripe your data partition with either RAID 0 (for speed writing and reading) or RAID 5 (for read speed and redundancy).

You should always do some checks to make sure that Samba is actually your bottleneck. Other areas to look at include checking the operating system for problems—some runaway processes might be causing your problem. Check for higher than normal network utilization, and make sure your hardware is not the problem.

The chapter also explained some Samba configuration parameters that may improve performance (or indeed may reduce performance!). Remember that there is no one way to make Samba perform faster. It depends quite heavily on each individual environment, especially what hardware is running and what sort of data you are sharing out with Samba.

Finally, the chapter looked at client-side tuning. Many Samba problems are in fact not Samba issues but problems with the client setup. If you are getting slow performance and you rule Samba out as best you can, you should then look at your client, perhaps as a first step reinstalling the TCP/IP protocol and seeing whether that makes a difference.

Review Questions

1. You are buying a system for a small company to run Linux and Samba on. What could be a possible configuration for the server given that the company has about 20 employees?

2. Your users are complaining about Samba being too slow. What should you do?

3. What are opportunistic locks and why are they useful?

4. How do Level II oplocks differ from normal oplocks?

## CHAPTER 12

DEBUGGING SAMBA

You will learn about the following in this chapter:

- Common mistakes people make when configuring their Samba server

- Methods of systematically troubleshooting your Samba server

- How to set up and view Samba debug logs

- How sniffing the SMB network traffic can help in the debugging process

- Other resources that are available for you to use if you still cannot get your problem sorted out

T his chapter is designed to help you debug any problems you may be having while trying to get your Samba configuration up and running the way you want it. The common mistakes people make are described. You will probably find that most of your questions are answered in this section. But if they aren't, the next section covers how to use network monitoring tools to help figure out problems with your Samba server. These tools really are not as scary as you might think, and they are very helpful. If you are still stuck after going through the first two sections, the rest of the chapter points you to the usual places to help fix your problem, which include mailing list archives, Web sites, and newsgroups.

Common Mistakes and Troubleshooting Techniques

This section has a question-and-answer format to help you debug your problem. But first, before you start any troubleshooting, perform the following simple network tests. This will pick up any simple network connectivity problems:

1. From the Windows box, ping the Samba box.

   You can do this by entering `ping sambaserver` from a command prompt. See Figure 12.1 for an example of how to do this.

FIGURE 12.1

Pinging the Samba Server.

2. From the Samba box, ping the Windows box (again, use the ping command).

3. On the Windows box, telnet to the Samba box on port 139. You can do this by going to Start, Run and entering `telnet sambaserver 139`. The telnet program should connect, although you will not see any output. If the cursor continues to display as an egg-timer, the Windows telnet program is not connecting.

If all the tests fail, check the following points:

- Verify that networking is enabled on the Windows box. You can do this by right-clicking Network Neighborhood. If you're using Windows 9x, you should see a network adapter and TCP/IP as a protocol as in Figure 12.2. If you're using Windows NT, click the Protocols tab and check that TCP/IP is there, as shown in Figure 12.3. If you want, click on adapters and there should be an entry for your network adapter in there.

FIGURE 12.2

Windows 9x networking with TCP/IP correctly bound.

FIGURE 12.3

Windows NT networking
with TCP/IP correctly
bound.

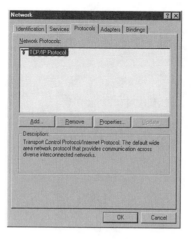

- If TCP/IP networking is enabled, check that you have a correct IP address/subnet mask
  and default gateway on both your Samba server and Windows machine. On your Samba
  server, use the `ifconfig` command to interrogate your network card:

```
# ifconfig eth0
eth0      Link encap:Ethernet  HWaddr 00:C0:A8:47:F1:1F
          inet addr:192.168.66.4  Bcast:192.168.66.15  Mask:255.255.255.240
          UP BROADCAST RUNNING MULTICAST  MTU:1500  Metric:1
          RX packets:70264035 errors:4 dropped:0 overruns:0 frame:211
          TX packets:121332245 errors:0 dropped:0 overruns:0 carrier:0
          collisions:8205
          Interrupt:10 Base address:0x300
```

For Windows, click your TCP/IP protocol and click Properties. This is shown for
Windows 9x in Figure 12.4 and Windows NT in Figure 12.5.

FIGURE 12.4

Windows 9x networking
TCP/IP properties.

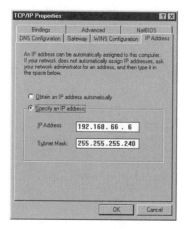

FIGURE 12.5

Windows NT networking TCP/IP properties.

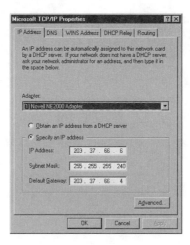

- If you are sure all your addressing is correct, check that you have DNS servers set up. If you don't, set them up now! Otherwise, make sure there is no firewall software between your Windows machine and Samba server. It is possible that your pings or connection attempts to port 139 are being filtered. Also try pinging other workstations in your area and other servers that you know are up. This might help you narrow your problem.

If your networking layer is functioning incorrectly, fix it before going any further. Networking issues are usually the problem in many situations.

If you are still having problems, work through the following questions and answers. Hopefully your problem is listed here. But don't despair if it is not—other resources are available to help you fix your problem!

Q: My Samba server does not start.

A: The most obvious problem you may encounter is that **smbd** fails to start or does not work as you expect. This could be due to some other process using port 139. The **smbd** daemon cannot bind to this port if another process is already using it. You can check if this port is being used already by using the **netstat** command:

```
# netstat -a | grep LISTEN
tcp        0      0 *:netbios-ssn            *:*                     LISTEN
tcp        0      0 *:smtp                   *:*                     LISTEN
tcp        0      0 192.168.66.4:domain      *:*                     LISTEN
tcp        0      0 *:swat                   *:*                     LISTEN
tcp        0      0 *:3000                   *:*                     LISTEN
tcp        0      0 *:nntp                   *:*                     LISTEN
tcp        0      0 *:22                     *:*                     LISTEN
tcp        0      0 goofey.here.com :domain  *:*                     LISTEN
tcp        0      0 localhost:domain         *:*                     LISTEN
tcp        0      0 *:2049                   *:*                     LISTEN
tcp        0      0 *:635                    *:*                     LISTEN
tcp        0      0 *:printer                *:*                     LISTEN
tcp        0      0 *:linuxconf              *:*                     LISTEN
```

```
tcp        0        0 *:auth                *:*                  LISTEN
tcp        0        0 *:time                *:*                  LISTEN
tcp        0        0 *:finger              *:*                  LISTEN
tcp        0        0 *:login               *:*                  LISTEN
tcp        0        0 *:shell               *:*                  LISTEN
tcp        0        0 *:gopher              *:*                  LISTEN
tcp        0        0 *:telnet              *:*                  LISTEN
```

Note that the first entry in this list is the `netbios-ssn` port. If you `grep` this text in `/etc/services`, you get port 139:

```
# grep netbios-ssn /etc/services
netbios-ssn      139/tcp           nbssn
```

If you get something like this on your server before you start Samba, you have another daemon that talks SMB on your server. It could be another version of Samba that you did not even know was there, Digital Pathworks, or any number of other commercial packages. Find it and kill it! After you have done that, Samba should start.

If it still does not start, or it starts but behaves not quite as expected, you may have a problem with your `smb.conf` file. There is a utility called `testparm` that is designed to check your `smb.conf` file for you and find any syntax errors. You would execute it like this:

```
[/usr/local/samba/lib]# testparm smb.conf
```

If there are any lines that make no sense to `testparm`, you will see something like this:

```
params.c:Parameter() - Ignoring badly formed line in configuration file: blah
```

If `testparm` picks up any problems, fix them and try starting `smbd` again.

Q: I am connecting from Windows 9x or Win 3.11 and I am getting an "Access Denied" message.

A: There is one thing you need to make sure of when connecting from non-Windows NT clients: The username you are logged in as should be the username that is passed to Samba when you are logging in. Unfortunately, you cannot specify a different user name unless you are running Windows NT. So you have two options. First, you can create an account on the Samba server that matches your Windows 9x login name. Secondly, you can create a `username map` file that maps the WFW or Windows 9x login name to a valid UNIX username. For example, if you are logged on to WFW as Brian Williams, the contents of the username map file might be:

```
# cat /usr/local/samba/lib/user.map
brianw = "Brian Williams"
```

Make sure there is an account called `brianw` on your UNIX system, and that this line appears in `smb.conf`:

```
username map = /usr/local/samba/lib/user.map
```

Q: I am trying to connect from my Windows NT workstation, but I get "Access Denied."

A: You most likely have a username or password problem. That is, either the password you are supplying is incorrect or the username is incorrect, or perhaps both. Check and try again. You could also try setting Samba's debug level to something higher, perhaps 5 or 6 and that may also point to your problem (see "Turning On Logging" later in this chapter). With Windows NT, you can connect to a share as a different user than what you are currently logged in as, so you can do something like this:

```
C:\> net use * \\goofey\tmp /user:root
```

This will connect you to the `tmp` share as root (after you supply the correct password). This may be all you need to get a connection up and running.

Q: I am trying to connect from Windows NT, but I get this message, `You are not authorized to login from this station`. Or from Windows 95sr2 and Windows 98 I get this message: `The password is incorrect. Try again`.

A: You are probably not using encrypted passwords and not setting the registry key on Windows NT or Windows 9x to not use encrypted passwords by default. The appropriate registry entries again are as follows.

For Windows 98 or Windows 95, follow this registry tree after running regedit:

```
[HKEY_LOCAL_MACHINE\System\CurrentControlSet\Services\VxD\VNETSUP]
```

And add this value:

```
"EnablePlainTextPassword"=dword:00000001
```

For Windows NT 4.0, run regedt32 and follow this tree:

```
[HKEY_LOCAL_MACHINE\SYSTEM\CurrentControlSet\Services\Rdr\Parameters]
```

And add this value:

```
"EnablePlainTextPassword"=dword:00000001
```

For Windows 2000, run regedt32 and follow this registry tree:

```
[HKEY_LOCAL_MACHINE\SYSTEM\CurrentControlSet\Services
\LanmanWorkStation\Parameters]
```

And add this value:

```
"EnablePlainTextPassword"=dword:00000001
```

Q: I am trying to connect from Windows, but I get "The network path was not found."

A: Most likely you have a name resolution problem. Let's say you are trying to connect to `\\goofey\tmp`. If you are running Windows NT and have a DNS server available, verify that the Enable DNS For Windows Resolution check box is checked in your network properties, and try this instead:

```
C:\> net use * \\goofey.full.domain.name\tmp
```

If this works, your DNS lookups are fine and your NetBIOS lookups are the problem. Add this to your `%SYSTEMROOT%\system32\drivers\etc\lmhosts` file:

```
192.168.66.4     goofey
```

Then try connecting to the NetBIOS name again:

```
C:\> net use * \\goofey\tmp
```

If this works, the problem was due to Windows NT not being able to resolve the NetBIOS name, goofey. Because using lmhosts files is not scalable, I recommend setting up your Samba server with

```
wins support = yes
```

And pointing all your PCs WINS settings at your Samba machine so NetBIOS names will be resolved properly.

If the previous command still did not work, check that the Samba daemons are running. If they aren't, that can cause the same error as well.

Q: I am trying to use SWAT with my Web browser, connecting to http://sambaserver:901, but I get a message no data when trying to connect.

A: This is almost certainly due to tcpd wrappers denying connections to the SWAT port. Some Linux distributions (namely Red Hat) secure their systems by default quite tightly, and this stops SWAP from working the way you expect it. But this is in fact the way it should be. You do not want random Joe connecting to your Samba server and checking out your Samba configuration! If you are using the Web browser on your Linux system, you can most likely get to your SWAT Web site by connecting to http://127.0.0.2:901. This is one of the local loopback network devices that cannot be accessed directly from the network. Your /etc/hosts.allow file will probably contain something like this:

```
# cat /etc/hosts.allow
SWAT: 127.0.0.2
```

Q: I try to change my password on the SWAT Web page, but it does not work.

A: The password-changing feature on the SWAT Web page requires smbpasswd to be in use (that is, encrypted passwords = yes). You are probably not using encrypted passwords and that is why it is failing.

Q: I try to connect my NT server/workstation to the Samba PDC by clicking the Change button and entering the Samba domain name. It says it cannot find a domain controller for the domain.

A: Make sure that if you are changing the Windows NT Server or Workstation from another domain to the Samba domain that you reboot after you remove it from the first domain before putting it in the Samba domain, and then reboot once again. This is the way you have to do it.

If you still have problems, your Windows NT machine is having problems resolving the NetBIOS name for the domain. Check that you have WINS running on Samba and the NT machine is using your Samba server as its WINS server. If you do not want to use WINS, add this entry to your %SYSTEMROOT%\system32\drivers\etc\lmhosts file:

```
192.168.66.4    SAMBADOMAIN
```

Of course, replace *SAMBADOMAIN* with the name of your domain, *not* Samba server. The IP address is the address of your Samba server. When trying to join the new domain, Windows tries to contact the NetBIOS name of the domain. Adding this entry will allow it to resolve the domain name to an IP address so it can contact your Samba server.

Q: I try to connect my NT server/workstation to the Samba PDC by clicking the Change button and entering the Samba domain name. It complains about not being able to change the domain password.

A: You probably do not have `encrypted passwords` set to `yes` in your `smb.conf` file.

Q: For some reason my Samba server cannot talk to any Windows machine with `smbpasswd` or `smbclient`.

A: Name resolution is probably the culprit here as well. Try using the `nmblookup` command on your Samba system:

```
$ nmblookup -B windowsbox '*'
```

This should return the IP address of the Windows client you are trying to access. If it doesn't, and your Samba server is acting as a WINS server, check that the Windows machine is correctly configured with the right IP address for the WINS server entry.

Q: When adding an account to the `smbpasswd` file (`smbpasswd -a fred`), you get the error `User fred was not found in system password file`.

A: Before you add usernames to `smbpasswd`, they must already exist in the system `/etc/passwd` file first. Add new Samba users to the system as you normally would, possibly through the `useradd` command, and then add them to `smbpasswd`.

Hopefully your problem was answered by one of the preceding questions. If not, there is a good documentation file that comes with the Samba distribution called DIAGNOSIS.txt. This gives you some step-by-step guidelines on helping pinpoint the exact problem.

Sniffing

One way to know exactly what is happening in the network and to help debug your Samba problems is to use a network sniffer. There are a few different ways to go about this. One is to use the tool, Network Monitor, that comes with Windows NT. This is probably the best, and the one with the most user-friendly display. There is also a modified version of the old favorite for UNIX sysadmins, `tcpdump`. The modified version is called `tcpdump-smb` and contains the information required to break out all the information in an SMB packet. Finally, there is an Open-Source product, ethereal, which is X Windows-based and has a lot of potential. It breaks out many different protocols in a very user-friendly format, and this tool will probably be in every System Administrator's toolbox in the near future to help track down those nasty network problems.

Network Monitor

Network Monitor comes in two versions. There is the version that comes with Windows NT Server and the one that comes with SMS. The former only allows you to monitor traffic to and from the system it is running on, whereas the other allows you to see all traffic passing by the server that it is running on. If you only have Windows NT Workstation, you will need to get your hands on Windows NT Server or SMS to be able to use Network Monitor.

Now take a look at two traces. Both traces depict the servers DAFFY and GOOFEY. DAFFY is a Windows NT Server and GOOFEY is a Samba box. DAFFY is trying to connect to a file service on GOOFEY called \\GOOFEY\TMP. The first trace is shown in Figure 12.6.

FIGURE 12.6

A Network Monitor Trace in which an SMB server cannot be found.

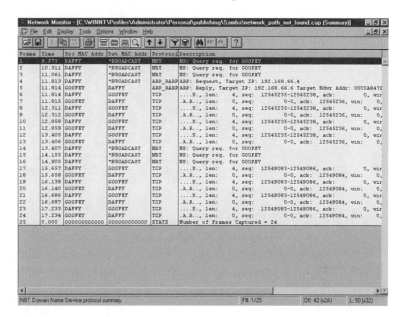

In this trace, Samba is not running on GOOFEY. DAFFY does three NS: Query req. for GOOFEY NetBIOS requests. This will provide a quick way to map any existing NetBIOS sessions to the NetBIOS name GOOFEY if it exists. There are none, so it does a Reverse ARP request looking for who belongs to the IP address 192.168.66.4. In this particular configuration, there is an lmhosts file that contains the mapping between GOOFEY and this IP address. The Reverse ARP request is to satisfy the IP layer that it can actually talk to GOOFEY. It then attempts a TCP connection to Samba on GOOFEY four times. You will notice a number of packets with the protocol type set to TCP. Directly next to the protocol is the TCP options, and each initiating connection has the S option set. So as you can see in Figure 12.6, four connections attempt to be initiated, but each time they fail because there is nothing listening on port 139 on the server. It tries again another four times, then fails, and then you get the resulting error message The network path was not found.

The next trace is of an SMB connection being established for the first time. This is shown in Figure 12.7.

FIGURE 12.7

A Network Monitor Trace of a NetBIOS session being set up, then a resource being connected to.

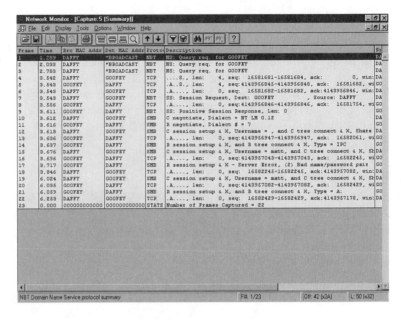

This time, the NetBIOS session setup occurs in frames 4–9. Now that a NetBIOS session is successfully set up, it can set up the SMB connection over this NetBIOS session. First of all, the dialect of the LAN Manager protocol is selected by the client, the server agrees with this dialect, and then the connection to the actual share is initiated from DAFFY in frame 12. The first is the IPC$ share, which is the Inter Process Communication connection. Then the connection to the TMP share is attempted in frame 15. Because I specified no password, SMB tells the client a password must be specified, and then the SMB connection attempts to connect again in frame 19. The SMB setup is successful in frame 21, and the drive is connected to the client.

Hopefully, now that you know what a real SMB session setup looks like, you will be able to compare what you are seeing with what it should look like and make an informed judgement about what could be wrong.

tcpdump-smb

If you have no access to the NT Network Monitor, fear not! Use the SMB extensions to tcpdump. You can find the patch at `ftp://ftp.samba.org/pub/samba/tcpdump-smb` called `tcpdump-3.4a5-smb.patch`, which you can apply to the standard tcpdump source distribution. There are also precompiled binaries in the binaries directory for Solaris, SunOS, and Linux.

After you have installed the patch on your system, it is just a matter of running it to capture your SMB packets on the network. Try something like this:

```
# tcpdump -l -I eth0 -s 1500 'port 139'
```

This says listen to interface eth0, break out the packets to 1500 bytes, and capture all traffic that is going to or from TCP/IP port 139. The output of tcpdump is not quite as nice as Network Monitor, but it certainly does the job. In some respects it is slightly better, as it breaks out all the important SMB variables so that you (or one of the Samba team members) know exactly what is going on.

A sample SMB packet using `tcpdump` will look something like this:

```
22:15:09.870000 daffy.here.com.1495 > 192.168.66.4.netbios-ssn: . ac
k 83 win 8047 (DF)
22:15:14.100000 daffy.here.com.1495 > 192.168.66.4.netbios-ssn: P 82
:266(184) ack 83 win 8047
>>> NBT Packet
NBT Session Packet
Flags=0x0
Length=180 (0xb4)

SMB PACKET: SMBsesssetupX (REQUEST)
SMB Command   =  0x73
Error class   =  0x0
Error code    =  0 (0x0)
Flags1        =  0x18
Flags2        =  0x3
Tree ID       =  0 (0x0)
Proc ID       =  51966 (0xcafe)
UID           =  0 (0x0)
MID           =  704 (0x2c0)
Word Count    =  13 (0xd)
Com2=0x75
Res1=0x0
Off2=152 (0x98)
MaxBuffer=61440 (0xf000)
MaxMpx=50 (0x32)
VcNumber=1 (0x1)
SessionKey=0x6290
CaseInsensitivePasswordLength=24 (0x18)
CaseSensitivePasswordLength=24 (0x18)
Res=0x0
Capabilities=0xD4
Pass1&Pass2&Account&Domain&OS&LanMan=
[000] AA B4 ED 49 BD A5 37 BA  33 65 6D B1 62 59 8C A1  ...I..7. 3em.bY..
[010] DE 96 87 3D C5 31 DF B1  1A A7 CF AD 0C 76 A0 6F  ...=.1.. .....v.o
[020] BF 4D 7C B8 F6 62 35 8A  30 2B 57 B9 37 6B 77 60  .M|..b5. 0+W.7kw`
[030] 6D 61 74 74 00 48 4F 4D  45 00 57 69 6E 64 6F 77  matt.HOM E.Window
[040] 73 20 4E 54 20 31 33 38  31 00 00 57 69 6E 64 6F  s NT 138 1..Windo
[050] 77 73 20 4E 54 20 34 2E  30 00 00                 ws NT 4. 0..
```

It is probably best to capture all that you need to a file, then look at it later with a text editor.

Ethereal

This is probably one of the more exciting open source products available today. The home page for the product is at `http://ethereal.zing.org`. From here you can click the Download button. Note that you need to have a few different libraries installed if you want to compile from scratch. There are some links for precompiled binaries, which I heartily recommend if your system is listed. I downloaded the precompiled Linux version and had no major problems. If you are running Red Hat Linux 6.1 or greater, download ethereal version 0.8.1 or higher. This fixed quite a number of bugs that caused it not to work with this particular distribution of Linux.

Once you have downloaded and installed Ethereal, you can start it with a command like this (subsititute the path with where you installed it):

```
# /usr/sbin/ethereal &
```

A screen should pop up on your display like that in Figure 12.8.

FIGURE 12.8
Starting Ethereal.

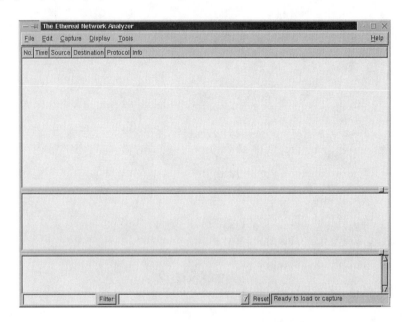

Once you have started it, you can start doing some sniffing. Click on Capture, Start and a secondary window will pop up. Here you can specify the interface you want to sniff. If none are listed, you have probably started Ethereal as a user, rather than root. By default, and for obvious security reasons, only root can put the network interfaces in promiscuous mode, which is the mode that allows you to look at all the traffic passing the interface. Log in to your system as root and then start Ethereal again. For the moment, click on Update List of Packets in Real Time, which will show you various statistics on what sort of packets are floating by, and also how many have been captured. When you have done that click on OK. Now, you should be collecting network data from your network. An example is shown in Figure 12.9. In this example you will see a lot of SMB network traffic. This was done deliberately to show you what SMB traffic looks like using Ethereal. Notice that the SMB packets are broken out into SMB commands—very handy when you are debugging problems.

FIGURE 12.9

Capturing data with
Ethereal.

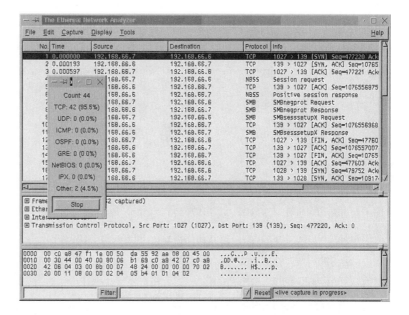

Turning On Logging

A debugging resource that is probably not used often enough is the logging capability of the
Samba server. You can specify the debug level in **smb.conf** with a line like this:

```
debug level = 3
```

Usually, level 3 or 4 is the best level to use. Anything higher than that is there for the Samba
developers to really see what is going on behind the scenes. If you have a problem that you
cannot solve, you probably want to choose one of the higher levels (maybe 6 or 7), and then
send the debug logs to one of the technical mail lists (see the later section "Samba Help
Resources").

You also need to know where your Samba logs will be put. Check your **smb.conf** file for a line
like this:

```
log file = /var/log/samba-log.%m
```

This says that all logs are separated for each machine that Samba talks to. For example, when
it talks to the machine DAFFY, the logfile will be:

```
log file = /var/log/samba-log.daffy
```

An example of debug output when using **smbclient** might look something like this:

```
[root@goofey var]# smbclient //daffy/goofey -d 4
Added interface ip=192.168.66.4 bcast=192.168.66.15 nmask=255.255.255.240
Client started (version 2.0.5a).
resolve_name: Attempting lmhosts lookup for name daffy<0x20>
getlmhostsent: lmhost entry: 127.0.0.1 localhost
resolve_name: Attempting host lookup for name daffy<0x20>
```

```
Connecting to 192.168.66.6 at port 139
 session request ok
Password:
```

More complex output at debug level 6 from **smbd** looks like this:

```
[....]
[1999/12/05 17:30:43, 5] lib/util.c:show_msg(502)
  smb_tid=1
  smb_pid=51966
  smb_uid=100
  smb_mid=256
  smt_wct=2
[1999/12/05 17:30:43, 5] lib/util.c:show_msg(507)
  smb_vwv[0]=255 (0xFF)
[1999/12/05 17:30:43, 5] lib/util.c:show_msg(507)
  smb_vwv[1]=152 (0x98)
[1999/12/05 17:30:43, 5] lib/util.c:show_msg(512)
  smb_bcc=0
[1999/12/05 17:30:43, 3] smbd/process.c:switch_message(402)
  switch message SMBulogoffX (pid 25746)
[1999/12/05 17:30:43, 3] smbd/reply.c:reply_ulogoffX(1647)
  ulogoffX vuid=100
[1999/12/05 17:30:43, 5] lib/util.c:show_msg(496)
  size=39
  smb_com=0x74
  smb_rcls=0
[....]
```

Note that with these higher levels you get variable values, which helps the developers debugging the problem to find out exactly what is going on.

A nifty feature is that you can temporarily change the debug level of the running Samba session by sending it a UNIX signal. Namely, each signal SIGUSR1 increases the debug level, and the signal SIGUSR2 decreases the debug level.

Here's an example to increase the debug level by two of the Samba server:

```
# ps auwx | grep smbd
root     25087  0.0  1.8  2184   856  ?   S    Dec  3   0:00 smbd
# kill -USR1 25087
# kill -USR1 25087
```

Then you can leave it at this debug level as long as you like, perhaps while you try to replicate a problem. Then you can decrease the debug level to what it was before:

```
# kill -USR2 25087
# kill -USR2 25087
```

Use the Samba logging function, It can tell you quite a few things, which may in fact solve your problem!

Samba Help Resources

Of course, there are many different places you can go if you are really stuck with a particular problem and you have tried all you can to fix it yourself.

Samba mailing lists are also available. Yes, that's list plural. Ten Samba lists are shown on the Samba Listproc Archives page. Go to `http://www.samba.org` and choose the mirror closest to you, click Archives in the top-left corner, and they are all listed there. You can search all archives or just one list and also browse the lists. For most Samba problems, you would use the general Samba list, but if your problem is related to the NT Domain Controller functionality, you would probably want to use `samba-ntdom`.

Many helpful resources are available from the main Samba home page. On the documentation link, there are a number of FAQs and other bits and pieces that also may contain a solution to your problem. Countless Web pages are available on the Net made by people sharing their hints and tips on how they got Samba to work well for them.

There are also newsgroups. If you have a newsreader, look at the `comp.protocols.smb` newsgroup. This is where SMB servers are discussed, most often Samba. If you want to search the archives of this newsgroup, set your browser up and point it to `http://www.deja.com`. Click Power Search on the top-right corner. Enter the keywords to your problem, for example:

`samba and "slow performance"`

Then in the forum section, enter

`comp.protocols.smb`

You should get a list of results back, which hopefully contain relevant information!

There are also organizations providing commercial Linux support these days. If you go to `http://au1.samba.org/samba/support/`, there is a list of companies around the world sorted by country that can help you with your Samba problems. Also, Hewlett Packard has just announced support of Samba on its line of HP9000 servers. Of course, Red Hat supports Samba on its Linux distribution, as do most of the major distributions that provide Linux support.

Summary

In this chapter, you have learned some techniques to help debug any Samba problems that you may come across. Remember the number one tip—make sure that your network is operating correctly. Try some simple ping tests between the Windows machine and the Samba server. Also, check that you have WINS set up correctly, or if you are using `lmhosts` files, check that the correct entries are in there for the servers you need to access.

You also learned about network sniffing and how you can use it to look at an entire SMB session. After using Network Monitor for a while (or another Network sniffer of your choice), you will get the feel of how SMB sessions are supposed to look, and hopefully be able to diagnose any problems you are having yourself.

You also found out how to use Samba's debugging features. You can set debugging in the Samba configuration file, or set the debug level dynamically while Samba is running to fix those on-the-fly problems.

Finally, the last section of the chapter explained where to go for support. Most of your online Samba support will be through the Samba Web site at `http://www.samba.org`. There are archives of all the Samba mailing lists, as well as copious amounts of documentation. There is also a list of commercial companies who support Samba, and these companies are listed on the Samba home page. You can also get a lot of help from the newsgroup `comp.protocols.smb`. Archives of this newsgroup are available at `http://www.deja.com`.

Review Questions

1. I have a problem connecting my Windows NT 4.0 Workstation to my Samba server. What is wrong?

2. How do you increase the debugging level of your Samba server on the fly without stopping and restarting `smbd`?

3. How do you get support for Samba when you have run out of ideas of what could be wrong?

CHAPTER 13

SAMBA SECURITY

You will learn about the following in this chapter:

- What you should know about security

- The differences between proactive security and reactive security

- Why you should use a firewall to partition your local network from the Internet

- Security procedures to follow when setting up a Samba server

- Where to go to get the latest security advisories for popular UNIX/Linux variants

T his chapter covers a topic that you as a system administrator should be concerned with, no matter what applications you run. The focus of this chapter is security in relation to your Samba server, or in fact any SMB server. The chapter gives you hints on how to make sure that your Samba installation is as secure as possible, while still providing the functionality required for your users. After going through the reasons why security is important, the chapter covers two major topics: proactive security and reactive security. There are some guidelines included on how to go about securing your Samba installation, then toward the end of the chapter there is a section on where to go for more information on good security practices, including Web sites and books to read.

Why Is Security So Important?

A security chapter has been included in this book for a very simple reason—nobody seems to care as much about security these days as they should! Time and time again systems get broken into because of poor systems administration practices. Because of the importance of security, it should be high on your list of priorities as a system administrator to make it as hard as possible for the bad guys to get in. This chapter concentrates on good security practices you should follow if you have Samba servers in your network. Throughout the chapter, any references that are made to Samba can safely be used for other SMB servers such as Windows NT. Toward this chapter's end is a section on "Other Resources" that gives you an idea where to find more information on this topic.

Two major methodologies that you can keep in mind to keep your system secure are covered. The first is proactive security, the most overlooked aspect of security. Proactive security involves looking for problems and potential security issues before they actually arise. The second methodology is reactive security. This is when you are notified of a particular problem and are given the tools or patches to fix it, thereby reacting to a security issue.

Proactive Security

Proactive security involves making your network infrastructure as secure as you possibly can using the tools you have available to you at the time. This includes (but is not limited to):

- Installing the latest patch levels of security patches for the operating system

- Installing the most secure and stable version of Samba currently released (at the time of this writing, this is 2.0.6)

- Making sure you have a firewall at the perimeter of your network to stop the bad guys from trying to hack into your network

- Making sure you have configured your operating system to run only the services that are actually needed

- Configuring your Samba server to accept connections only from the machines it is supposed to be servicing

Each of these tools is discussed in turn.

Get the Latest Patch Levels for Your Operating System

Whatever operating system you are running, you should always make an effort to keep up to date with the latest security patches as they are released. All the major commercial UNIX vendors have security sections on their Web pages. Similarly, all the Linux vendors have security-related pages. Table 13.1 shows you where to find most of the popular security sites for major operating system releases.

TABLE 13.1   A List of the Security Web Pages of the Various Popular UNIX Variants

Operating System	Web Page
Sun Solaris	http://www.sun.com/security
HP-UX	http://us-support.hp.com
IBM AIX	http://www.ibm.com/servers/aix/support
Red Hat Linux	http://www.redhat.com/corp/support/errata/
Caldera OpenLinux	http://www.calderasystems.com/support/security/
SuSE Linux	http://www.suse.de/de/support/security/

If your operating system is not listed in Table 13.1, don't worry. Just go to the vendor's home page and the security section will probably be emphasized. Most vendors also provide security notifications by email. This information will be advertised on your vendor's home page if they provide such a service. The major vendors (Sun, HP, IBM, and all the Linux vendors) offer these services.

Install the Latest Stable and Secure Version of Samba

You should always make sure you are installing the most up-to-date production-quality version of Samba for two reasons. The first is that the latest production version is usually the most bug-free and stable. The second reason is that it usually has all the latest security patches applied, which makes it less likely that you will have any security-related problems. But don't take this for granted! Follow the directions in the "Reactive Security" section of this chapter, and stay up to date!

Have an External Router That Filters the NetBIOS Ports

Having an external router that filters the NetBIOS ports is an obvious precaution that many sites do not follow for some reason. There have been many denial of service (DoS) attacks in the past that have affected Windows hosts as well as Samba systems through the NetBIOS ports (137-139). A DoS attack happens when a cracker exploits a bug in an application that either causes the application to terminate, or to use huge amounts of resources, which prevents your system from doing what it was intended to do. DoS attacks are not the only thing you are protecting against. If you have unprotected SMB servers, it is easy for crackers to remotely find out information about your servers that will allow people outside your company to connect to your file resources and either delete data or copy it and sell it to your competitors.

So, at a minimum, you should protect your Windows and Samba hosts with some sort of exterior router or some other port filtering device that stops traffic destined for NetBIOS ports from hosts out on the Internet. This infrastructure is commonly referred to as a *firewall*. A sample firewall setup is depicted in Figure 13.1.

The network diagram in the figure is a typical firewall infrastructure that many organizations use. First, there is a perimeter router, which is the first line of defense from the Internet. This router contains many access control lists (ACLs) that stop all unwanted traffic from entering the network at all. Connected to the perimeter router is a network segment commonly referred to as a Demilitarized Zone (DMZ). In this area, Web servers, public FTP servers, and other servers that will need to be accessed from the Internet are commonly placed. There are rules on the perimeter router to let the appropriate traffic through. Then at least one final router separates the DMZ from the internal network. This router also has ACLs that stop unwanted DMZ traffic from entering the organization's internal network.

FIGURE 13.1

The internal network is being isolated from the Internet.

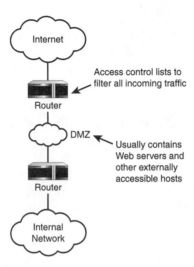

The idea behind the DMZ is that if an intruder finds a security problem that gives him full access to that network, he should not be able to get any further without getting through this second router. A cracker would have to get through both routers before he could access the internal network. Many companies have many more levels of complexity than this, but the simple design in the figure demonstrates the principles of why a firewall is important to your company's data security.

Here's another way of looking at it: Think of your organization's computer network as your personal home, and your firewall as your deadlocked front door. You don't leave your home with the door open all the time; if you did, chances are that you would get robbed! It is the same with your network.

Some sites even filter Windows NT servers from other parts of the corporate network, perhaps between divisions of the same company if those other areas are considered untrustworthy. This is commonly the case when two companies merge or there is a takeover. In the early stages of this process, when upper management directs that the computer networks should merge, the different IT departments might not trust each other, so they put up their own internal fire-walls. Yes, this does happen!

Run Only the Services That You Require

A simple rule of thumb to follow is to run only the services that you require. If your Samba server is used purely for file and print resource sharing, you should only be running the Samba daemons **smbd** and **nmbd** and not much else. This serves two purposes. Your server is not doing tasks that would be taking resources away from the Samba server, and also, there are fewer entry points for a would-be intruder to break into your system. Make sure your Samba server is not running services such as your intranet, performing mail hub duties, running an NNTP server, or other such tasks. As you are probably aware, there are always new security bugs found in sendmail, for example. The fewer services you run, the better.

Implementing Security Measures on Your Samba Server

You can minimize the incidence of unauthorized users connecting or attempting to connect to your Samba server by following some simple techniques in building your Samba configuration file, `smb.conf`. This section covers the use of the `hosts allow` and `hosts deny` options where you can reduce the exposure of your Samba server to unauthorized networks by making sure that guest access is disabled, removing anonymous access to your Samba server, and turning on encrypted passwords.

hosts allow/hosts deny

You should use the `hosts allow` parameter to restrict which hosts can connect to your Samba server. You can do this as a global setting that is used for all file services, or on a per file service basis. If you use the latter method, you can restrict access to particular file services on a per IP address basis. In a secure environment, this may be what you want. The use of this parameter is best shown with an example:

```
hosts allow = 192.168.,10.10.
```

This allows access for all hosts in the `192.168.*.*` network, and all hosts in the `10.10.*.*` network to access the Samba server. Note that the trailing dots are important. They signify to Samba that you are specifying the network address of a subnet. Another way of saying the same thing is to use the IP address/subnet mask format instead:

```
hosts allow = 192.168.0.0/255/255.0.0,10.10.0.0/255.255.0.0
```

You can also include exceptions. You can either do this as part of the `hosts allow` statement:

```
hosts allow = 192.168.,10.10. EXCEPT 10.10.3.4
```

Or as part of a `hosts deny` statement:

```
hosts deny = 10.10.3.4
```

In this case you are allowing everyone in those named networks, except the host 10.10.3.4, to access the Samba server. You can use any mix of `hosts allow` and `hosts deny` that you like, and remember that you can use them either as global parameters, or on a per file service basis.

Guest Access

Windows NT systems have a guest account, which is disabled by default. Samba also has a guest account where the default is to have it disabled. When a user connects as a guest, the SMB connection ignores any username or password specified. This should make it obvious to you that you generally don't want this. It makes auditing who accessed the system almost impossible!

Make sure that `guest ok` is set to no. It may be mentioned in some fileservice definitions for some reason. If it is not needed, remove it. Another option to look out for is `guest only`. When set, this option means that you can only connect to a particular service as a guest rather than as a normal user.

Anonymous Access

Sometimes in a Windows environment, machines access an SMB server without a username to get certain information such as userlists or sharelists. This is called an *anonymous connection*. If you have a Windows NT machine handy and it is logging security log messages, scroll through them. You will almost certainly see some messages logged by the username ANONYMOUS. In a purely NT environment there is no real reason why you should let an anonymous process connect. All users have a domain account anyway and can be authenticated if additional information about the domain is required. Like Windows NT, you can turn off anonymous access to your Samba server with the `restrict anonymous` parameter. By default, this is switched to false because it could cause communications to fail when Samba interoperates with NT servers. However, if you are only running Windows NT and Samba, you can safely switch this to `true`. You may find that you cannot log on properly if you log out and log in to the domain again from a Windows NT workstation. If you find this happening, choose to restart your machine and then log in again rather than just logging out.

Encrypted Passwords

A topic that was discussed in Chapter 5, "Integrating Samba into an Existing Windows Network," is encrypted passwords. Remember that the default behavior of Samba is to use cleartext passwords in the authentication process. Chapter 5 showed you how simple it was to use encrypted passwords, which will make it harder for a would-be intruder to find out your users' passwords. If you are unsure about turning encrypted passwords on, reread the section "Samba and Encrypted Passwords" in Chapter 5.

Reactive Security

When a security bug is found in a product or operating system, it is either fully published on certain mailing lists, or an overview of the problem is published with information on where to get the bug fix, or patch. Reactive security, as the name implies, means that a system administrator makes changes to a system configuration or applies patches to an operating system or software package to repair a security vulnerability (usually because it was found and reported on one of the many mailing lists that exist for this very purpose). This section gives you information on where to get reactive information not just on Samba security issues but other system security problems as well.

Samba Announcement Mailing List

The Samba Announcement mailing list is the mailing list you should be subscribed to to get information on new releases of Samba, security patches for any Samba security problems as they arise (not very often), and any other announcements that are seen as important to the general Samba community. You subscribe by sending a message to `majordomo@samba.org` with no subject, and in the message body including `subscribe` *`your email address`*. Here's an example of how to do this easily on a UNIX host:

```
$ echo "subscribe samba-announce matt@foo.com" | mail majordomo@samba.org
```

Of course, replace my email address with yours. Soon after, you should get the mailing list introduction that tells you certain important things like how to unsubscribe if you don't want to be on the list any more.

CERT

Numerous Computer Emergency Response Teams (CERTs) around the world specialize in collating information about system break-ins, new security holes in both operating systems and software, and other related topics. The CERT home page is at `http://www.cert.org`. CERT has sister organizations around the world; for example, in Australia it is called AusCERT. Most CERT organizations are members of the Forum of Incident Response and Security Teams (FIRST). All CERT organizations have a mailing list where security tips and vulnerabilities are posted. Some of these lists are free and some, such as AusCERT, require a fee. The fee is required because in some countries CERT organizations receive little government funding and therefore need subscription costs to keep them running. If you are responsible for looking after computer systems, you should be a member of the appropriate organization in your country to be up to date on what is considered a threat in your area of the world. If you are based in the United States, the U.S.-based CERT is free and you can subscribe to their alert mailing list by sending a mail message to their list server:

```
$ subscribe matt@foo.com | mail cert-advisory-request@cert.org
```

Security-Related Linux Mailing Lists

If you are running Samba, chances are you are running Linux. If you are, as a matter of course you should be subscribed to the announcement mailing list for your particular Linux distribution. For Red Hat you would use this one:

```
$ echo "subscribe matt@foo.com" | mail
➡redhat-announce-list-request@redhat.com
```

For SuSE:

```
$ echo "subscribe matt@foo.com" | mail suse-security-announce@suse.com
```

For Slackware:

```
$ echo "subscribe slackware-security matt@foo.com" | mail
➡majordomo@slackware.com
```

If your distribution was not mentioned, the distribution vendor is sure to have a similar service, which should be documented on the vendor's home page.

BugTraq and NTBugTraq Mailing Lists

BugTraq is a moderated list where security exploits for just about any operating system or software package are posted. NTBugTraq is also a moderated security bug mailing list; however, the focus here is on Windows-based systems. For both lists, the policy is generally full disclosure, so you get to see step by step how to exploit various security-related bugs. This should highlight how easy it is for someone to break into your system when a new security bug is found—so it should also make you aware of how important it is to repair any security holes as they are found. Subscription details and archives of the BugTraq list can be found at `http://www.securityfocus.org`. For NTBugTraq, go to `http://www.ntbugtraq.com`.

Other Resources

Many security-related resources are available. Go to the UNIX or Security section in your local bookstore and you will find many good titles on the topic of system security.

Numerous sites on the Internet offer all sorts of useful information. The main one you should go to is the BugTraq mailing list archives where you can get an idea of the number of security problems that arise each week! Go to `http://www.securityfocus.com` and click Forums, then BugTraq, then Archive, and a list of the most recent postings should appear.

Marcus Ranum maintains the Internet Firewalls FAQ at `http://www.clark.net/pub/mjr/pubs/fwfaq/`. There is also the ever-popular free firewall toolkit available at `http://www.fwtk.org`. The FWTK is probably the best and most comprehensive free firewall solution available today.

These are just a few of the best and most useful resources. Open up your Web browser and search if you are hungry for more security-related information.

Summary

In this chapter you learned about security, and more importantly, how it affects you if you run Samba servers. Remember that security is *not* "someone else's problem." If you are responsible for any servers, especially if they are running SMB services like Samba, you should tighten up the security as much as you can.

This security tightening should include a firewall between the Internet and your local area network. This keeps the average cracker from trying to exploit your internal systems. SMB servers are a favorite target, so you need to be extra careful that they are well protected.

You learned the differences between proactive and reactive security. Proactive security includes all your groundwork of getting the server up, updating it with all known patches, and installing the services for your users, in this case Samba. You should also make sure that Samba is up to date with any security patches applied. Reactive security, as the name implies, means reacting to a particular security problem. A security alert could be released that requires you to upgrade Samba to a newer version if a bug is found that gives an attacker root privilege, for example.

You will learn about new security alerts when you are subscribed to the appropriate mailing lists. You should be subscribed to samba-announce, where new versions of Samba are announced, and also to the security alerts list for your particular operating system. Subscription addresses for the common alerts lists were given.

Finally, some resources providing more information on security and securing your systems were discussed. Go to your local bookstore to find books on the topic of system security. There are also some good Web sites out there that have plenty of good security information.

Review Questions

1. Why is it important to have a firewall at the boundary between your company and the Internet?

2. If you have some important and highly confidential data on a particular Samba server in your organization, how could you go about protecting it?

3. What is the difference between reactive security and proactive security?

## CHAPTER 14

THIRD-PARTY SAMBA TOOLS

You will learn about the following in this chapter:

- How to use smbfs to mount SMB sharepoints onto the UNIX file system

- How to use LinPopUp to send and receive Windows messages

- What Pluggable Authentication Modules (PAMs) are

- How to use a PAM to send authentication to a Windows NT domain controller

- Where to find other useful SMB "add-on" utilities

T his chapter discusses tools that are beneficial to system administrators but are not included as part of the core Samba distribution. The great benefit of open source software projects like Samba is that they allow third-party add-ons to be easily created because there are no hidden hooks or proprietary protocols. There are many add-ons other than those that are discussed in this chapter, but the aim of this chapter is to cover the most popular ones to give you an insight into what is available and inspire you to investigate these tools further.

smbfs

Remember smbclient? You have probably noticed by now that using smbclient all the time can get a bit aggravating, especially if you use it frequently to access SMB systems. smbfs is a driver that allows you to mount an SMB drive under a directory on your Linux system. Currently, smbfs is available only on Linux systems. All the latest Linux kernels (2.2.x) have smbfs as part of the standard kernel build, so if you have one of the latest Linux distributions, you will find that smbfs is probably already installed for you as a loadable module. Two utility programs, smbmount and smbumount, which are part of the Samba distribution, also use smbfs.

Essentially, smbmount is a stripped-down version of smbclient. If you execute smbmount with no parameters, you will see what I mean:

```
# smbmount
Usage: smbmount //server/share mountpoint [options ...]
Version 2.0.5a
        -d debuglevel        set the debuglevel
        -n netbios name.     Use this name as my netbios name
        -N                   don't ask for a password
        -I dest IP           use this IP to connect to
        -E                   write messages to stderr instead of stdout
        -U username          set the network username
        -W workgroup         set the workgroup name
        -t terminal code     terminal i/o code {sjis|euc|jis7|jis8|junet|hex}
```

The options that you can use are very similar to smbclient, but there are not as many of them. Here is an example using smbmount to map a drive to a Windows system:

```
# smbmount //goofey/matt /windows_files -U matt
Added interface ip=192.168.66.6 bcast=192.168.66.15 nmask=255.255.255.240
Password:
```

As you can see, it is a fairly simple process. In the example, the connection is made as a specific user with the -U option. By default, as with smbclient, the connection is made using the currently logged in user's name. But if you happen to be logged in as someone else, you can override this with any username you like—just make sure that you know the corresponding password. Note that smbfs is dynamically loaded. You can find out which modules are loaded with the lsmod command:

```
# lsmod
Module              Size  Used by
smbfs              25976  1  (autoclean)
ne                  6512  1  (autoclean)
8390                5920  0  (autoclean)
aic7xxx           112208  0  (unused)
```

Execute the df command, and you will see the newly mounted directory:

```
# df
Filesystem         1k-blocks      Used Available Use% Mounted on
/dev/hdb5            1007960    897188     59568  94% /
//goofey/matt        199044    196936      2108  99% /windows_files
```

Now you can do a directory listing if you want:

```
# ls -l /windows_files
total 256
drwxr-xr-x   1 root     root           512 Nov 22 22:51 tmp
-rwxr-xr-x   1 root     root            54 Feb 17  1999 WORD.DOC
[...]
```

When you are done, simply smbumount the directory:

```
# smbumount /windows_files
# df
```

```
Filesystem          1k-blocks     Used Available Use% Mounted on
/dev/hdb5             1007960    897188    59568  94% /
```

In the past, administrators had a number of options for accessing Windows file systems from UNIX systems.

The first option was to use the `ftp` command from UNIX to Windows NT to retrieve files and put files. This is messy and time-consuming, primarily because it requires effort to start the `ftp` command, enter a valid username and password, change to the required directory, and retrieve or store the required files.

The next option was to install a Network File System (NFS) server product on the Windows server, which then allowed any UNIX machine to mount the Windows file system using NFS. That's okay for the UNIX systems because they have NFS installed as part of the operating system. But Windows NT does not come with NFS products—they must be purchased, and that costs money. At least with NFS, however, you can mount the Windows file system and write to it in real time; that is an advantage over the `ftp` method, in which files must be retrieved and stored individually.

A third option was to use the `smbclient` utility that comes as part of the Samba distribution. Again, this is similar to the `ftp` option described initially. You need to enter your password to access the resources, and you need to keep retrieving and storing files all the time, which isn't very practical for day-to-day work.

`smbfs`, as described in this section, provides a method to access your Windows file system via an SMB share interactively. The connection to your Windows server appears in the UNIX file system under a directory tree structure that you can access interactively just like any other UNIX file or directory. It is almost as easy as mounting an NFS exported directory, but without requiring the extra NFS server software at the other end.

LinPopUp

You are probably familiar with the programs WinPopUp in Windows 9x and Windows Messenger in Windows NT/2000. You can send messages with these utilities to particular usernames or computernames on your network. An example of this was given in Chapter 8, "Using `smbclient`," utilizing the `smbclient` utility and its `-M` option. A third-party application is now available that is a wrapper to `smbclient` and acts just like the WinPopUp program, but does so on a Linux system in the X Windows environment. Currently the source is designed for Linux, but it may work on other UNIX variants.

You can download the binary distribution of LinPopUp from `ftp://ftp.samba.org/pub/samba/contributed/LinPopUp-0.9.1.bin.tgz`. There is a source distribution as well (`LinPopUp-0.9.1.src.tgz`), but the binary one is recommended. After you have downloaded LinPopUp and expanded the tarfile contents, you will be left with a few documentation files and the executable LinPopUp. It is recommended that you install the executable to `/usr/local/bin`. There is one change you need to make to your Samba configuration so that it can execute LinPopUp when it receives a message. Open up `smb.conf` and add this line:

```
message command = /usr/local/bin/LinPopUp "%f" "%m" %s; rm %s
```

All this does is tell Samba to execute LinPopUp when it receives an SMB datagram with a Windows message inside it. You can send a message from your Windows 9x machine by running the program WinPopUp. Or, if you are running Windows NT/2000, you can drop to an MS-DOS prompt and type a command like this:

```
C:\>net send computername "Message"
```

An example of LinPopUp receiving a message is shown in Figure 14.1.

FIGURE 14.1

LinPopUp receiving a Windows message from the network.

If you know how to use WinPopUp, you should be a natural at LinPopUp. All the main buttons are along the top. You can reply, delete, scroll through older messages, and send new ones. An example of sending a new message is shown in Figure 14.2.

FIGURE 14.2

Using LinPopUp to send a message to a Windows machine.

It is a simple matter of filling in the destination (either a username in use on the network or a computername) and the message, and then clicking Send (or Cancel if you change your mind). Remember that the normal rules of NetBIOS name resolution apply. Both usernames and computernames are classed as NetBIOS names, and if you have a multisubnetted network, you really should have some sort of WINS name resolution in place. See Chapter 5, "Integrating Samba into an Existing Windows Network," for instructions on how to do this in a Samba environment.

This utility is an excellent example of some of the good work that is being done to make Linux able to seriously compete with Windows as a desktop operating system. The more utilities developed that mimic the Windows environment that people are so used to, the greater the chance that companies will give Linux a chance on the desktop. LinPopUp is quite useful if your users want to send messages to each other.

The SMB Authentication Module

You may have heard of the term Pluggable Authentication Module (or PAM, as it is commonly known). PAMs are authentication modules that can be *plugged* into the login processes of a UNIX system. This means that rather than the system authenticating users logging in with the telnet protocol via the system /etc/passwd or /etc/shadow files, the system administrator can define how authentication is to occur. For example, a system administrator might prefer that all remote telnet logins to a server be done using authentication with S/Key (a method of implementing one-time passwords) for security reasons. However, local logins using the standard `login` program can use the regular UNIX login methods. All UNIX system applications that accept some form of authentication are written to the PAM standard, which has a defined set of APIs. When a new PAM is written, it just has to be written to a standard; all the required API functions should be implemented, and it should be ready to be plugged in when required. PAM is now standard with many UNIX platforms including all varieties of Linux, HP-UX, and Solaris.

As the name suggests, the SMB PAM allows authentication of UNIX users via a Windows NT domain controller or Samba domain controller. This means that you can set up your UNIX system to authenticate to a Windows NT domain controller if your organization requires a unified login. Your users only need to remember one password, their NT domain one, which gives them access to UNIX systems as well.

You can download the PAM for SMB from `ftp://ftp.samba.org/pub/samba/pam_smb/pam_smb-1.1.5.tar.gz`. When you unpack it, you'll find installation instructions in the `README` file. A shortened version of the installation process follows:

1. Run the `configure` program:

   ```
   [root@myhost pam_smb] # ./configure
   ```

2. Run `make`:

   ```
   [root@myhost pam_smb] # ./make
   ```

3. Copy the resulting **pam_smb_auth.so** file to **/lib/security** (or on Solaris to **/usr/lib/security**).

4. Configure a **pam_smb.conf** file with the name of the Windows NT domain, and two domain controllers for authentication purposes. Put this file into **/etc**. Here's an example:

```
NTDOMAIN
NTPDC
NTBDC1
```

5. Now you need to configure PAM to use the SMB PAM. Copy **/etc/pam.d/login** to **/etc/pam.d/login.old**, and create a new one with these entries:

```
auth       required    /lib/security/pam_securetty.so
auth       required    /lib/security/pam_smb_auth.so
auth       required    /lib/security/pam_nologin.so
account    required    /lib/security/pam_pwdb.so
password   required    /lib/security/pam_cracklib.so
password   required    /lib/security/pam_pwdb.so shadow nullok use_authtok
session    required    /lib/security/pam_pwdb.so
```

If you are using Solaris, you need to make a change to **/etc/pam.conf** instead:

```
other   auth required   /usr/lib/security/pam_smb_auth.so.1
```

That's all there is to it. However, there are a few extra things to look out for. The user must still exist in the **/etc/passwd** file, and if the user has a password entry, it will be used instead. Replacing a user's password with a star (*) forces the **pam_smb** module to be used, and the user is authenticated off the Windows NT server specified in the configuration file.

There are many situations in which setting up the SMB PAM module may be useful. Say that you have many users who use Oracle databases. They may use a dumb terminal program such as telnet to access the text-based version of the Oracle application. To be able to do this, they need a login name and password for the UNIX server where the Oracle database is stored. Instead of having separate usernames and passwords for logging in to the NT domain (via his workstation) and for logging in to Oracle, the user would surely appreciate having a single username and password to use to log in to everything! Setting up the UNIX server with the SMB PAM module allows you to configure the UNIX server to direct all login requests to a Windows NT server for authentication, thus giving users their single username and password combination.

Other SMB Utilities

Countless other SMB-type utilities are available, and going through them all would fill a book in itself! There are, however, a couple of others that deserve mention, both of which are available on the Samba FTP site. The first is called **smb2www**. This program allows you to access Windows machines through your Web browser. You can download **smb2www** from the FTP directory **ftp://ftp.samba.org/pub/samba/smb2www**. When you uncompress **smb2www**, install instructions are provided. The main thing you do need, obviously, is a functioning Web server. If you would like to know what it will look like before you go to the trouble of installing it, there are sample images in the download directory. It is basically like having a Network Neighborhood in your Web browser.

Another tool that has been superseded by SWAT, but is still useful is called `smbedit`. You can download this from `ftp://ftp.samba.org/pub/samba/smbedit`. It allows configuration of your Samba configuration file via a Windows machine, which could be useful if you want to delegate that responsibility to someone else who does not know UNIX very well—perhaps to someone who just needs to add new shares to an existing Samba installation. It takes a little effort to set up, but the install instructions are provided and may be worth the effort. It requires a couple of new shares to be created, one of which will be the Samba configuration file's location. The rest of it runs as an executable on a Windows machine.

LinNeighborhood

A feature that is predominant on Windows desktops is the Microsoft Network Neighborhood concept. It is a way for users to traverse the Windows computers (and optionally Netware servers as well) to find out what resources are available. These resources can be either printers or shared directories. This makes it easy to find and connect to shared resources throughout the network. Think about what would happen if you placed a Linux PC in front of a user and expected him to use it. The Linux desktop would be more appealing to him if it had the same or similar features as an equivalent Windows desktop PC. Open source developers throughout the world are trying to make this happen by developing Linux utility equivalents for those Windows applications that make our lives easier. LinPopUp, described earlier in this chapter, provides Windows Messaging functions much like WinPopUp. Another useful utility to put on those Linux desktops is called LinNeighborhood. LinNeighborhood is a Linux application that mimics the Windows Network Neighborhood functionality. An example of what LinNeighborhood looks like is shown in Figure 14.3.

FIGURE 14.3
LinNeighborhood in action on a Red Hat Linux machine.

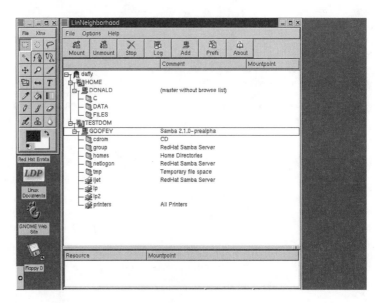

Notice that LinNeighborhood is similar to what you are used to seeing on Windows machines. You get a good snapshot of your CIFS/SMB servers (Windows and Samba) and which resources are available.

You can download LinNeighborhood from `http://www.bnro.de/~schmidjo/download/index.html`. If you have a distribution of Linux that uses the rpm package manager, download the precompiled rpm package on that Web page. Installation is then just a matter of typing the following:

```
# rpm -i LinNeighborhood-0.4.3-1.i386.rpm
```

After that, just type **LinNeighborhood** to bring it up on your X Windows session. Read the documentation on the Web site for more detailed system requirements and installation instructions, especially if you want to compile it yourself.

When you start LinNeighborhood for the first time, you may need to enter the name of the master browser for your network for LinNeighborhood to see your network. You can do this by clicking on the Prefs button, clicking on Primary Master Browser, and entering the NetBIOS name of the PDC in your main domain. This can be a Windows NT PDC or a Samba PDC. This screen is shown in Figure 14.4.

FIGURE 14.4

Setting up LinNeighborhood preferences.

Optionally, you can put in a WINS server as well. This will help when the browser tries to resolve names to which to connect if you want to mount a share.

Mounting a share is very easy. First make sure the `smbmnt` and `smbumount` commands are both `setuid root`. On some systems they are not, but they need to be. Execute this command:

```
# ls -l /usr/bin/smbmnt
-rwxr-xr-x   1 root     root          235768 Sep 26 03:12 /usr/bin/smbmnt
```

If you get the same output, you need to make `smbmnt setuid root` like this:

```
# chmod u+s /usr/bin/smbmnt
# ls -l /usr/bin/smbmnt
-rwsr-xr-x   1 root     root          235768 Sep 26 03:12 /usr/bin/smbmnt
```

Do the same thing for `smbumount`. Now you can mount a share using LinNeighborhood. Click on the share you want to mount, and then click on the Mount button. You will get a dialog box that looks like Figure 14.5.

FIGURE 14.5

Mounting an SMB share using LinNeighborhood.

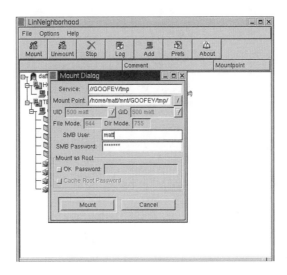

Enter a valid SMB username and password and then click on the Mount button. A file manager–like program will start up, allowing you to browse the new file share you just connected to. In LinNeighborhood, to the right of the share name is a display of where the share is mounted. If you execute the `df` command, you will see the SMB share mounted:

```
$ df
Filesystem            1k-blocks      Used Available Use% Mounted on
/dev/hdb5               1007960    927228     29528  97% /
//GOOFEY/tmp              40953     36070      4883  88%
➥/home/matt/mnt/GOOFEY/tmp
```

Notice that LinNeighborhood is a tool that uses other tools to provide the features that have been discussed. It uses Samba (`smbmnt` and `smbumount`) as well as `smbfs` to mount and unmount the remote SMB file systems. Overall, LinNeighborhood is quite a useful tool for easy connection to remote SMB resources, especially if you have a large and complex Windows/Samba network.

Summary

You have learned in this chapter how to use `smbmount` and `smbumount` to mount and unmount SMB resources in the UNIX file system. These commands are part of the Samba distribution, and they work in conjunction with the `smbfs` file system driver, which is usually compiled as an installable module with most Linux distributions these days. The command to mount a resource is

```
# smbmount //goofey/matt /windows_files -U matt
```

Remember that `smbmount` automatically installs the `smbfs` driver into the kernel if it is available and not already installed. The command to unmount the resource when you are finished is

```
# smbumount /windows_files
```

You also learned that LinPopUp was created to mimic the functionality of the Windows NT messaging service and Windows 9x's WinPopUp program. You can configure Samba to execute LinPopUp when it receives a Windows message, which is handy when you are using Linux/UNIX workstations in your environment instead of Windows clients and you need to be able to have an easy-to-use interface for your users. LinPopUp also supports sending messages and records all messages received unless you explicitly delete them.

Using PAMs allows you to specify methods of authentication other than the standard UNIX authentication through /etc/passwd or /etc/shadow files. This chapter went through the addition of SMB authentication as a PAM module on PAM-compatible systems.

You were also pointed to a couple of other useful SMB add-on programs that are not part of the standard Samba distribution. The first, smb2www, allows you to look at your Windows network through a Web browser. The second, smbedit, allows you to edit your Samba configuration from a Windows machine (although it requires you to add a new share).

Finally, the tool LinNeighborhood was discussed. It is an add-on to Samba that provides Microsoft Network Neighborhood functionality to Linux. It is an essential tool to put on your Linux desktops to provide easy traversal of your heterogeneous UNIX and Windows SMB network.

Review Questions

1. What is smbfs and what would you use it for?

2. How do you mount an SMB file system onto a Linux file system?

3. What is LinPopUp?

4. What is a Pluggable Authentication Module, and what is pam_smb?

Exercises

1. Using the tools mentioned in this chapter, along with a version of Linux (Red Hat, Caldera, Corel, or any other distribution of your choice), attempt to create a desktop environment that mimics the Windows user interface. For any later versions of the utilities mentioned in this chapter, check http://www.freshmeat.net and do a search by name.

## CHAPTER 15

A LOOK AT SAMBA'S FUTURE

You will learn about the following in this chapter:

- Which PDC functions are to be completed for the next release of Samba

- When Samba 2.1 is likely to be released

- When Windows 2000 support is likely to be implemented, and what features it will contain

- The new philosophy on the Samba development team

T his chapter gives you an insight as to what features will be implemented in Samba over the next few years. The chapter covers such areas as the missing PDC functionality, Windows 2000 support, LDAP support, and where the future of Samba development is going. The information in this chapter is based on the author's research and what he thinks will happen next in the Samba development cycle.

When Will Samba 2.1 Be Released and What Features Will It Contain?

The question on everyone's lips is: "When will version 2.1 of Samba be released?" No one can really answer that one. Samba 2.1 should be out sometime in the first half of 2000.

One of the most awaited aspects of Samba 2.0 was its ability to be a Primary Domain Controller (PDC). Unfortunately, the release version of Samba 2.0 did not behave quite as expected and a lot of things that were supposed to be working were not. Additionally, there are quite a number of Windows NT functions that are not present in Samba 2.0. A list of features that do not exist or are broken in Samba 2.0 follows:

- *Ability to act as a full Primary Domain Controller (PDC)*. This was originally a feature planned for 2.0, but unfortunately it was not implemented. Never use the PDC functionality that is currently part of 2.0, or you may find that it does not behave as you expect or exhibits inconsistent behavior. The working version of the PDC functionality is a part of the 2.1 development (alpha) tree, which you can use until the production 2.1 code is released.

- *BDC replication.* Samba can operate as a Backup Domain Controller (BDC) in a Windows NT domain or a Samba domain. This means that you will be able to install Samba as a BDC in an existing Windows NT domain, so it can keep a backup copy of the accounts database like a regular Windows NT server. You can also run a Samba PDC and run Windows NT BDCs in the same domain, again so that you have backup copies of the accounts database.

- *User Manager for Domains and Server Manager support.* User Manager allows you to manage user accounts and groups on your Samba server, and Server Manager allows you to do domain-wide server administration tasks, such as viewing and modifying the various machine accounts that are members of the domain, seeing certain file statistics such as how many and what files are open and how many users are connected, and sending broadcast messages to all users connected.

- *Windows NT trust relationships.* Windows NT domains can interoperate with each other. When trust relationships support is included in Samba, you will be able to have two or more separate domains. An example could be a Samba domain and a regular Windows NT domain. When a trust relationship is put in place, these two domains will be able to share account information to allow one domain or the other to share resources with only one account required in either domain. More information on trust relationships is found in Chapter 7, "Samba in a Windows NT/2000 Domain Environment."

- *Ability to manipulate Access Control Lists (ACLs) on Samba file shares.* This is already partially implemented and allows a mapping of UNIX file system permissions to Windows NT, like ACLs. In the future you will be able to manipulate the file and directory permissions on a Samba file share just as if it were a regular NTFS file share, including being able to add any number of access control entries (ACEs).

- *Full Windows NT–like printing subsystem.* Currently Samba uses the old LANMAN method of printing. This method does not take advantage of the Windows NT method of printing, which uses a named pipe `\\PIPE\spoolss` to talk to the printing subsystem. The code for this feature is almost complete and should make it into Samba 2.1.

This list should give you some idea of what features Samba 2.0 was originally going to include that were left out due to lack of time.

There have been moves on the Samba developers mailing lists to define exactly what functionality should be included for a 2.1 release, and the general consensus has been to get the majority of the missing PDC functionality finished as just described.

Operating Samba with Windows 2000

The major Microsoft operating system that has finally been released, Windows 2000, is what people are talking about. Now people on the Samba mailing lists are wondering when Samba will interoperate properly with Windows 2000. The answer to that question is that it depends on your definition of "properly." Because there were public betas of Windows 2000 12 months before it was released, there have been many opportunities for people to try Windows 2000 and Samba together and see what happens. In the process of doing this, interoperability testing problems have been found and corrected. There have been reports of people successfully joining a Windows 2000 machine to a Samba domain and vice versa. By the time Samba 2.1 comes along, it should support Windows 2000 in the same way that it supports Windows NT 4.0 currently, hopefully with no outstanding issues.

New Windows 2000 Features in Samba

The next task that is receiving serious attention is to incorporate the new features of Windows 2000 into Samba. The main features that seem to be getting this attention include the new Active Directory support, Kerberos authentication support, Microsoft's Distributed Filesystem (DFS) support, and the ability to share file systems without requiring NetBIOS to be available for name resolution.

The new Active Directory functionality Microsoft has included with Windows 2000 should also be fairly easy to add support for. Active Directory is Microsoft's implementation of the ISO X.500 directory standards. This eliminates the original Security Accounts Manager in which usernames and password hashes were previously stored. Now, every entity in a Windows 2000 domain will have an entry in the Active Directory including machines, usernames, and resources. There is already Lightweight Directory Access Protocol (LDAP) support partially implemented in the Samba code; hopefully, it will only be the LDAP functions that need to be extended to allow communication with the Windows 2000 Active Directory.

Kerberos support allows a Samba server to authenticate to a Kerberos IV server rather than authenticate using regular UNIX methods such as NIS or plain /etc/passwd authentication. Support for Kerberos is already incorporated into Samba 2.0, although it is not well documented. Note that you have to configure Samba with the --with-krb4 option if you want your Samba server to authenticate to a Kerberos server. Support for authenticating against Kerberos V servers has been incorporated into the latest Samba development trees, both Samba 2.1 and Samba The Next Generation (TNG). Kerberos has been available as part of UNIX systems for at least the past 10 years. Now that Microsoft has gone the way of Kerberos, the Samba community and others are hoping that their Kerberos implementation is standard enough to allow Windows 2000 systems to communicate easily with UNIX Kerberos implementations.

A lot of work has been done over the last few years to get Distributed Filesystem (DFS) support into Samba. It is still a compile-time option with Samba 2.0 (--with-dfs), but hopefully this support will be complete for Samba 2.1. Microsoft's DFS concept allows you to create a sharepoint in which each subdirectory is really a share to some other machine. This is similar in concept to having a UNIX file system with mountpoints that have NFS mounts from many different UNIX NFS servers around the organization.

See Figure 15.1 for an example of what a DFS tree might look like.

FIGURE 15.1

An example DFS tree in an NT environment.

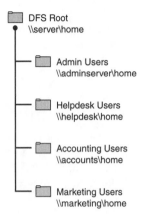

Note that you have a directory tree, but instead of directories on a filesystem, each entry could be a pointer to a resource on a remote machine. Using this methodology, you could in fact hide where the actual resource is located and give a common interface to all your shared resources. In this way you can move resources around servers internally any number of times, and there is no reconfiguring on the end client required.

DFS is provided as a download for Windows NT 4.0 environments (`http://www.microsoft.com/ntserver/nts/downloads/winfeatures/NTSDistrFile/default.asp`) and is shipped with Windows 2000.

Finally, CIFS in Windows 2000 promises to be able to have file sharing without requiring the dreaded NetBIOS to be around for name resolution. This means that for the first time, Windows will be able to use DNS directly to resolve names. This also means that CIFS will be able to be run over TCP as the transport, rather than using a NetBIOS session connection. This removes some of the complexity of the current SMB filesharing methods, and hopefully makes things a little more stable.

The Future Direction of Samba Development

As of December 1999, the Samba development has branched into three releases. The first is the CVS branch that is used to continue to work on the 2.0 series. Samba 2.0.7 should be released soon and fixes some problems that 2.0.6 created, such as a minor issue with user profiles. The second development version is Samba 2.1, which is the successor to 2.0. Finally, a new development branch called Samba The Next Generation (TNG), which will turn into Samba 3.0, is not expected to be released until sometime in 2001.

The current CVS branch used for the 2.0 series will continue to be used to create minor new releases in the 2.0.x Samba series. Stay on these versions if you want total stability of your system and are not too concerned about requiring PDC functionality.

As previously mentioned, Samba 2.1 will consist of the missing PDC functionality, other fixes for Samba to work with Windows 2000 correctly, and not much else. If not released already, it should be finished sometime in 2000. Once 2.1 is in production release, it is recommended that you test it in your environment and, if everything works, feel free to upgrade. You should then have a completely working PDC implementation that you can install on any UNIX box that Samba compiles on.

Samba TNG consists of bleeding-edge development, and is much more of a moving target than the other two CVS branches. Some of the more senior Samba developers are re-engineering certain functions of the Samba code to make it easier to upgrade in the future. One of the more interesting projects happening here is the changing of `smbd` to only do file sharing. All non–file-sharing functionality features, like authentication, print spooling, and other "sub-tasks," are being taken out and put into their own processes. This will mean that there will be separate processes for all the functionality that is now provided by two processes: `nmbd` and `smbd`. It also means that you will be able to upgrade a particular function without upsetting the rest, rather than downloading and installing a whole new `smbd` daemon. This is a plus for those times when you upgrade to get a particular feature, but something seemingly unrelated breaks.

Other work that is being done in Samba TNG is the tidying up of internal databases with a brand new database engine called TDB (Trivial Database). Samba developer Andrew Trigell has created this database to take care of a few internal data structures that Samba uses to store information. This will include a lot of the Samba WINS information as well. In the end, this makes the Samba code cleaner, and hopefully provides a performance boost as well.

Once all these changes have been implemented and when Samba 3.0 is released, it should be a fully working alternative to a Windows NT/2000 server. The amount of work that has been done by the Samba development team to get as far as they have is to be commended—especially because a lot of the implementation details are undocumented and have been figured out through trial and error and reverse engineering.

Summary

In this chapter you have read about the new features of Samba that should be implemented into Samba 2.1 by the time you read this book. Samba 2.1 will include working PDC functionality to allow you to use some Windows NT/2000 domain administration tools such as User Manager and Server Manager. These tools enable you to do a limited amount of administration, as well as creating trust relationships. Samba 2.1 should also provide support for including ACLs on Samba file shares. In addition, Samba should work with Windows 2000 systems as it does with earlier versions of Windows NT.

You have also learned that Windows 2000 brings with it new functionality such as Kerberos authentication, Active Directory, and DFS support. These features will be implemented in the 3.0 release (or later) of Samba.

This chapter also discussed the new development model that the Samba team is using. There used to be two Samba development trees: one for the current series of releases (2.0.x), and another for the next major version (called the 2.1 development head). The new CVS tree is called Samba TNG. It contains bleeding-edge work and many new features and will end up being Samba 3.0 sometime in the future. This splitting of the development Samba code into three development versions is good for the Samba community. Hopefully it will cause Samba development to speed up because there is a new development head for new features, and they can be tested sooner.

Review Questions

1. What features are likely to make it into Samba 2.1?

2. What is Samba TNG?

3. What are the major new features of Windows 2000?

PART IV

APPENDIXES

A   A Sample CIFS/SMB Session

B   Answers to Review Questions

A SAMPLE CIFS/SMB SESSION

T he purpose of this appendix is to introduce you to the Common Internet File System (CIFS) protocol, show a real-life CIFS session, and point you to other resources if you want to learn more. This appendix is designed for those readers who want to learn more about CIFS for analysis or debugging purposes.

A Summary of the Overall CIFS Process

As you are aware from reading this book, SMB (or CIFS, as it is now known), is basically a high-level protocol for accessing files across a network. CIFS can either be run via a NetBIOS transport over TCP, or it can be run directly over TCP without using NetBIOS at all (first implemented in Windows 2000).

CIFS supports all the usual operations you would expect when accessing files; these include open, close, read, write, and seek. CIFS also supports the batching of multiple CIFS messages into one single message, even if some CIFS messages depend on the results of earlier transactions. These batched requests are called *AndX* messages. This batching can be done because the results of earlier CIFS messages are passed down to the next chained command.

This appendix walks you through a simple CIFS session so that you can see how all the messages come together to get a specific task achieved. Certain main steps take place when a connection is established to a server for the first time. Here are the steps listed in sequential order:

- Dialect negotiation
- Authentication
- Connection to resource
- Accessing resource
- Disconnection of resource
- Logoff of user

First, the CIFS dialect is negotiated. As you are aware from Chapter 1, "What Is Samba?," there are many different dialects of the CIFS protocol, ranging from the earliest, PC NETWORK PROGRAM 1.0, to the most recent, NTLM 0.12. The client sends to the server a NULL terminated list of dialects it supports within the CIFS message SMB_COM_NEGOTIATE, and the server responds with the dialect to be used for the session. There are numerous security problems with the server choosing the dialect to use; however, this was designed for backward compatibility purposes and not for security reasons. An example of why this is a security risk follows: Say a bad guy replaces a legitimate server with one of his own, which is running his own modified CIFS server. This CIFS server responds to the **SMB_COM_NEGOTIATE** message with the earliest possible dialect, which by no mere coincidence uses plain text passwords. So when the user tries to connect to a resource using his password, the bad server stores the username and password combination to be used later. This is only one of many possible attacks.

If there is no existing connection, the next step is to set up a NetBIOS session and then authenticate the user. The CIFS message **SMB_COM_SESSION_SETUP_ANDX** is sent with the credentials of the requesting user to the server for authentication. If the user is authenticated, the response CIFS message from the server contains a User ID (UID) variable set to the UID of the user for this NetBIOS session. Any future CIFS message from this authenticated user uses this UID parameter to identify itself to the server. This saves having to authenticate each time when a new resource is required. However, this means that the client must *always* make sure that any CIFS message sent has a UID that matches the currently logged-in user.

Next, a resource can be connected to by using the CIFS message **SMB_COM_TREE_CONNECT**. This CIFS message contains the name of the resource, or disk share, that the user wants to access, as well as a current, valid UID. If the server successfully processes this command, it returns a Tree ID (TID) value, which is the identifier that will be used for subsequent access to this resource.

In the next step, all the accessing of the resource takes place. It can be opening a file (using **SMB_COM_OPEN**), reading or writing (**SMB_COM_READ** or **SMB_COM_WRITE**), closing a file (**SMB_COM_CLOSE**), or one of many other CIFS messages. All these commands use the previously set variables, TID, UID, and others.

When a share is disconnected (perhaps with the `net use \\server\resource /delete` command), the CIFS message **SMB_COM_TREE_DISCONNECT** is sent to the server to release access to the resource represented by the TID.

Finally, when a NetBIOS session times out or a user logs off, the CIFS message **SMB_COM_LOGOFF_ANDX** is sent to any servers that the client is still connected to. This means that any subsequent CIFS connection attempts will require authentication.

A Samba CIFS Session

This section shows you some real CIFS traffic and guides you through what it looks like step by step. The CIFS session being described is a Windows NT client called **DAFFY**, connecting to a Samba share located on a Linux box called **GOOFEY**. The resource being connected to is `\\GOOFEY\TMP`. The traffic was captured using Network Monitor located on the Windows NT machine. You should, however, note that you can use the network traffic capture program of your choice. Ethereal was mentioned in Chapter 12, "Debugging Samba," and is a fine graphical network traffic capture tool that displays traffic in a similar manner to Network Monitor. Alternatively, if command-line is your preference, `tcpdump-smb` will also do the job (it was also introduced to you in Chapter 12).

Figure A.1 shows the first part of the CIFS share connection transaction.

FIGURE A.1
The first section of the CIFS/SMB message transfer.

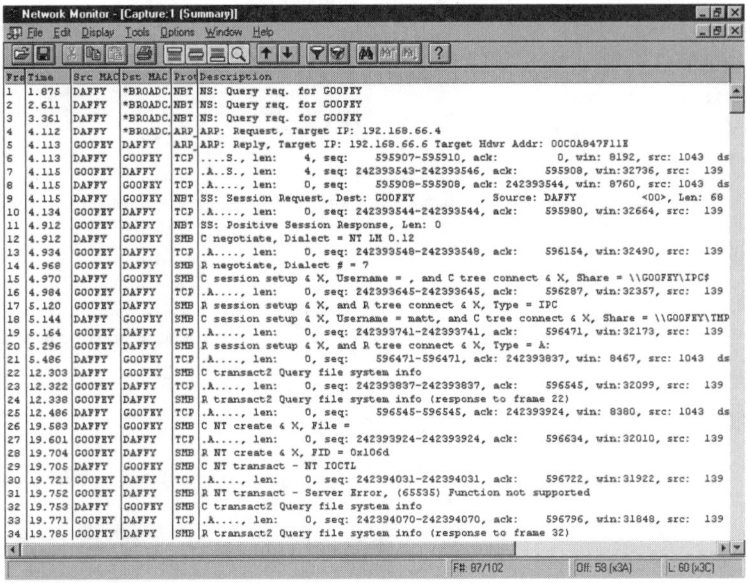

Fra	Time	Src MAC	Dst MAC	Prot	Description
1	1.875	DAFFY	*BROADC.	NBT	NS: Query req. for GOOFEY
2	2.611	DAFFY	*BROADC.	NBT	NS: Query req. for GOOFEY
3	3.361	DAFFY	*BROADC.	NBT	NS: Query req. for GOOFEY
4	4.112	DAFFY	*BROADC.	ARP_	ARP: Request, Target IP: 192.168.66.4
5	4.113	GOOFEY	DAFFY	ARP_	ARP: Reply, Target IP: 192.168.66.6 Target Hdwr Addr: 00C0A847F11E
6	4.113	DAFFY	GOOFEY	TCP	....S., len: 4, seq: 595907-595910, ack: 0, win: 8192, src: 1043 ds
7	4.115	GOOFEY	DAFFY	TCP	.A..S., len: 4, seq: 242393543-242393546, ack: 595908, win:32736, src: 139
8	4.115	DAFFY	GOOFEY	TCP	.A...., len: 0, seq: 595908-595908, ack: 242393544, win: 8760, src: 1043 ds
9	4.115	DAFFY	GOOFEY	NBT	SS: Session Request, Dest: GOOFEY , Source: DAFFY <00>, Len: 68
10	4.134	GOOFEY	DAFFY	TCP	.A...., len: 0, seq: 242393544-242393544, ack: 595980, win:32664, src: 139
11	4.912	GOOFEY	DAFFY	NBT	SS: Positive Session Response, Len: 0
12	4.912	DAFFY	GOOFEY	SMB	C negotiate, Dialect = NT LM 0.12
13	4.934	GOOFEY	DAFFY	TCP	.A...., len: 0, seq: 242393548-242393548, ack: 596154, win:32490, src: 139
14	4.968	GOOFEY	DAFFY	SMB	R negotiate, Dialect # = 7
15	4.970	DAFFY	GOOFEY	SMB	C session setup & X, Username = , and C tree connect & X, Share = \\GOOFEY\IPC$
16	4.984	GOOFEY	DAFFY	TCP	.A...., len: 0, seq: 242393645-242393645, ack: 596287, win:32357, src: 139
17	5.120	GOOFEY	DAFFY	SMB	R session setup & X, and R tree connect & X, Type = IPC
18	5.144	DAFFY	GOOFEY	SMB	C session setup & X, Username = matt, and C tree connect & X, Share = \\GOOFEY\TMP
19	5.164	GOOFEY	DAFFY	TCP	.A...., len: 0, seq: 242393741-242393741, ack: 596471, win:32173, src: 139
20	5.296	GOOFEY	DAFFY	SMB	R session setup & X, and R tree connect & X, Type = A:
21	5.486	DAFFY	GOOFEY	TCP	.A...., len: 0, seq: 596471-596471, ack: 242393837, win: 8467, src: 1043 ds
22	12.303	DAFFY	GOOFEY	SMB	C transact2 Query file system info
23	12.322	GOOFEY	DAFFY	TCP	.A...., len: 0, seq: 242393837-242393837, ack: 596545, win:32099, src: 139
24	12.338	GOOFEY	DAFFY	SMB	R transact2 Query file system info (response to frame 22)
25	12.486	DAFFY	GOOFEY	TCP	.A...., len: 0, seq: 596545-596545, ack: 242393924, win: 8380, src: 1043 ds
26	19.583	DAFFY	GOOFEY	SMB	C NT create & X, File =
27	19.601	GOOFEY	DAFFY	TCP	.A...., len: 0, seq: 242393924-242393924, ack: 596634, win:32010, src: 139
28	19.704	GOOFEY	DAFFY	SMB	R NT create & X, FID = 0x106d
29	19.705	DAFFY	GOOFEY	SMB	C NT transact - NT IOCTL
30	19.721	GOOFEY	DAFFY	TCP	.A...., len: 0, seq: 242394031-242394031, ack: 596722, win:31922, src: 139
31	19.752	GOOFEY	DAFFY	SMB	R NT transact - Server Error, (65535) Function not supported
32	19.753	DAFFY	GOOFEY	SMB	C transact2 Query file system info
33	19.771	GOOFEY	DAFFY	TCP	.A...., len: 0, seq: 242394070-242394070, ack: 596796, win:31848, src: 139
34	19.785	GOOFEY	DAFFY	SMB	R transact2 Query file system info (response to frame 32)

The first command executed on the Windows NT client was this:

```
C:\>net use * \\goofey\tmp
```

Because there is no current NetBIOS session from DAFFY to GOOFEY, DAFFY needs to find out the IP address of GOOFEY to be able to establish the NetBIOS channel of communication. That is what frames 1–5 show. The first three are NetBIOS broadcasts, basically DAFFY advertising that it wants GOOFEY's IP address. After the IP address is found, it then needs to do an ARP Request to find the physical address of GOOFEY (this is also known as the MAC address), so the lower network layers can talk to GOOFEY. Frame 5 shows GOOFEY replying to the ARP request; the MAC address will be in the data payload of that frame.

Frame 9 is the beginning of the NetBIOS session setup. DAFFY sends a NetBIOS Session Request to GOOFEY; GOOFEY replies in the affirmative in frame 11. This indicates that a valid process that speaks NetBIOS is listening on port 139.

Next you see the first CIFS/SMB protocol packet where the dialect of the protocol to be used is negotiated (frame 12) and the server responds with its chosen dialect in frame 14. Immediately after, in frame 17, you see a connection to the share \\GOOFEY\IPC$ with a null username. This interprocess communication (or IPC) share is connected to if the remote system is detected as being NT-compatible and is used to transfer IPC requests of the various NT IPC-compatible applications like Server Manager and User Manager for Domains. Because GOOFEY is running a version of Samba with PDC support, it is detected as an NT server, so the IPC$ share connection is attempted. After that, you see in frame 18 the two SMB commands chained

(ANDX'd) together to authenticate the username `matt`, and perform a tree connect to the share `\\GOOFEY\TMP`. The reply from the server in frame 20 contains the allocated TID and UID for the specific username and share combination. This is shown in Figure A.2.

FIGURE A.2

The share connection SMB internal variables are set with this SMB reply.

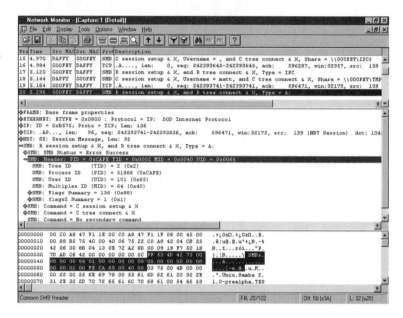

Notice how Network Monitor nicely lays out the contents of the different sections of the frame. The TID is clearly displayed as 2 and the UID is 101. The **IPC$** share connection got a TID value of 1 and a UID value of 100. The next share connection would have a TID value of 3, and so on. If you like, you can go deeper into the SMB frame and delve into the Flags part (to find out whether specific flags have been set for the session) or any other part that you like.

After the share was successfully connected to drive letter E: on the NT machine, I waited a bit then changed to drive E: on the NT command line. Notice the time that elapsed between the share connecting and the next SMB packet, between frames 20 and 22. That was done deliberately so you could easily distinguish the different sets of SMB packets for each command that was typed. As the current working directory was changed to E:, one SMB packet was sent out to get the system information from the share, and the reply was sent back in frame 24 with the information that the client required. The system information in this example is shown in Figure A.3.

This information is required so that the client can update certain pieces of information about the current directory that it is in. This information includes creation time, volume serial number, and volume name, as you can see in Figure A.3.

Next the **DIR** command was typed at the command prompt on NT. This caused a sequence of SMB messages to be sent out from frame 26 to frame 68. The network capture from Figure A.1 continues in Figure A.4.

FIGURE A.3

The system information on the resource is set with this SMB reply.

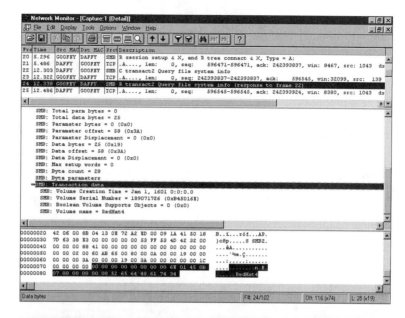

FIGURE A.4

The second part of the CIFS/SMB capture.

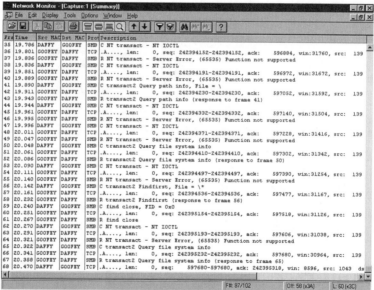

You will notice that there are a lot of NT IOCTL messages sent to the server GOOFEY. The version of Samba that was running does not support these kinds of messages, so it responds with Server Error, (65535) Function not supported. The rest of the frames are used to build up the directory listing on the client by getting the information required such as filename and file modification time and date. The directory listing is built up by using the TRANSACT2 SMB message with subtype Findfirst. The last thing you see in a directory listing is the amount of hard disk used and free. Frame 65 is a **TRANSACT2** message with a subtype **Query file system info**, which is the SMB transaction to get this file system utilization information.

The next command typed on the command line of the NT client was:

`E:\>type interesting.txt`

Frame 72 in Figure A.5 shows the SMB command being sent to find required information about the file `interesting.txt`. Then if you drop down to frame 86 through to frame 96, you see the file being opened, read, and then closed.

FIGURE A.5
The final part of the CIFS/SMB capture.

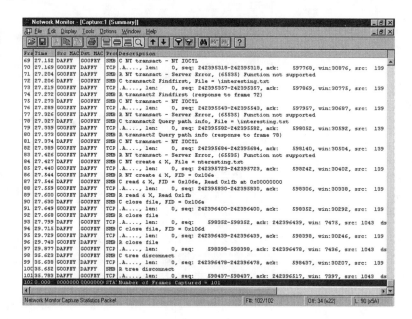

The final command executed on the NT client was this:

`C:\>net use e: /delete`

This removes the resource connection. The relevant SMB message is frame 98 in Figure A.5, the tree disconnect SMB.

Summary

The aim of this appendix was to show you what a valid CIFS/SMB transaction looks like and to walk you through the different messages that are transferred between server and client. You now have enough information to be able to analyze and debug your own CIFS logs if you discover you have SMB problems.

APPENDIX B

ANSWERS TO REVIEW QUESTIONS

Chapter 1

1. Samba is a file and print server that runs on any UNIX operating system, and is designed to be a plug-in replacement for Windows NT.

2. SMB stands for Server Message Block. It is the protocol that is used when a Windows client connects to a resource provided by an SMB server (such as Windows, Samba, or some other commercial server). The protocol consists of a number of commands, just like an operating system. A subset of the commands includes `CREATE DIRECTORY`, `OPEN FILE`, `CLOSE FILE`, and `DELETE FILE`.

3. • SMB file-sharing services

   • NetBIOS Name Resolution

   • User Authentication

   • Provides Computer Browser service

   • Performs domain login capabilities for Windows 9x and Windows NT clients

4. CIFS is the latest version of the SMB protocol. It is designed so that it does not require NetBIOS name services, which previous versions did require. Any compatible name service effectively can be used instead, and in Windows 2000, DNS is the recommended name service to use.

Chapter 2

1. If you have a Linux system, you would choose a precompiled package. This would be on your Linux vendor's CD-ROM or FTP site. Otherwise, if you have a UNIX system that has no precompiled packages available, as long as you have an ANSI C compiler, your best bet is to download the source code and compile it yourself.

2. In your Samba distribution, there is a `docs` directory. Or if you used a precompiled package, these docs will be found in `/usr/doc/samba-2.0.6` (or whatever version you installed).

3. `$ configure --prefix=/opt/samba --mandir=/opt/local/share/man`

4. You can put the script that normally goes into `/etc/rc.d/init.d` into `/sbin/init.d`. Then the link files to this script go in `/sbin/rc3.d` and `/sbin/rc1.d`. Optionally, you can put a file in `/etc/rc.config.d` with some environment variables that get processed on bootup that control whether or not a service should be started.

5. If you put Samba in `inetd`, it saves memory; however, there is a longer delay between a connection being established to the Samba server as it has to start up first. Also, putting it into `inetd` is quicker and less complicated. Putting Samba in a startup file is more efficient—`smbd` is already running, so there is no delay between a connection request being sent and a connection being established to the client. However, even if Samba is not being used, it does take up some memory. Today, memory is relatively cheap, so this is not normally considered to be a problem. The preferred option to start `smbd` and `nmbd` these days is via startup scripts.

Chapter 3

1. SWAT provides a framework to edit `smb.conf` easily without having to use a text editor.

2. Freeware `smb.conf` editors are available at `ftp.samba.org`. Or you can manually edit the `smb.conf` file with `vi`.

3. Assuming DNS is set up, you can do `net use * \\sambaserver.com\resource`. Or, if no DNS is available, you can use the IP address `net use * \\192.168.3.4\resource`.

4. The problem is most likely an incorrect subnet mask on the Samba server. Always check that your networking parameters are correct.

Chapter 4

1. Workgroups are just a collection of machines labeled as being in the same resource group. Security is distributed between all machines in a workgroup, and any machine can be connected to the network and theoretically can access any resource. A domain is a group of machines that has been set up by an administrator to provide resources to all client machines that can be authenticated by the domain. Security is centralized, which makes it easier to control who has access and who does not.

2. In share-level security, there is just a password on a particular share that users need to know to be able to connect to it. Windows 9x and Windows 3.x clients can do share-level security. In user-level security, a resource needs a valid domain username and password to be able to connect to a resource. Windows NT and Windows 9x can perform user-level security.

3. NT can be a PDC, BDC, member server, or standalone server. Samba can perform all of these except for BDC functionality as of version 2.0.6.

4. NetBIOS is the transport protocol that is used by NetBIOS applications to communicate with each other. SMB is a NetBIOS application, and needs an existing NetBIOS channel to travel through.

5. The roles can be a potential browser, backup browser, master browser, or domain master browser.

6. An election is forced, which will decide who will be the next master browser.

Chapter 5

1. Samba can do all sorts of things. An incomplete list could include the following:

   - Acts as file and print server

   - Can perform in the various computer browsing roles

   - Can act as both a WINS client and server

   - Supports encrypted passwords

   - Can send all authentication requests to a password server (Windows NT domain controller)

2. Using an lmhosts file is like using a hosts file instead of DNS. When a host changes IP address, you have to go into all the lmhosts files and change the entry. However, if you are using WINS, computer names are stored dynamically in a centralized database and no manual updating needs to be done.

3. Use the following command:

   ```
   # kill -HUP `cat /var/lock/samba/nmbd.pid`
   ```

   This will dump the info you need into the file /var/lock/samba/namelist.debug. Filenames may be different for other flavors of UNIX. This answer is correct for Linux.

4. A domain master browser is usually the PDC of a Windows NT domain, and it takes care of gathering machine names from all the master browsers on each subnet and building the browselist.

   ```
   domain master = no
   ```

5. The methods include user, share, server, or domain. They are set with the security parameter.

6. The smbpasswd command is used for manipulating the smbpasswd file that contains the NTLM password hashes for each user, changing passwords, and adding users. It also allows you to change the password for users on remote SMB servers such as Samba or Windows NT servers.

   ```
   $ smbpasswd -r oyster -U mikec
   ```

7. In `smb.conf`, define "`load printers = no`".

8. In Windows:

   ```
   C:\>net send bbq "This is a message!"
   ```

   With Samba:

   ```
   $ echo "This is a message!" | smbclient -M bbq
   ```

Chapter 6

1. a. Domain authentication for users as they log in

   b. Support for login scripts

   c. Support for user home directories

   d. Support for roaming profiles

   e. Support for Windows 95/98 policies

2. Any answer that mentions the main points in the section "Configuring Samba as a Domain Login Server" from Chapter 6 is valid as an answer.

3. ```
   local master = yes
   domain logins = yes
   wins server = <ip of windows nt WINS server>
   logon script = logonscripts\%U.bat

   [netlogon]
       path = /samba/netlogon
       read-only = yes
   guest ok = no
   ```

4. Roaming profiles allow users to keep all their preferences and Start menu items available regardless of which PC they log in to. User profiles are saved back to a central point.

5. Add the following in `smb.conf`:

   ```
   logon path = \\ronald\profiles\%U
   ```

6. Password encryption is turned on in the client and not turned on in Samba, or the user's password is incorrect.

7. See the "System Policies" section at the end of Chapter 6.
   ```

Chapter 7

1. A machine trust account is required on the PDC for each member server and workstation that is a part of the domain. It is a method of verifying that all the clients are actually who they say they are.

2. Make sure your `smb.conf` has the following settings:

```
encrypted passwords = yes
security = domain
password server = NTDC1 NTDC2 NTDC3
workgroup = DOMAIN
```

Before you start the Samba daemons, add a machine trust account for the Samba server on the domain's PDC with Server Manager, and then execute this command on the Samba server: `smbpasswd -j DOMAIN -r PDC` where `DOMAIN` is the name of the `DOMAIN` you are joining and `PDC` is the NetBIOS name of the `PDC`.

3. Make sure these values are set in `smb.conf`:

```
encrypted passwords = yes
domain logons = yes
domain master = yes
security = user
workgroup = DOMAIN
```

Remember to add accounts in `/etc/passwd` for all Windows NT workstations/servers that will be members of the domain (their NetBIOS names with a "$" at the end). Also, create accounts for them in `/etc/smbpasswd` with this command:

 # smbpasswd -a -m MACHINENAME$.

4. Edit `/etc/group` and put a group in here called `manufac` or some other shortened abbreviation of Manufacturing.

Create a file called `domain_group.map` and put in an entry that looks like this:

`manufac = Manufacturing`

Put this in `smb.conf` if it isn't already there:

`domain group map = /usr/local/samba/lib/domain_group.map`

On the Windows NT server, right-click the directory to which you want to add the permission and click Properties, and then click the Security tab. Click Add, select the Manufacturing global group and choose the rights you want to give the group, and then click OK.

5. Yes. Although these tools are not fully implemented, you can use Server Manager and User Manager for Domains to view your Samba PDC.

6. Yes. Create a policy file called `NTconfig.pol` and put it on your Samba server's `netlogon` share.

7. Create a user called `profile`.

   Log in as that user and create the environment the way you would like the users to see it.

   Log out, log back in as an Administrative user, go to Control Panel, System, User Profiles, and copy the profile you just created from the `\\pdc\netlogon` share to a directory called `Default User` using the Copy To button.

   Make sure that everyone has read access to this directory.

   This profile will now be used by default when new users log in.

   Optionally, include a policy file, created using the System Policy Editor (`POLEDIT.EXE`), which has policies that disallow users from modifying their own background/screen saver.

8. Each user has this file under his profile directory. `NTuser.DAT` contains the details to populate the registry tree `HKEY_CURRENT_USER`, which has all of the user's Windows and application preferences.

9. `rpcclient` is a tool developed by the Samba development team to access the different RPC services provided in NT from the UNIX platform.

Chapter 8

1. `$ smbclient \\alfred\apps`

2. `$ smbclient -U anotheruser \\alfred\apps`

   OR

   ```
   $ export USER=anotheruser
   $ smbclient \\alfred\apps
   ```

3. In this case, you turn on debugging with the `-d 3` option.

4. `$ smbclient -L //rhino -U username`

5. `$ smbclient -W accounts \\int60239\documents`

6. In previous versions of Samba (pre-2.0), the `-P` option was needed to connect to Windows print shares. In the latest versions of Samba, `smbclient` is smart enough to determine whether it has connected to a file share or print share.

Chapter 9

1. SSL, together with the authentication handshake, provides a secure means of communicating through an unsecure network such as the Internet. SSL has many applications, an example of which is that a user can connect to an online shop to purchase an item with his credit card, and he is guaranteed that the shop is who it says it is through the use of certificates.

2. A CA is a Certification Authority. CAs are entrusted by the public to digitally sign certificates. By signing certificates, they indicate that they have done the necessary background checks to make sure that the organization supplying the certificate is who it says it is so that the public will be able to do secure business with it.

3. A certificate signing request (CSR) is an unsigned certificate that is sent to the CA for signing. The CSR contains both the Distinguished Name (DN) and the public key of the organization. The public key is derived from the private key, which *must* be kept private. This process involves some complex mathematics.

4. Client-side certificates would be most important with Samba. In conventional SSL applications, they are used with the Web where the server must authenticate to the client so the client knows exactly who it is talking to. Samba, however, will probably be storing sensitive files on it—you don't want just anyone accessing them with an SSL SMB client, even if it is encrypted! So with Samba, the client must authenticate to the server so that only valid SSL-enabled SMB clients are allowed to access the Samba server.

5. You would compile and install OpenSSL (source from `www.openssl.org`), and then compile and install Samba yourself from scratch with SSL support (source from `www.samba.org`).

   You would create a CA, generate a certificate for your Samba server, and then generate individual certificates for Samba clients. All these certificates should be signed using the CA you created.

   You would configure Samba to enable SSL for all connections, or possibly for only certain IP address ranges. Then you would configure Samba with its server-side certificate, and configure your SSL clients (`smbclient`) with their client-side certificate (still in `smb.conf` but on the client machine).

   Finally, you would start Samba, enter the passphrase, and Samba would be ready to use SSL.

Chapter 10

1.
```
[cdrom]
path = /mnt
read only = yes
root preexec = sh -c /usr/local/bin/mount_cd.sh
root postexec = sh -c /usr/local/bin/umount_cd.sh
```

2. When a Windows 3.11 or DOS user connects to a resource on a Windows NT machine or a UNIX machine with Samba on it, chances are some of the filenames will not comply with DOS's limitation on filenames to 8 characters and a 3 letter extension (8.3). Name mangling is the process by which Samba (and Windows NT systems) change a non-complying name, like `long filename.txt`, to the appropriate format. Windows 95 and higher can handle long filenames, so it is not much of an issue these days.

3. `hide files = /~*/$*/`

4. Add `max connections = 4` to the share definition for the graphic designing software.

5. The keyword here is *minimal*. Access can be granted in a number of ways. The first is to use `force user`:

```
[scratch]
comment = "Temporary file share space"
force user = scratch
path = /scratch
writable = yes
```

An alternative is to use `public = yes`:

```
[scratch]
comment = "Temporary file share space"
public = yes
path = /scratch
writable = yes
```

This last solution causes all connections to be made as the user defined in guest account.

6. Simply include this option in your `smb.conf` file:

```
hide dot file = yes
```

Chapter 11

1. • Entry-level Pentium II or Celeron

   • Minimum of two IDE hard disks (9GB each)

   • First hard disk has operating system on it

   • Second hard disk has user data on it

2. • Find out when it started being slow.

   • Check your records to see if you changed anything on the server at that time.

   • Check that the client machines have not had anything installed on them lately that may have corrupted the TCP/IP stack.

- Check that there are no weird processes that could be out of control on the server.

- Check network utilization and collisions.

- Play with Samba performance parameters to see if they make a difference.

3. oplocks are a method of caching file data when a single network client has a file. Using the cached data, a client can make changes to a file or read various parts of it locally without having to do separate SMB requests each time it needs to access the file.

4. As soon as multiple clients need to access a file read-only, their local clients can all cache the file data locally, which lowers the amount of network traffic when all the clients are accessing the file.

Chapter 12

1. There is no one answer to this question. The idea is to come up with some diagnostic steps as outlined in the chapter. These steps are examples of logical things to check:

   Check the network configuration on both the client and the server (IP address/subnet mask/default gateway).

   From Windows, ping the Samba server to make sure network connectivity is okay.

   From the Windows machine, try the following command:

   `C:\>nbtstat -a sambaserver`

   You should get the NetBIOS name table on your Samba server.

   If you don't, NetBIOS name resolution is the problem; check **lmhosts** or WINS entries.

   Check that **smbd** is running on the server.

   Check that **nmbd** is running on the server.

2. Use `kill -USR1 <PID>` to increase log level, and `kill -USR2 <PID>` to decrease it.

3. You get support through Samba mailing list archives, Samba Web pages, and the `comp.protocol.smb` newsgroup. There are also commercial support organizations you can turn to.

Chapter 13

1. There are actually several reasons:

   - To stop people from poking around in your file services when what they may find does not concern them. Consider a firewall an investment in the security of your data.

   - To stop possible denial of service attacks on your Samba servers.

- To stop potential crackers from entering your network completely; it is a way of locking people out.

- You can control access from inside to outside as well. You don't generally want people filling all the available bandwidth by pulling any data they like from the Internet. You can put in a proxy server and force all outgoing traffic to pass via the proxy server to cut costs.

2. First, you would add a `hosts allow` entry to your `smb.conf` file with the name of the subnet that was allowed to have access to the server. Something like

```
hosts allow = 192.168.3.0/255.255.255.240
```

would allow all hosts from `192.168.3.0` to `192.168.3.15` access. If it is highly confidential information you don't want anyone else in the company looking at, you would probably put some kind of packet filter in front of it to stop all traffic to the server, except for legitimate SMB traffic to and from the valid hosts.

3. Reactive security refers to administrators responding to specific holes that should be plugged. Proactive security is related to administrators doing all they can to minimize any security problems by installing the latest patches, making sure the latest Samba version is running, and so on.

Chapter 14

1. `smbfs` is a file system driver that is included as part of the standard Linux source distribution. It is usually compiled as an installable module that is installed on-the-fly when needed. It is used as part of the process when you are mounting SMB file systems onto your Linux system.

2. You first need a compiled version of the `smbfs` file system driver either as part of your running kernel or available as a module (most Linux distributions use this method). You also need the executables `smbmount` and `smbumount` from the Samba distribution. To mount a file system, you would do this:

```
# smbmount //goofey/resource /mountpoint -U matt
```

Substitute a valid username for `matt`, a valid resource, and a mountpoint (an empty directory).

3. LinPopUp is a program that runs on Linux in the X-Windows environment to replicate the behavior of WinPopUp, which is available on Windows 9x. You can send messages to other SMB-compatible machines, receive messages, reply to messages, and have a message history.

4. On newer UNIX systems, programs that run on the UNIX system are written using a special API for the authentication functionality. A number of plug-in modules are available to provide different methods of user authentication rather than the common `/etc/passwd` or `/etc/shadow` methods. These alternative methods can include S/Key,

one-time key, smart cards, fingerprint, and of course, SMB authentication. SMB authentication can be done using a package called **pam_smb**. It allows you to authenticate UNIX users using a Windows NT domain controller.

Chapter 15

1. The most likely features are remainder of PDC functionality, full Windows NT printing (using **PIPE****spoolss**), trust relationship support, BDC support, and read-only use of User Manager. The ability to manage ACLs on Samba file shares should also be there.

2. At the time of this writing, it is effectively Samba 3.0, and contains all the new cutting-edge Samba development code for the next major release of Samba.

3. The major new features include Active Directory, Kerberos authentication support, DFS support, and removal of the requirement to have NetBIOS with CIFS.

GLOSSARY

Access Control Entry—Each ACL is made up of access control entries that control who has access to the particular file system resource (file or directory).

Access Control List—A list of ACEs that control who has access to file system resources.

ACE—*See* Access Control Entry.

ACL—*See* Access Control List.

Asymmetric Cryptosystems—Public key cryptography.

Backup Domain Controller—A specific type of Windows NT server that contains a backup of the accounts database that lives on the primary domain controller.

BDC—*See* Backup Domain Controller.

CA—*See* Certification Authority.

Certificate Signing Request—A file containing an organization's public key that is sent to the CA for signing and is turned into an X.509 certificate.

Certification Authority—A trusted entity that signs certificates so they can be used in authentication.

Challenge/Response Authentication—The method of authentication used by Samba and Windows NT servers.

CIFS—*See* Common Internet File System.

Ciphertext—Text that has been encrypted.

Client-Side Certificate—An X.509 certificate that is used for authentication of a client.

Common Internet File System—A revised version of the SMB protocol.

Daemon—A process (sometimes called a server process) that listens on a particular TCP/IP port and services requests to do a specific task.

Denial of Service Attack—Occurs when someone on a network consumes the server's resources in such a way that it affects the server's intended purpose.

DHCP—*See* Dynamic Host Configuration Protocol.

Digital Signature—A unique sequence, or hash, of characters that uniquely identifies a piece of text.

Distinguished Name—Tree-like unique identification of an object.

DN—*See* Distinguished Name.

Dynamic Host Configuration Protocol—A protocol that allows a computer to get its TCP/IP configuration from a DHCP server.

File Transfer Protocol—A method of block-by-block transfer of files between two machines on the Internet.

Firewall—An infrastructure that is used to separate an organization's internal network from the Internet. Its purpose is to stop crackers from breaking into systems they should not be accessing.

FTP—*See* File Transfer Protocol.

Interprocess Communication—A method of communication that processes can use to communicate with each other.

IPC—*See* interprocess communication.

LAN Manager—The name given to the Microsoft implementation of the SMB/CIFS protocol.

LANMAN—*See* LAN Manager.

Login Scripts—Batch files that are executed when a user logs in to a system.

Name Mangling—A method of shortening long filenames so that older versions of Windows and DOS that use only filenames in 8.3 format can use the filename.

NetBIOS—*See* Network Basic Input and Output System.

Network Basic Input and Output System—A programming API that is used extensively with the SMB; however, it is now optional with CIFS.

nmbd—The Samba daemon that implements the NetBIOS API.

PDC—*See* Primary Domain Controller.

Primary Domain Controller—Contains the System Account Manager or master user database in a Windows NT domain. This is replicated to all the domain BDCs for backup and fallback purposes.

Public Key Cryptography—Unlike conventional cryptography, in which encryption and decryption is done using a single key, this method allows encryption to occur using a well-known public key, and the resulting decryption to occur using a private key.

Remote Procedure Call—A piece of code contained on one machine (A) but whose code, or procedure, is called by another machine (B). Execution of the code occurs on A.

RPC—*See* Remote Procedure Call.

rpcclient—A program included in the Samba distribution that allows testing of the various RPC interfaces on a Windows NT/2000 server.

SAM—*See* System Account Manager.

Server Message Block—The file-sharing protocol used by Microsoft LAN Manager systems and Samba.

Server-Side Certificate—An X.509 certificate that is used for authentication of a server.

Share-Level Security—A form of security in which access to a resource on an SMB server is restricted by two different passwords: one for read access, and one for write access.

SMB—*See* Server Message Block.

smbclient—A program included with the Samba distribution that allows connection to SMB/CIFS resources from the UNIX platform.

smbd—The Samba daemon that implements the SMB/CIFS protocol.

Symmetric Cryptosystems—Single shared key cryptography.

System Account Manager—The main account database that contains all the user/group/machine accounts for a Windows NT domain. It is stored on a PDC.

System Policy Editor—A Microsoft-provided utility used to set system policies on client computers. The policy file is read during the logon process from a share that is available on all domain controllers.

User-Level Security—Access to resources on an SMB server that must be authenticated using a valid username/password pair.

Windows Domain—A method of centralized and secure Windows management. Consists of one PDC and one or more BDCs.

Windows Internet Name Service—A central database of IP addresses and NetBIOS naming mappings.

Windows Workgroup—An uncentralized method of resource sharing.

WINS—*See* Windows Internet Name Service.

X.509 Certificates—These contain a public key of an organization, as well as a signature to prove that the public key actually belongs to the given organization.

INDEX

SYMBOLS

@ (at symbol), 90
/ (forward slash), 145
. (period), 42
(pound sign), 77

A

access control
    Access Denied messages, 203-204
    ACEs (Access Control Entries), 261
    ACLs (Access Control Lists)
        definition of, 261
        Samba configuration parameters, 122
        Samba users, adding, 130
    anonymous access, 220
    guest access, 219
    permissions, controlling users' changes to, 128-129
    Samba configuration parameters
        guest ok, 219
        guest only, 219
        hosts allow, 219
        hosts deny, 219
        restrict anonymous, 220
    share-level options, 183
        force group, 184
        force user, 184
        invalid users, 183-184
        read list, 184
        valid users, 183-184
        write list, 184

Access Control Entries (ACEs), 261
Access Control Lists (ACLs)
    definition of, 261
    Samba configuration parameters, 122
    Samba users, adding, 130
Access Denied messages, 203-204
accounts
    domains, 116
    machine trust accounts
        creating, 118-119
        definition of, 112
ACEs (Access Control Entries), 261
ACLs (Access Control Lists)
    definition of, 261
    Samba configuration parameters, 122
    Samba users, adding, 130
Active Directory, 237
adapters, troubleshooting, 51-52
administration
    Server Manager, 130-131
        connected users, listing, 133
        messages, sending to connected users, 132
        open files, viewing, 134
        share connections, viewing, 133
        SMB server statistics, viewing, 132-133
    User Manager for Domains, 134-136, 236
administration tools
    LinNeighborhood, 231-233
    LinPopUp, 227-229
    SMB PAM (Pluggable Authentication Module), 229-230
    smb2www, 230
    smbedit, 231
    smbfs, 225-227

anonymous connections, 220
APIs (application programming interfaces),
    NetBIOS, 10-11, 64-65
        datagram service, 70
        name service, 65-69
        session service, 69-70
asymmetric cryptosystems, 162, 262
at symbol (@), 90
auditing, 123
authentication, 11
        Challenge/Response Authentication, 261
        SMB PAM (Pluggable Authentication Module),
            229-230

B

b-node mode (NetBIOS), 68
backup browsers, 71
backups, creating, 155-156
BDCs (Backup Domain Controllers), 63, 72, 236,
    261
blocking locks parameter (shares), 186
broadcast mode (NetBIOS), 68
broadcasting. *See* sending messages
broadcasts (NetBIOS), 68
browsers, 71
        backup browsers, 71
        computer browsing services, 11-12
        domain master browsers, 71
        elections, 72
        master browsers, 71-72
        non-browser role, 71
        potential browsers, 71
browsing. *See* computer browsing
BugTraq mailing list, 221
buttons, SWAT (Samba Web Administration Tool),
    34
        Globals, 34-36
        Home, 34
        Password, 39
        Printers, 37-38
        Shares, 36-37
        Status, 38
        View, 39

C

c option (smbclient program), 151
CAs (certification authorities), 163
        configuring yourself as, 168-171
        definition of, 261
case sensitive parameter (Samba configuration),
    182
CERT (Computer Emergency Response Team), 221
certificate signing requests (CSRs), 164, 261
certificates, 163
        creating, 166-168
        installing, 171-172
        server-side, 163
        signing, 164
        verifying, 164-165
Certification Authorities, 163
        configuring yourself as, 168-171
        definition of, 261
Challenge/Response Authentication, 261
changing
        directories, 150-151
        passwords, 87
chosen plaintext attacks, 9
CIFS (Common Internet File System), 12, 243
        definition of, 261
        dialects, 243
        sample session, 243-248
                dialect negotiation, 243
                share connection transaction, 245-246
                system information, setting, 246
                user authentication, 244
ciphertext, 261
client-side certificates, 261
clients
        performance tuning, 197
        troubleshooting, 55
        Windows 98 configuration, 43-45
        Windows NT configuration, 45-47, 120-121
code (Samba). *See* source code Samba distributions
code listings
        configure program options, 22-23
        Samba startup script, 27
        username.map files, generating, 83-84
command-line programs. *See also* programs;
    scripts
        configure, 21-24
                advantages, 21

options, 22-23
running, 21
cvs, 117
gunzip, 20
killall, 78
make, 24
nbtstat, 10, 66
nmblookup, 66-67
ping, 48, 199
pwdump, 88-89
rpcclient, 139-140
rpm, 19
running multiple, 151
smb2www, 230
smbclient, 40-42, 94, 143
    debugging, 148-150
    default directories, 150-151
    environment variables, 152
    multiple commands, 151
    NetBIOS names, specifying, 150
    options, 143-144
    printing, 154-155
    server IP addresses, specifying, 150
    sessions, 144-146
    share connections, 147
    tar archives, creating, 151-152
    troubleshooting, 206
    user interface, 152-154
    Windows backups, creating, 155-156
    WinPopUp messages, sending, 147
smbedit, 231
smbmount, 225-226
smbpasswd, 86
    adding users, 87
    changing passwords, 87
    multiple passwords, 86
    password synchronization, 87-88
    troubleshooting, 206
smbtar, 156
smbumount, 226
tcpdump-smb, 208-209
testparm, 54, 85, 203
UNIX commands, ls, 42
Common Internet File System. See CIFS
compiling Samba, 21-24, 172
computer browsing
    services, 11-12
    Windows NT networks, 70-71
        backup browsing, 71
        domain master browsing, 71
        elections, 72

        master browsing, 71-72
        non-browsing, 71
        potential browsing, 71
Computer Emergency Response Team (CERT), 221
config.pol file, 98
configuration parameters. See also smb.conf file
    access control, 219
        guest ok, 219
        guest only, 219
        hosts allow, 219
        hosts deny, 219
        restrict anonymous, 220
    ACL support parameters, 122
    file shares
        blocking locks, 186
        case sensitive, 182
        copy, 186
        default case, 182
        delete readonly, 187
        delete veto files, 187
        dont descend, 187
        force group, 184
        force users, 184
        hide dot files, 187
        hide files, 187
        invalid users, 183-184
        locking, 186
        mangle case, 182
        mangled map, 183
        mangled names, 183
        mangled stack, 183
        max connections, 185
        postexec, 181-182
        preexec, 181-182
        preserve case, 182
        read list, 184
        short preserve case, 183
        valid users, 183-184
        veto files, 187
        veto oplock files, 188
        volumes, 185
        write list, 184
    file/directory permission parameters, 128-129
    SSL (Secure Sockets Layer), 172-176
        ssl CA certDir, 175
        ssl CA certFile, 175
        ssl ciphers, 175
        ssl client cert, 175
        ssl client key, 175
        ssl compatibility, 176
        ssl hosts, 176

ssl hosts resign, 176
ssl require clientcert, 176
ssl require servercert, 176
ssl version, 176
configure program, 21-24
advantages, 21
options, 22-23
running, 21
configuring Samba. *See also* SWAT (Samba Web Administration Tool)
as domain member, 111-114
directory permissions, 127-129
domain members, 112-114
file permissions, 122-129
PDCs (Primary Domain Controllers), 114-121
roaming profiles, 136-139
Server Manager, 130-131
User Manager for Domains, 134-136
users, 130
browsing clients, 81
domain login servers, 101-105
global variables, 34-36
passwords, 39
performance tuning
compile options, 194
debug level parameter, 196
getwd cache parameter, 197
max xmit parameter, 196
oplocks (opportunistic locking), 195-196
read raw parameter, 197
read size parameter, 196
socket options, 194-195
strict sync parameter, 196
sync always parameter, 196
widelinks parameter, 197
print servers
global printer configuration, 91-92
share-level printer configuration, 92-93
UNIX side configuration, 90-91
printers, 37-38
roaming user profiles, 105-107
shares, 36-37
smbedit tool, 231
status screen, 38-39
testing configuration, 40-42
troubleshooting, 51
client configuration, 55
name servers, 52-54
network adapter problems, 51-52

network configuration problems, 52
server configuration, 54
user home directories, 89-90
Windows 98 clients, 43-45
Windows NT clients, 45-47
connecting to Samba servers, 47-48
through mapped network drives, 49-51
through Network Neighborhood, 48
copy parameter (shares), 186
create mask parameter (smb.conf file), 128
cryptoanalysis, 8
cryptography, 162
public key, 162, 262
SSL (Secure Sockets Layer), 162-163
symmetric, 162
CSRs (certificate signing requests), 164
cvs command, 117

D

d option (smbclient program), 148-151
daemons
inetd, running Samba from, 25-26
smbd, 10
troubleshooting, 202-203
viewing files, 134
datagram service (NetBIOS), 70
debug level parameter (Samba configuration), 196
debugging
networks
Access Denied messages, 203-204
connectivity problems, 199-202
help resources, 213
log files, 211-212
login problems, 204
network path problems, 204-205
network sniffers, 206-210
no data when trying to connect, 205
password changes, 205-206
unable to find domain controller, 205-206
Samba server, 199, 202-203
smbclient, 148-150, 206
smbpasswd, 206
default case parameter (Samba configuration), 182
del command (smbclient program), 152
delete readonly parameter (shares), 187

delete veto files parameter (shares), 187

deleting read-only files, 187

denial of service attacks, 261

DFS (Distributed File System) support, 237-238

DHCP (Dynamic Host Configuration Protocol), 262

digital signatures, 262

dir command (smbclient program), 152

directories
    Active Directory, 237
    docs, 21
    examples, 21
    packaging, 21
    permissions
        controlling users' changes to, 128-129
        editing, 127-128
    smbclient default directories, changing, 150-151
    source, 21
    swat, 21
    user home directories
        configuring, 89-90
        restricting, 90

directory mask parameter (smb.conf file), 129

directory security mask parameter (smb.conf file), 129

disabling pwl files, 101

disk drives, mapping, 49-51

Distinguished Names (DNs), 262

Distributed File System (DFS) support, 237-238

DNs (Distinguished Names), 262

DNS (Domain Name System)
    alternatives to, 54
    enabling, 53

docs directory, 21

domain controllers
    BDCs (Backup Domain Controllers), 63, 72, 236, 261
    PDCs (Primary Domain Controllers), 63, 72, 114, 235
        capabilities, 115
        definition of, 262
        login servers, 117-121
        troubleshooting, 121
        trust relationships, 115-116
    troubleshooting, 205-206

domain environments (Samba configuration), 62-63, 100-101, 111-112, 263
    BDCs (Backup Domain Controllers), 63, 72, 236, 261
    computer browsing, 80-81
        services, 11-12
        Windows NT networks, 70-72
    directory permission
        controlling users' changes to, 128-129
        editing, 127-128
    domain members, configuring Samba as, 112-114
    file permission
        controlling users' changes to, 128-129
        editing, 123-124, 126-127
    file permissions, 122-123
    login servers
        configuring Samba as, 101-105
        troubleshooting, 108-109
    logins, 12
    PDCs (Primary Domain Controllers), 63, 72, 114, 235
        capabilities, 115
        definition of, 262
        login servers, 117-121
        troubleshooting, 121
        trust relationships, 115-116
    roaming profiles, 136-139
    Samba users, adding to ACLs (Access Control Lists), 130
    Server Manager, 130-131
        connected users, listing, 133
        messages, sending to connected users, 132
        open files, viewing, 134
        share connections, viewing, 133
        SMB server statistics, viewing, 132-133
    servers, 64
    User Manager for Domains, 134-136
    workstations, 64

domain master browsers, 71

domain member, configuring Samba as, 112-114

Domain Name System (DNS)
    alternatives to, 54
    enabling, 53

dont descend parameter (shares), 187

downloading
    LinNeighborhood, 232
    LinPopUp, 227
    Samba
        precompiled packages, 17-18
        source code distributions, 19-20

drivers, smbfs, 225-227
drives, mapping, 49-51
Dynamic Host Configuration Protocol (DHCP), 262

E

editing
    permissions
        directory permissions, 127-128
        file permissions, 123-127
    registry, 47
    smb.conf file, 34-36
elections (browsers), 72
email mailing lists, 213
    BugTraq/NTBugTraq lists, 221
    CERT (Computer Emergency Response Team), 221
    Samba Announcement list, 220-221
    security-related Linux lists, 221
enabling
    DNS lookups, 53
    encrypted passwords, 85-86
    logging, 211-212
    plaintext passwords, 47-48
encrypted passwords, 84-86
encryption
    passwords, 84-86
    public key, 162
    SSL (Secure Sockets Layer), 162-163
    symmetric cryptography, 162
environment variables (smbclient program), 152
error messages
    Access Denied, 203-204
    no data when trying to connect, 205
    The network path was not found, 204-205
    The password is incorrect, 204
    You are not authorized to login, 204
Ethereal, 209-210
examples directory, 21
executing. *See* running
extensions (filename), 20

F

file share connections, viewing, 133
file shares, 181
    maximum number of connections, setting, 185
    name mangling, 182-183
    parameters
        blocking locks, 186
        case sensitive, 182
        copy, 186
        default case, 182
        delete readonly, 187
        delete veto files, 187
        dont descend, 187
        force group, 184
        force users, 184
        hide dot files, 187
        hide files, 187
        invalid users, 183-184
        locking, 186
        mangle case, 182
        mangled map, 183
        mangled names, 183
        mangled stack, 183
        max connections, 185
        postexec, 181-182
        preexec, 181-182
        preserve case, 182
        read list, 184
        short preserve case, 183
        valid users, 183-184
        veto files, 187
        veto oplock files, 188
        volumes, 185
        write list, 184
file systems
    CIFS (Common Internet File System), 12
        definition of, 261
        dialects, 243
        sample session, 243-248
    DFS (Distributed File System), 237-238
File Transfer Protocol (FTP)
    definition of, 262
    Samba download sites, 18
filenames
    filename extensions, 20
    name mangling, 182-183, 262
files
    config.pol, 98
    hiding, 187-188
    lmhosts, 76-77
    log files, 211-212

names
  filename extensions, 20
  name mangling, 182-183
open files, viewing, 134
passwd, 87-88
permissions, 122-123
  controlling users' changes to, 128-129
  editing, 123-127
pwl files
  creating, 99
  disabling, 101
smb.conf. *See* smb.conf file
smbpasswd, 85
  adding users to, 87
  creating, 88-89
  synchronizing with passwd files, 87-88
  trust account settings, 119
startup, running Samba from, 26-28
tar files, 151-152
username.map, 83-84
filtering NetBIOS ports , 217-218
firewalls, 217-218, 262
force create mode parameter (smb.conf file), 128
force directory mode parameter (smb.conf file),
  129
force directory security parameter (smb.conf file),
  129
force group parameter (shares), 184
force security mode parameter (smb.conf file), 129
force users parameter (shares), 184
forward slash (/), 145
FTP (File Transfer Protocol)
  definition of, 262
  Samba download sites, 18
future of Samba, 235
  development, 238-239
  version 2.1, 235-236
  Windows 2000 interoperability, 236-238

G

get command (smbclient program), 152
getwd cache parameter (Samba configuration), 197
global groups, 125
global printer configuration, 91-92
global variables, 34-36

Globals button (SWAT), 34-36
groups, 125
guest ok parameter (smb.conf file), 219
guest only parameter (smb.conf file), 219
guests, 219
gunzip command, 20
.gz filename extension, 20

H

h-node mode (NetBIOS), 69
handshake process (SSL), 164-165
hardware, performance tuning, 191-192
hashes, 119
help command (smbclient program), 152
help resources, 213
hide dot files parameter (shares), 187
hide files parameter (shares), 187
hiding files, 187-188
historical overviews
  Samba, 5-6
  SMB (Server Message Block) protocol, 7-9
Home button (SWAT), 34
home directories
  configuring, 89-90
  restricting, 90
hosts allow parameter (smb.conf file), 35, 219
hosts deny parameter (smb.conf file), 219

I

I option (smbclient program), 150
inetd daemon, running Samba from, 25-26
input filters, 154
installing Samba, 15
  certificates, 171-172
  precompiled packages
    advantages, 16-17
    disadvantages, 17
    downloading, 17-18
    installation, 19
  source code distributions
    compiling, 21-24
    directory structure, 20-21

downloading, 19-20
installation, 24-25
SWAT (Samba Web Administration Tool), 32
Internet
FTP sites, Samba download site, 18
Web sites
CERT (Computer Emergency Response Team), 221
OpenSSL, 166
operating system security, 216
Samba download sites, 18
Internet Firewalls FAQ (Web site), 222
invalid users parameter (shares), 183-184
IPC (interprocess communication), 262

J-K-L

Kerberos, 237
killall command, 78
known plaintext attacks, 8

LAN Manager, 262
LANMAN protocol, 7-8
LinNeighborhood tool, 231-233
LinPopUp tool, 227-229
Linux, 6, 221
listings
configure program options, 22-23
Samba startup script, 27
username.map files, generating, 83-84
lmhosts files, 76-77
local groups, 125
locking parameter (shares), 186
locks, oplocks (opportunistic locking), 195-196
log files, enabling, 211-212
logins
domain logins, 12
login servers, configuring Samba as, 101-105, 117-118
machine trust accounts, 118-119
NT client configuration, 120-121
smb.conf file, 118
troubleshooting, 108-109
scripts, 262
troubleshooting, 204
Windows 95/98 networks, 98
Windows NT networks, 73

lookups (DNS), 53
ls command, 42

M

M option (smbclient program), 147
m-node mode (NetBIOS), 68
mailing lists, 213
BugTraq/NTBugTraq lists, 221
CERT (Computer Emergency Response Team), 221
Samba Announcement list, 220-221
security-related Linux lists, 221
make command, 24
mandatory user profiles, 98
mangle case parameter (Samba configuration), 182
mangled map parameter (Samba configuration), 183
mangled names parameter (Samba configuration), 183
mangled stack parameter (Samba configuration), 183
mangling names, 182-183, 262
mapping network drives, 49-51
master browsers, 11, 71-72
max connections parameter (shares), 185
max xmit parameter (Samba configuration), 196
member servers, 72
messages
CIFS (Common Internet File System)
SMB_COM_NEGOTIATE, 244
SMB_COM_SESSION_SETUP_ANDX, 244
SMB_COM_TREE_CONNECT, 244
SMB_COM_TREE_DISCONNECT, 244
error messages
Access Denied, 203-204
no data when trying to connect, 205
The network path was not found, 204-205
The password in incorrect, 204
You are not authorized to login, 204
receiving, 95
sending, 93-95, 147
LinPopUp tool, 227-229
Server Manager, 132
mget command (smbclient program), 152
migrating to Samba, 88-89. *See also* installing Samba; configuration parameters

mkdir command (smbclient program), 152

modified b-node mode (NetBIOS), 69

modifying. *See* editing

monitoring performance, 193

mounting shares

    LinNeighborhood tool, 232-233

    smbfs tool, 226-227

mput command (smbclient program), 152

N

n option (smbclient program), 150

name mangling, 182-183, 262

name resolution

    DNS (Domain Name System)

        alternatives to, 54

        enabling, 53

    lmhosts files, 76-77

    NetBIOS, 10-11, 65

        broadcasts, 68

        limitations, 69

        name tables, 66

        nodes, 68-69

        remote machines, interrogating, 66-67

        resource types, 67-68

    WINS (Windows Internet Name Service), 76-78, 263

name servers, troubleshooting, 52-54

name service (NetBIOS), 65

    broadcasts, 68

    limitations, 69

    name tables, 66

    nodes

        b-node, 68

        h-node, 69

        m-node, 68

        modified b-node, 69

        p-node, 68

    remote machines, interrogating, 66-67

    resource types, 67-68

name tables (NetBIOS), 66

names

    filenames

        filename extensions, 20

        name mangling, 182-183

    NetBIOS names, 10, 65

navigating SWAT (Samba Web Administration Tool), 34

    Globals, 34-36

    Home, 34

    Password, 39

    Printers, 37-38

    Shares, 36-37

    Status, 38

    View, 39

nbtstat command, 10, 66

NetBEUI, 64

NetBIOS (Network Basic Input/Output System), 64-65

    datagram service, 70

    name resolution, 10-11

    name service, 65

        broadcasts, 68

        limitations, 69

        modes, 68-69

        name tables, 66

        remote machines, interrogating, 66-67

        resource types, 67-68

    ports, filtering (firewalls), 217-218

    session service, 69-70

network adapters, troubleshooting, 51-52

Network Basic Input/Output System. *See* NetBIOS

Network Monitor, 207-208

Network Neighborhood, connecting Samba servers to, 48

network path was not found (error message), 204-205

network sniffers, 206

    Ethereal, 209-210

    Network Monitor, 207-208

    tcpdump-smb, 208-209

networks. *See also* security; shares

    domains. *See* domain environments (Samba configuration)

    drives, mapping, 49-51

    sniffers, 206

        Ethereal, 209-210

        Network Monitor, 207-208

        tcpdump-smb, 208-209

    troubleshooting, 52, 199-202

        Access Denied messages, 203-204

        help resources, 213

        log files, 211-212

        login problems, 204

network paths, 204-205
    no data when trying to connect, 205
    password changes, 205-206
    unable to find domain controller, 205-206
verifying configuration of, 48
Windows 95/98. *See* Windows 95/98 networks
Windows NT networks. *See* Windows NT
    networks
newer command (smbclient program), 153
newsgroups, 213
nmblookup command, 66-67
no data when trying to connect (error message),
    205
non-browsers, 71
NT. *See* Windows NT networks
nt acl support parameter (smb.conf file), 122
NT LM protocol, 9
NTBugTraq mailing list, 221

O

obtaining Samba
    precompiled packages, 17-18
    source code distributions, 19
one-way trust relationships, 115-116
online resources, 222
    CERTs (Computer Emergency Response Teams),
        221
    mailing lists
        BugTraq/NTBugTraq lists, 221
        CERT (Computer Emergency Response
            Team), 221
        Samba Announcement list, 220-221
        security-related Linux lists, 221
open files, viewing, 134
OpenSSL, 166
oplocks (opportunistic locking), 195-196
optimizing performance. *See* performance tuning
options. *See* configuration parameters

P-Q

p-node mode (NetBIOS), 68
packaging directory, 21
packet sizes, configuring, 196

PAMs (Pluggable Authentication Modules), SBM
    PAM, 229-230
parameters. *See* configuration parameters
passwd files, 87-88
Password button (SWAT), 39
password is incorrect (error message), 204
password servers
    choosing, 82-83
    username.map files, 83-84
passwords, 220
    changing
        remote servers, 87
        troubleshooting changes, 205-206
        user controls, 87
    encrypted, 84-86
    multiple, 86
    password servers
        choosing, 82-83
        username.map files, 83-84
    Password view, 39
    plaintext, 47-48
    security
        chosen plaintext attacks, 9
        known plaintext attacks, 8
    smbpasswd command, 86
    synchronizing, 87-88
    Windows NT passwords, migrating to Samba,
        88-89
patches, 216-217
paths (network), troubleshooting, 204-205
PCLAN protocol, 7
PDCs (Primary Domain Controllers), 63, 72, 114,
    235
    capabilities, 115
    definition of, 262
    login servers, 117-118
        machine trust accounts, 118-119
        NT client configuration, 120-121
        smb.conf file, 118
    troubleshooting, 121
    trust relationships, 115
        one-way, 115-116
        two-way, 116
performance monitoring, 193
performance tuning, 191
    client-side tuning, 197
    hardware, 191-192
    Samba configuration
        compile options, 194
        debug level parameter, 196

getwd cache parameter, 197
max xmit parameter, 196
oplocks (opportunistic locking), 195-196
read raw parameter, 197
read size parameter, 196
socket options, 194-195
strict sync parameter, 196
sync always parameter, 196
widelinks parameter, 197

period (.), 42

permissions
directory permissions
controlling users' changes to, 128-129
editing, 127-128
file permissions, 122-123
controlling users' changes to, 128-129
editing, 123-127

ping command, 48, 199

plaintext attacks
chosen, 9
known, 8

plaintext passwords, 47-48

Pluggable Authentication Modules (PAMs), SBM
PAM, 229-230

point-to-point mode (NetBIOS), 68

poledit tool, 107

policies, System Policy Editor, 98, 107-108

pop-up messages, sending, 147

porting software, 17

ports, filtering, 217-218

postexec parameter (shares), 181-182

potential browsers, 71

pound sign (#), 77

precompiled Samba packages
advantages, 16-17
disadvantages, 17
downloading, 17-18
installing, 19

preexec parameter (shares), 181-182

preserve case parameter (Samba configuration),
182

Primary Domain Controllers. See PDCs

print servers, 90
global printer configuration, 91-92
printing to, 154-155
share-level printer configuration, 92-93
UNIX side configuration, 90-91

printer configuration, 37-38
global, 91-92
share-level, 92-93

Printers button (SWAT), 37-38

proactive security
anonymous access, 220
definition of, 216
firewalls, 217-218
guest access, 219
operating system patches, 216-217
passwords, 220
Samba configuration parameters, 219
guest ok, 219
guest only, 219
hosts allow, 219
hosts deny, 219
restrict anonymous, 220
Samba versions, 217
services, 218

profiles, roaming
configuring, 105-107
definition of, 98
Windows NT, 136-139

program listings
configure program options, 22-23
Samba startup script, 27
username.map files, generating, 83-84

programs. See also command-line programs; scripts
Ethereal, 209-210
LinNeighborhood, 231-233
LinPopUp, 227-229
running when users connect/disconnect from file
shares, 181-182

protocols
CIFS (Common Internet File System), 243
definition of, 261
dialects, 243
sample session, 243-248
DHCP (Dynamic Host Configuration Protocol), 262
DNS (Domain Name System)
alternatives to, 54
enabling, 53
FTP (File Transfer Protocol), 262
LANMAN, 7-8
NetBEUI, 64
NT LM, 9
PCLAN, 7
SMB (Server Message Block), 6-7
definition of, 263
history of, 7-9

public key cryptography, 162, 262
put command (smbclient program), 152
pwdump command, 88-89
pwl files
    creating, 99
    disabling, 101

R

reactive security, 222
    BugTraq/NTBugTraq mailing lists, 221
    CERT (Computer Emergency Response Team), 221
    definition of, 220
    Samba Announcement mailing list, 220-221
    security-related Linux mailing lists, 221
read list parameter (shares), 184
read raw parameter (Samba configuration), 197
read size parameter (Samba configuration), 196
read-only files, deleting, 187
receiving messages, 95
recurse command (smbclient program), 152
registry
    editing, 47
    pwl files, disabling, 101
rename command (smbclient program), 152
resolving names. *See* name resolution
resource domains, 116
restrict anonymous parameter (smb.conf file), 220
restricting user home directories, 90
roaming profiles
    configuring, 105-107
    definition of, 98
    Windows NT, 136-139
routers, 217-218
rpcclient program, 139-140
rpm command, 19
running
    command-line programs
        multiple commands, 151
        when users connect/disconnect from file
            shares, 181-182
    Samba, 25
        from inetd, 25-26
        from startup file, 26-28

S

Samba configuration. *See also* SWAT (Samba Web
Administration Tool)
    as domain member, 111-114
        directory permissions, 127-129
        domain members, 112-114
        file permissions, 122-129
        PDCs (Primary Domain Controllers),
            114-121
        roaming profiles, 136-139
        Server Manager, 130-131
        User Manager for Domains, 134-136
        users, 130
    browsing clients, 81
    domain login servers, 101-105
    global variables, 34-36
    passwords, 39
    performance tuning
        compile options, 194
        debug level parameter, 196
        getwd cache parameter, 197
        max xmit parameter, 196
        oplocks (opportunistic locking), 195-196
        read raw parameter, 197
        read size parameter, 196
        socket options, 194-195
        strict sync parameter, 196
        sync always parameter, 196
        widelinks parameter, 197
    print servers
        global printer configuration, 91-92
        share-level printer configuration, 92-93
        UNIX side configuration, 90-91
    printers, 37-38
    roaming user profiles, 105-107
    shares, 36-37
    smbedit tool, 231
    status screen, 38-39
    testing configuration, 40-42
    troubleshooting, 51
        client configuration, 55
        name servers, 52-54
        network adapter problems, 51-52
        network configuration problems, 52
        server configuration, 54
    user home directories, 89-90
    Windows 98 clients, 43-45
    Windows NT clients, 45-47

Samba installation, 15
    certificates, 171-172
    precompiled packages
        advantages, 16-17
        disadvantages, 17
        downloading, 17-18
        installation, 19
    source code distributions
        compiling, 21-24
        directory structure, 20-21
        downloading, 19-20
        installation, 24-25
    SWAT (Samba Web Administration Tool), 32
Samba, future of, 235
    development, 238-239
    version 2.1, 235-236
    Windows 2000 interoperability, 236-238
Samba, overview of, 181
    advantages, 75-76
    compiling, 172
    connecting to, 47-48
        through mapped network drives, 49-51
        through Network Neighborhood, 48
    debugging, 199, 202-203
    history of, 5-6
    precompiled packages
        advantages, 16-17
        disadvantages, 17
        downloading, 17-18
        installing, 19
    server connections, 48
    source code distributions
        compiling, 21-24
        directory structure, 20-21
        downloading, 19-20
        installing, 24-25
    starting, 25
        from inetd, 25-26
        from startup file, 26-28
    TNG (The Next Generation), 238-239
    versions, 217
Samba Announcement mailing list, 220-221
Samba Web Administration Tool. See SWAT
scripts
    login scripts, 98, 262
    running when users connect/disconnect from file
        shares, 181-182
    Samba startup scripts, 26-28
    smbprint, 154-155
    smbtar, 155-156

Secure Sockets Layer. See SSL
security, 215
    access control
        Access Denied messages, 203-204
        ACEs (Access Control Entries), 261
        ACLs (Access Control Lists), 122, 130, 261
        anonymous access, 220
        guest access, 219
        permissions, controlling users' changes to,
            128-129
        Samba configuration parameters, 219-220
        share-level options, 183-184
    anonymous access, 220
    authentication, 11
    cryptoanalysis, 8
    denial of service attacks, 261
    directory permissions
        controlling users' changes to, 128-129
        editing, 127-128
    file permissions, 122-123
        controlling users' changes to, 128-129
        editing, 123-127
    firewalls, 217-218, 262
    guest access, 219
    importance of, 215-216
    Kerberos, 237
    online resources, 222
        BugTraq/NTBugTraq mailing lists, 221
        CERT (Computer Emergency Response
            Team), 221
        Samba Announcement mailing list, 220-221
        security-related Linux mailing lists, 221
    operating system patches, 216-217
    password servers
        choosing, 82-83
        username.map files, 83-84
    passwords, 220
        changing, 87
        chosen plaintext attacks, 9
        encrypted, 84-86
        known plaintext attacks, 8
        multiple, 86
        plaintext, 47-48
        smbpasswd command, 86
        synchronizing, 87-88
        troubleshooting, 205-206
        Windows NT passwords, migrating to
            Samba, 88-89
    proactive/reactive, 216, 220
    Samba versions, 217
    services, 218

share-level, 8, 263
SSL (Secure Sockets Layer), 161-162
    alternatives to, 163
    CAs (certification authorities), 163, 168-171
    certificates, 163-168, 171-172
    client support for, 177
    configuration parameters, 172-176
    encryption, 162-163
    handshake process, 164-165
    Samba support, enabling, 172-174
user-level, 8, 62, 263
Windows 95/98 networks, 98, 106-108
security mask parameter (smb.conf file), 129
Security tab (Windows NT), 122-123
security variable (smb.conf file), 35
security-related Linux mailing lists, 221
sending messages, 93-95
    LinPopUp tool, 227-229
    Server Manager, 132
Server Manager, 130-131
    connected users, listing, 133
    messages, sending to connected users, 132
    open files, viewing, 134
    share connections, viewing, 133
    SMB server statistics, viewing, 132-133
Server Message Block Protocol. *See* SMB
server-side certificates, 163-165, 263
servers, 64
    connecting to, 47-48
        through mapped network drives, 49-51
        through Network Neighborhood, 48
    debugging, 202-203
    domain login servers
        configuring Samba as, 101-105
        troubleshooting, 108-109
    password servers
        choosing, 82-83
        username.map files, 83-84
    print servers, 90
        global printer configuration, 91-92
        share-level printer configuration, 92-93
        UNIX side configuration, 90-91
    Server Manager, 130-131
        connected users, listing, 133
        messages, sending to connected users, 132
        open files, viewing, 134
        share connections, viewing, 133
        SMB server statistics, viewing, 132-133
    troubleshooting, 54
    UNIX, 6
    Windows NT, 72

session service (NetBIOS), 69-70
sessions (CIFS), 243-248
setmode command (smbclient program), 153
share-level printer configuration, 92-93
share-level security, 8, 263
sharepoints, mounting, 226-227
shares, 181
    configuring, 36-37
    connecting to, 147
    maximum number of connections, 185
    mounting, 226-227, 232-233
    name mangling, 182-183
    parameters
        blocking locks, 186
        case sensitive, 182
        copy, 186
        default case, 182
        delete readonly, 187
        delete veto files, 187
        dont descend, 187
        force group, 184
        force users, 184
        hide dot files, 187
        hide files, 187
        invalid users, 183-184
        locking, 186
        mangle case, 182
        mangled map, 183
        mangled names, 183
        mangled stack, 183
        max connections, 185
        postexec, 181-182
        preexec, 181-182
        preserve case, 182
        read list, 184
        short preserve case, 183
        valid users, 183-184
        veto files, 187
        veto oplock files, 188
        volumes, 185
        write list, 184
    viewing connections, 133
Shares button (SWAT), 36-37
short preserve case parameter
  (Samba configuration), 183
signatures (digital), 262
signing certificates, 164
sites, Web. *See* Web sites
slash (/), 145

SMB (Server Message Block Protocol), 6-7
   definition of, 263
   history of, 7-9
   server statistics, viewing, 132-133
   SMB PAM (Pluggable Authentication Module),
    229-230
smb.conf file, 34
   access control parameters, 219
      guest ok, 219
      guest only, 219
      hosts allow, 219
      hosts deny, 219
      restrict anonymous, 220
   ACL (Access Control List) support parameters, 122
   editing, 34-36
   file/directory permission parameters, 128-129
   login server options, 118
   share-level parameters
      blocking locks, 186
      case sensitive, 182
      copy, 186
      default case, 182
      delete readonly, 187
      delete veto files, 187
      dont descend, 187
      force group, 184
      force user, 184
      hide dot files, 187
      hide files, 187
      invalid users, 183-184
      locking, 186
      mangle case, 182
      mangled map, 183
      mangled names, 183
      mangled stack, 183
      max connections, 185
      postexec, 181-182
      preexec, 181-182
      preserve case, 182
      read list, 184
      short preserve case, 183
      valid users, 183-184
      veto files, 187
      veto oplock files, 188
      volume, 185
      write list, 184
   SSL (Secure Sockets Layer) parameters, 172-175
      ssl CA certDir, 175
      ssl CA certFile, 175
      ssl ciphers, 175
      ssl client cert, 175

      ssl client key, 175
      ssl compatibility, 176
      ssl hosts, 176
      ssl hosts resign, 176
      ssl require clientcert, 176
      ssl require servercert, 176
      ssl version, 176
    WINS (Windows Internet Name Service)
    configuration options, 77-78
SMB_COM_NEGOTIATE message, 244
SMB_COM_SESSION_SETUP_ANDX message,
 244
SMB_COM_TREE_CONNECT message, 244
SMB_COM_TREE_DISCONNECT message, 244
smb2www tool, 230
smbclient program, 40-42, 94, 143
   debugging, 148-150
   default directories, changing, 150-151
   environment variables, 152
   multiple commands, running, 151
   NetBIOS names, specifying, 150
   options, 143-144
      -c, 151
      -d, 148-151
      -I, 150
      -M, 147
      -n, 150
      -T, 151-152
      -W, 147
   printing, 154-155
   server IP addresses, specifying, 150
   sessions, 144-146
   share connections, 147
   tar archives, creating, 151-152
   troubleshooting, 206
   user interface, 152-154
   Windows backups,creating, 155-156
   WinPopUp messages, sending, 147
smbd (Samba daemon), 10
   open files, viewing, 134
   troubleshooting, 202-203
smbedit tool, 231
smbfs tool, 225-227
smbmount command, 225-226
smbpasswd command, 86
   passwords
      adding multiple, 86
      changing, 87
      synchronizing, 87-88
   troubleshooting, 206

smbpasswd files, 85
    adding users to, 87
    creating, 88-89
    synchronizing with passwd files, 87-88
    trust account settings, 119
smbprint script, 154-155
smbtar script, 155-156
smbumount command, 226
sniffers, 206
    Ethereal, 209-210
    Network Monitor, 207-208
    tcpdump-smb, 208-209
sockets
    Samba configuration options, 194-195
    SSL (Secure Sockets Layer), 161-162
        alternatives to, 163
        CAs (certification authorities), 163, 168-171
        certificates, 163-168, 171-172
        client support for, 177
        configuration parameters, 172-176
        encryption, 162-163
        handshake process, 164-165
        Samba support, enabling, 172-174
software porting, 17
source code listings
    configure program options, 22-23
    Samba startup script, 27
    username.map files, generating, 83-84
source code Samba distributions
    compiling, 21-24
    directory structure, 20-21
    downloading, 19-20
    installing, 24-25
source directory, 21
SSL (Secure Sockets Layer), 161-162
    alternatives to, 163
    CAs (certification authorities), 163
        configuring yourself as, 168-171
    certificates, 163
        creating, 166-168
        installing, 171-172
        server-side, 163
        signing, 164
        verifying, 164-165
    client support for, 177
    configuration parameters, 172-175
        ssl CA certDir, 175
        ssl CA certFile, 175
        ssl ciphers, 175

        ssl client cert, 175
        ssl client key, 175
        ssl compatibility, 176
        ssl hosts, 176
        ssl hosts resign, 176
        ssl require clientcert, 176
        ssl require servercert, 176
        ssl version, 176
    encryption, 162-163
    handshake process, 164-165
    Samba support, enabling, 172-174
ssl CA certDir parameter, 175
ssl CA certFile parameter, 175
ssl ciphers parameter, 175
ssl client cert parameter, 175
ssl client key parameter, 175
ssl compatibility parameter, 176
ssl hosts parameter, 176
ssl hosts resign parameter, 176
ssl require clientcert parameter, 176
ssl require servercert parameter, 176
ssl version parameter, 176
standalone servers, 72
starting
    command-line programs
        multiple commands, 151
        when users connect/disconnect from file
          shares, 181-182
    Samba, 25
        from inetd, 25-26
        from startup file, 26-28
startup files, running Samba from, 26-28
statistics, viewing, 132-133
Status button (SWAT), 38
strict sync parameter (Samba configuration), 196
SWAT (Samba Web Administration Tool), 31-34
    buttons
        Globals, 34-36
        Home, 34
        Password, 39
        Printers, 37-38
        Shares, 36-37
        Status, 38
        View, 39
    installing, 32
swat directory, 21
symmetric cryptography, 162, 263
sync always parameter (Samba configuration), 196

synchronizing passwords, 87-88
System Policy Editor, 98, 107-108, 263

T

T option (smbclient program), 151-152
tables, NetBIOS name tables, 66
tar command (smbclient program), 152
.tar filename extension, 20
tar files, creating, 151-152
tcpdump-smb program, 208-209
testing
    network connectivity, 199-202
    Samba configuration, 40-42
testparm command, 54, 85, 203
The Next Generation (TNG), Samba, 238-239
third-party tools
    LinNeighborhood, 231-233
    LinPopUp, 227-229
    SMB PAM (Pluggable Authentication Module),
        229-230
    smb2www, 230
    smbedit, 231
    smbfs, 225-227
TNG (The Next Generation), Samba, 238-239
tools. See command-line programs; programs
Tridgell, Andrew, 5
troubleshooting
    doman controllers, 121
    domain login servers, 108-109
    help resources, 213
    log files, 211-212
    make command, 24
    name servers, 52-54
    network connectivity, 199-202
    networks
        Access Denied messages, 203-204
        login problems, 204
        network paths, 204-205
        no data when trying to connect, 205
        password changes, 205-206
        sniffers, 206-210
        unable to find domain controller, 205-206
    Samba configuration, 51
        client configuration, 55
        network adapter problems, 51-52
        network configuration problems, 52
        server configuration, 54

smbclient, 206
smbpasswd, 206
startup problems, 202-203
trust accounts
    creating, 118-119
    definition of, 112
trust relationships, 115
    machine trust accounts
        creating, 118-119
        definition of, 112
    one-way, 115-116
    two-way, 116
    Windows NT networks, 236
tuning performance, 191
    client-side tuning, 197
    hardware, 191-192
    Samba configuration
        compile options, 194
        debug level parameter, 196
        getwd cache parameter, 197
        max xmit parameter, 196
        oplocks (opportunistic locking), 195-196
        read raw parameter, 197
        read size parameter, 196
        socket options, 194-195
        strict sync parameter, 196
        sync always parameter, 196
        widelinks parameter, 197
turning on. See enabling
two-way trust relationships, 116

U

UNIX
    advantages, 6
    filenames, changing to 8.3 format, 182-183
    ls command, 42
Usenet newsgroups, 213
user authentication, 11
    Challenge/Response Authentication, 261
    SMB PAM (Pluggable Authentication Module),
        229-230
User Manager for Domains, 134-136, 236
user profiles (roaming), 136-139
    configuring, 105-107
    definition of, 98
user-level security, 8, 62, 263

username.map files, 83-84
users
    adding to ACLs, 130
    groups, 125
    home directories
        configuring, 89-90
        restricting, 90
    listing connected users, 133
    roaming profiles, 136-139
        configuring, 105-107
        definition of, 98

V

valid users parameter (shares), 183-184
variables
    environment variables (smbclient), 152
    globals, 34-36
verifying
    network connections, 48
    server-side certificates, 164-165
versions of Samba, 235-236
veto files parameter (shares), 187
veto oplock files parameter (shares), 188
View button (SWAT), 39
viewing connected users, 133
volumes parameter (shares), 185

W

W option (smbclient program), 147
Web sites
    CERT (Computer Emergency Response Team), 221
    OpenSSL, 166
    operating system security, 216
    Samba download sites, 18
widelinks parameter (Samba configuration), 197
Windows 2000
    Active Directory, 237
    Kerberos, 237
    Samba interoperability, 236-238
Windows 95/98 networks, 98
    advantages of Samba integration, 75-76
    clients
        configuring, 43-45
        troubleshooting, 55

computer browsing, 78
    client configuration, 81
    in domains, 80-81
    in workgroups, 78-80
domains. *See* domain environments (Samba configuration)
login scripts, 98
name resolution, 76
    lmhosts files, 76-77
    WINS (Windows Internet Name Service), 77-78
registry
    editing, 47
    pwl files, disabling, 101
security, 106
system policies, 98, 107-108
troubleshooting
    Access Denied messages, 203-204
    login problems, 204
    network paths, 204-205
    no data when trying to connect, 205
    password changes, 205-206
    unable to find domain controller, 205-206
user profiles, 136-139
    configuring, 105-107
    definition of, 98
Windows messages. *See* messages
workgroups, 61-62, 99-100
    computer browsing, 78-80
    definition of, 263
Windows Internet Name Service. *See* WINS
Windows messages. *See* messages
Windows NT networks
    advantages of Samba integration, 60-61, 75-76
    clients
        configuring, 45-47
        troubleshooting, 55
    computer browsing, 70-71, 78
        backup browsers, 71
        browsing client configuration, 81
        domain master browsers, 71
        elections, 72
        in domains, 80-81
        in workgroups, 78-80
        master browsers, 71-72
        non-browsers, 71
        potential browsers, 71
    disadvantages, 60-61
    domains. *See* domain environments (Samba configuration)
    groups, 125
    login process, 73

name resolution
lmhosts files, 76-77
WINS (Windows Internet Name Service),
76-78
NetBIOS, 64-65
datagram service, 70
name service, 65-69
session service, 69-70
Network Monitor, 207-208
passwords, migrating to Samba, 88-89
registry
editing, 47
pwl files, disabling, 101
Server Manager, 130-131
connected users, listing, 133
messages, sending to connected users, 132
open files, viewing, 134
share connections, viewing, 133
SMB server statistics, viewing, 132-133
servers, 72
troubleshooting
Access Denied messages, 203-204
login problems, 204
network paths, 204-205
no data when trying to connect, 205
password changes, 205-206
unable to find domain controller, 205-206
trust relationships, 236
User Manager for Domains, 134-136
user profiles, 136-139
configuring, 105-107
definition of, 98
Windows messages. *See* messages
workgroups, 61-62, 99-100
computer browsing, 78-80
definition of, 263
WinPopUp messages. *See* messages
WINS (Windows Internet Name Service), 76-78
263
wins proxy option (smb.conf file), 78
wins server variable (smb.conf file), 36
workgroup variable (smb.conf file), 35
workgroups, 61-62, 99-100
computer browsing, 78-80
definition of, 263
workstations, 64
write list parameter (shares), 184

X-Y-Z

X.509 certificates, 263

You are not authorized to login (error message),
204

The IT site
you asked for...

It's
Here!

InformIT is a complete online library delivering
information, technology, reference, training, news
and opinion to IT professionals, students
and corporate users.

Find IT Solutions Here!

www.informit.com

ABOUT THE CD-ROM

Windows 95/98/NT/2000 Installation Instructions

1. Insert the CD-ROM disc into your CD-ROM drive.

2. From the Windows desktop, double-click the My Computer icon.

3. Double-click the icon representing your CD-ROM drive.

4. Double-click the file README.TXT to find out what's on the CD-ROM.

Linux and Unix Installation Instructions

These installation instructions assume that you have a passing familiarity with UNIX commands and the basic setup of your machine. As UNIX has many flavors, only generic commands are used. If you have any problems with the commands, please consult the appropriate man page or your system administrator.

1. Insert the CD-ROM into the CD-ROM drive.

   If you have a volume manager, mounting of the CD-ROM will be automatic. If you don't have a volume manager, you can mount the CD-ROM by typing

   ```
   mount -tiso9660 /dev/cdrom /mnt/cdrom
   ```

   NOTE: /mnt/cdrom is just a mount point, but it must exist when you issue the mount command. You may also use any empty directory for a mount point if you don't want to use /mnt/cdrom.

2. Navigate to the root directory of your CD-ROM. If your mount point matches the example listed above, type

   ```
   cd /mnt/cdrom
   ```

3. Open the file readme.txt with your favorite text editor to find out what's on the CD-ROM.